بسم اللہ الرحمن الرحیم

THE MAKING OF PAKISTAN

A Study in Nationalism

BY

K. K. AZIZ

SANG-E-MEEL PUBLICATIONS

25-SHAHRAH-E-PAKISTAN (LOWER MALL) LAHORE

320.512 Aziz, K.K.
The Making of Pakistan : A study in Nationalism / K.K.Aziz.— Lahore : Sang-e-Meel Publications, 1998.
223p.
Bibliography : p . 211-218
1. Politics. I. Title.

1998
Published by:
NIAZ AHMAD
Sang-e-Meel Publications
Lahore

Rs. 250.00

Sang- e-Meel Publications
Chok Urdu Bazar Lahore. PAKISTAN. Phone : 7667970
Showroom : 25-Shahrah-e-Pakistan (Lower Mall),
Lahore. Pakistan. Phones: 7220100 - 7228143 fax : 7245101
Email lhr01660 @ paknet1. Ptc.pk http://www.sang-e-meel.com

Printed at : Combine Printers, Lahore.

To

The Memory of My Mother

for whom the heart aches with a sense above all language

PREFACE

THIS book deals with Muslim nationalism in Imperial India in its four aspects. The first stage in the growth of a nationalism is the evolution of a group into a nation. This is mainly an historical development and occurs on the time-level. Chapters 1, 2, and 3 describe how the Indian Muslims came to look upon themselves as a separate national group, how this affected 'Indian' nationalism and how it was consummated by the establishment of an independent Muslim state. In brief, they deal with the Muslim nationalist movement in its historical and political aspects. The second stage (which, in terms of time, may sometimes coincide with the first stage) arrives when the national group begins to enunciate the principles and ideals on which it claims a separate existence. The nation justifies its nationhood on the philosophical plane. This may take two shapes: religion and culture. These two arguments are the theme of Chapters 4 and 5, which deal, respectively, with the religious element and the cultural background of Muslim nationalism. The last aspect chosen for study is the psychological factor in nationalism. How the Indian Muslims took pride in being one nation, how they invented symbols to represent their nationalism and created myths to reflect their aspirations, how they persuaded themselves of their own solidarity: this is the subject of Chapter 6. Chapter 7 examines the two-nation theory on which the creation of Pakistan was professedly based.

The Introduction describes the subject of the book and defines its terms of reference. The Epilogue sums up the argument and raises some questions.

My wife has helped me in the writing of this book by checking the references, reading the proofs and in sundry other ways. I am very grateful to her.

I should like to thank my literary agents, Messrs. A. P.

Watt & Son, and in particular Mr. J. H. McLaughlin of the firm, for their valuable help in the publication of this work.

K. K. Aziz

The University,
Khartoum
April 1966

CONTENTS

INTRODUCTION

'NATION', 'nationality', 'nationalism'—there is no more explosive set of words in modern political vocabulary, nor more polemical. Whether you are a political philosopher in search of a definition of 'nation' or a mere agitator claiming nationhood for your people, the concept eludes you. But elusiveness is one thing, inertness quite another. When nationalism is on the rampage no semantic defences will hold the storm; people make their own definitions and die for them. No other word is so heavily charged with emotional overtones; the discussion of no other concept attracts so many loaded phrases. To define any controversial term is notoriously difficult, to try to do so in such a disputatious field is to court disaster. For the curious there is a vast literature on the subject in which he can wallow to his heart's content.

To illustrate this confusion as well as to indicate the difficulties of precise definition let us briefly see how at different times different people have played games with this triad.

'Nation' is essentially a European concept, and it is interesting to recall that during the Middle Ages groups of students from one country working in the European universities were called nations. The University of Prague, for example, was divided into four nations: Bavarians, Bohemians, Poles and Saxons. Medieval Oxford made the Trent a national barrier: students belonged to different nations according as they came from north or south of the river. Then people also spoke of a nation of physicians, of smiths, of lawyers, and so on; we know Ben Jonson's line, 'You are a subtile nation, you physicians.' A day came when the raw facts of power eclipsed the narrow importance of the profession, and Martin Luther was quick to distinguish between folk and nation: the common people, the lowly mortals, were the folk; the princes, the knights and the bishops, the patricians who wielded political power, were the nation. Henceforth political power and nationhood were to keep company. The modern age had arrived.

Medieval Prague or Oxford might have had 'nations' amid their students, but they certainly had no 'nationalities'. The new word itself came into use in the second half of the nineteenth century. But youth did not save it from multiplicity of meaning. Some people used it in the sense of a group of people who have certain things in common: you *are* a nationality if you have national aspirations, if you are a group potentially but not actually a nation. Others made it a spiritual or abstract or subjective aspect of nationhood: you *have* nationality if you feel that you are one of a separate group. This subtle distinction between 'being' and 'having' makes for ambiguity, and we need not go any further with nationality.

We may be deceiving ourselves, but 'nationalism' seems to lend itself to better handling. We may not be able to agree on a definition acceptable to all. But there is substantial agreement on the point that it is a sentiment, a consciousness, a sympathy, which binds a group of people together. It is the desire of a group of individuals, who are already united by certain ties, to live together and, if necessary, to die together. It is the wish of a people, who feel that they are one, to go on living as one. Admittedly this is not very illuminating. Rigorous reasoning can pick many holes in it. But must we define before we can know? We know what toothache is without sitting down to define it. We can know something even without understanding it. If understanding must come first, who among us dare say that he ever loved a woman! Who among us will pause to define the ecstasy of love, the personal tragedy of death, the smell of a rose, or the glow of a star!

This is not a flight of fancy. The argument presented here is that nationalism, like so many other human experiences, is a state of mind. We know that we are a nation, therefore we are a nation. It is not logic, it is intuition. It is not dialectics, it is instinct. It is not a thought process approved by the laws of reasoning. It is a conviction born of insight. It is a vision, an awareness, which comes to us in the flash of a moment. That is what makes it irresistible. People die for their faith; they rarely die in defence of reason.

What are the articles of this strange faith which has made

and remade modern history, which has drawn lines across maps upon its own responsibility, which has killed millions in national wars, and which has also made millions free? A study of modern nationalism points to thirteen conditions or beliefs which seem to make up its creed.

The first and the most pre-eminent is the common group feeling which inspires the members of a nation. 'We all belong to one nation' expresses this sentiment. The second, flowing from the first, is the love for fellow nationals. This certainly does not mean that, say, every Pakistani loves or likes every other Pakistani; but it does mean that in a foreign country Pakistanis will tend to get together, or, on a personal level, in a quarrel with a Pakistani and a foreigner, other Pakistanis will normally side with their compatriot. The third, which is a consequence of the first two, is common hostility to other like groups. Before 1947 the Muslims of India, who considered themselves a nation, looked with hostility upon the Hindus and the Sikhs. This hostility is in proportion to the threat which one national group poses to the existence of the other. This feeling is inevitable in a country or geographical area occupied by more than one nation, particularly if one national group feels that its existence is denied or opposed or threatened or even criticized by the other, for example, in the pre-1947 Imperial India or in the pre-1919 Ottoman Empire.

The fourth is a common territory possessed or coveted by a nation. Once the emotion of nationalism has been aroused, territory is the first and an indispensable step towards the establishment of a State. In India the Muslims claimed the Muslim-majority provinces as their homeland. The Jews have similarly claimed and won Israel as their historical and national home. The fifth is the existence of a common sovereign government or the desire for it. This is the second step after a territory has been mentally demarcated and the claim to it staked. Sovereignty, or politically speaking independence, is usually the final goal of all nationalist movements. Freedom is the open sesame which has been invoked by all colonial peoples struggling to be their own masters. The sixth is the existence of common moral, social or economic institutions or ideas. Medieval history provides some examples of nationalism (though this word was then not used to describe the movement) based on the Christian religion. In our age nationalism has had such formidable inspirations as Communism, National Socialism and Fascism. On a less powerful scale radicalism and reformism have been the ingredients of many nationalist movements.

The seventh is the possession of some common cultural characteristics, such as language, customs, manners, literature, art, music and folk-lore. If a person shares these with others and wants to go on sharing them he is a member of that nation. Culture, in its broader sense, is the most lasting foundation of nationalism. The eighth is common religion. In the secularism of the twentieth century religion has lost much of its force, yet it has produced the two most controversial nation-states of the post-war period—Pakistan and Israel. The ninth is common history or common origin. Whether this history is real or invented is pointless so long as the members of a nation believe in it and look upon certain common historical figures as national heroes. Similarly, though modern science rejects both the theory and the purity of races, the feeling of common racial origin may lead to solidarity of sorts, as the modern Arab movements and the idea of pan-Africanism illustrate. The tenth is a common character shared by the national group. Geography, history, religion and culture combine to mould the contours of national character.

The eleventh is a common pride in national achievements and a common sorrow in national tragedies. Traditionally this pride attached to feats of arms and this sorrow to military reverses. But in our technological age, scientific competition, economic rivalry and even educational jealousy are largely replacing the race for armaments. The twelfth is simple devotion to the nation. 'My country, right or wrong' is one expression, an extreme one perhaps, of this feeling. The last is the hope that the nation will one day be great, or, if it is already that, the greatest in the world. This aspiration may work in many directions, depending on the nation's mood and background: territorial expansion, military power, scientific advance or, in rare cases, academic glory.

The order in which these conditions have been given reflects the nature and composition of nationalism. Each of the four preceding paragraphs describes one stage in its evolution. The first enumerates the three feelings (oneness, love for fellow nationals, and hostility to other groups) which make up the emotional basis of nationalism. The second mentions the three factors (territory, sovereignty, and social ideas) which form its political and social apparatus. The third lists the four beliefs (culture, religion, history, and character) which constitute its spiritual equipment. The fourth portrays the sentiment of nationalism on three time-levels: pride in historical achievements relates to the past, devotion to the national cause concerns the present, the wish to achieve greatness is a hope of the future.

Nationalism can be a sentiment, or a policy, or a myth, or a dogma, or a doctrine. It is a sentiment when it is the love of a common soil, race, language or culture. It is a policy when it is a desire for independence, security or prestige. It is a myth when it is a mystical devotion to a vague social whole, the nation, which is more than the sum of its parts. It is a dogma when it is a belief that the nation is an end in itself and that the individual lives exclusively for the nation. It is a doctrine when a nation considers itself dominant among other nations or aggressively strives to be supreme among them (the German *Nationalismus*).

These are different aspects of nationalism, not its definitions. As a description each of them is narrow, inadequate and misleading. As an aspect each represents one facet and concentrates attention on it. Every nationalism is *sui generis* and takes on its character and shape from its context and environment. Each is a mixture of all these ingredients—but never in equal proportions. It is a compound of all these in varying combinations. One nationalism will emphasize the element of dogma, another that of sentiment, still another that of policy. The same nationalism may appear sometimes to underline its doctrinal foundation and sometimes to over-accentuate its mythical content. However, it is unwise to underestimate or ignore the role of myths in nationalism. They are liable to obsess the minds of their creators and thus to become not true but real. And a real myth is a sword which few know how to sheath.

Chapter 1

THE HISTORICAL FACTOR: I

THE first Muslim conqueror to invade India was Muhammad bin Qasim, who entered the sub-continent through the sands of Sind in the eighth century, and opened the way to waves of subsequent Muslim incursions. But it was not till the end of the twelfth century that Qutbuddin Aibak established the first proper Muslim Empire in India when he founded the Slave Dynasty. His successors ruled for a hundred years before giving way to the Khaljis, who occupied the seat of imperial authority for another hundred years. The fourteenth and fifteenth centuries were a period of uncertainty in Indian history and of decline in the prestige and power of the Delhi Sultanate. It is quite possible that had the Sultanate completely collapsed and left a vacuum behind it, a Hindu revival might have taken heart and either driven the alien conqueror out of India or absorbed him within its expansive fold.

India was rescued from this suspense and the Muslims from this threat to their supremacy by the adventurous exploits of a descendant of Tamurlane and Chingiz Khan. A hardy Chaghtai Turk by the name of Babur crashed through the northwest frontier and swept everything before his courage and zeal. After a convincing victory over Ibrahim Lodhi, the last representative of the tottering Delhi Sultanate, at Panipat in 1526, he met the Rajputs, a foe worthy of his steel, at Khanua in 1527 and crushed them in a decisive combat. With the two most dangerous enemies thus disposed of, he proceeded to found the so-called Mughul Empire—one of the greatest and the most brilliant imperial pageants of all history. Babur the lion-hearted, Humayun the wanderer, Akbar the great, Jahangir the just, Shah Jahan the magnificent, Aurangzeb the puritan—the world has nothing to match Babur and his five lineal descendants who gave India peace and glory and fame for nearly two centuries.

For the first time Muslim culture flooded the Hindu land of India. Persian became the language of the court and, in conjunction with the Hindu languages, gave pith and point to Urdu. Islamic forms of architecture mingled with the Hindu tradition and flowered into the glorious Indo–Islamic art of the builder. The Taj Mahal was born to regale the art lovers of posterity. Under the inspiration of the Persians miniature painting reached the acme of its perfection. In every sphere, from revenue administration to culinary taste, the Mughuls set a standard and bequeathed traditions and systems from which the later rulers were not chary of borrowing on a large scale.

THE ALIGARH MOVEMENT

The Mughuls were succeeded by the British and one imperialist sat in the seat of another. With the advent of the British, and particularly after the Mutiny of 1857, the Muslims awoke to the realization of their true position in India. So far they had either ruled the country or 'enjoyed' the illusion of doing so. The exit of the last Mughul monarch from the throne of Delhi was not only a symbol of their downfall (which in effect had begun much earlier) but also an end to their existence as a separate and dominant group in Indian political life. The British believed that the 1857 uprising had been staged by the Muslims, and this added the discomfiture of retaliation to the humiliation of defeat. For many years the Indian Muslim community floated in the minatory atmosphere of suspicion, suffering and impotence. They had not yet reconciled themselves to the changed political conditions, not yet convinced that their innings was played out. They were not very friendly with the Hindus, whom they considered beneath equal privilege. They were distrusted by the new masters, secretly and at times openly humiliated by the Hindus, and disowned by both. They lost their moorings, their confidence, their hope. And, for the first time, they realized with the anguish of bitterness that they were nothing but a weak, powerless, supine minority. This was the first casting of the seeds of nationalism, the first kindling of a feeling of loneliness and prostration, the first awakening to the need of solidarity.

Every political phenomenon is caused by two agents: circumstances and personalities. The circumstances under which the Muslim began to have a glimmering of his nationhood have been sketched in the last paragraph. The man who moulded the circumstances, or acted with the tide of events (for in fact both are the same things), was Sir Sayyid Ahmad Khan. Born in 1817 in a highly respectable family of Delhi, he entered the service of the East India Company and rose to be a judge. During the Mutiny he did yeoman service for the English by saving many British lives, by refusing to lend his ears to the blandishments and threats of Muslim 'rebels', and by persuading many petty chieftains to give up their refractory attitude. In 1858 he wrote a pamphlet, *Essay on the Causes of the Indian Revolt* (English translation 1860, 1873), in which he attributed the Mutiny to British ignorance of the Indian mind This was a brave thing to do in that dark hour of bias and vindictiveness. In a well-argued narrative he tried to show that there might have been no revolt had the British rulers been less isolated from their Indian subjects and had they kept in touch with Indian opinion and sentiment through some sort of representative institutions, however rudimentary in character. In his next work, *The Loyal Muhammadans of India,* he defended the Muslims against the British charge of disloyalty. Retiring from service in 1876, he sat as a member of the Governor-General's Legislative Council from 1878 to 1883. He died in 1898.[1]

Sayyid's services to his community may be summarized in three terse phrases: loyalty to the British, devotion to education, aloofness from politics. He preached and practised loyalty to the British rule. From his speeches, writings and letters it is not difficult to read his mind. He based his pro-British attitude on three strong foundations. First, the only way of wiping off the stigma of Muslim instigation of the Mutiny was to make friends with the British and thus to make them disabuse their minds of the idea that Muslims were their traditional enemies. He was sagacious enough to realize that British control would not cease in any foreseeable future. It was ordinary common sense to be on good terms with the rulers. In the second place, his sense of loyalty sprang from his

[1] For a contemporary and sympathetic account of Sayyid's life see G. F. I. Graham, *The Life and Work of Sir Sayyid Ahmad Khan,* London, first ed. 1885, rev. ed. 1909.

reading of the Hindu–Muslim problem. Hindus and Muslims were two unequal 'nations', and the latter would ever remain a minority in India. Every advance towards democracy would mean the depression of the Muslims under the rule of the Hindu majority. Therefore he opposed the introduction of parliamentary institutions as well as the increase in the recruitment of Indians to public service by open competition. Such political principles, he said, could only be applied to a country inhabited by one nation. In India every step towards a representative goal would be one more rivet in Muslim chains. In the third place, he was sincerely convinced of the infinite superiority of the British (and European) way of life to the Indian or Oriental. In his letters written from London he paid magnificent, almost cringing, tributes to the English and went so far as to declare that in his opinion Indians were no better than animals and brutes. Such sentiments, expressed with frank vehemence, dispose of the suspicion that he advocated a Muslim–British *rapprochement* for purely political and strategic reasons. His call to the Muslims to cultivate the British and to be faithful to them was not just a matter of making amends for the Mutiny or of protecting the Muslim minority against Hindu domination, but a genuine conviction that it was only from and through the British that Muslims could learn to improve their status and to stand on their own feet.

His second slogan was: 'devote yourself to education; this is your only salvation.' He saw that now that the Muslims had lost their imperial sway over India they must compete with other Indians for jobs and preferments. Good education was the only key to political and economic progress. Education was an obsession with him, and records show that he went about his self-imposed task of providing avenues of education to his people with almost insane perseverance. In 1875 he established the Muhammadan Anglo–Oriental College at Aligarh with money collected through mendicant tours, begging letters and supplicant speeches.

For Sayyid politics was an unnecessary and undesirable encumbrance. The Muslims were under a cloud. The British frowned upon them. The Hindus were fast inheriting the intellectual and material superiority which not so long ago belonged to the Muslims. They were poorly equipped for political adventure. Educationally and economically they had reached their nadir. With such crippling handicaps how could they dream of political agitation? They must keep themselves completely aloof from all political movements and devote themselves to educational uplift. When the Indian National Congress was founded in 1885 Sayyid used every ounce of his influence, prestige and reputation in keeping the Muslims away from it. Unless the Muslims had freed themselves of the suspicion of disloyalty and had educated themselves to the Hindu level, it was suicidal to join the Congress or any other political organization. Sayyid was so uncompromisingly critical of the Congress and its objectives as to declare that even if he heard that the Viceroy, the Secretary of State and the whole House of Commons had declared for the Congress, he would remain firmly opposed to it. 'It is my definite belief,' he said, 'that should the resolutions of the native Congress be carried into effect, it would be impossible for the British Government to preserve the peace, or control in any degree the violence and civil war which would ensue.'[1]

Converting the people to such a creed was an immense undertaking. For his pro-British attitude Sayyid was dubbed a sycophant and dismissed as a toady. His enlightened views on education earned him the wrath of many a Muslim who passed *fatwas* (religious doctrinal decisions) declaring that his innovations were corrupting the Muslim youth. For his criticism of the Congress ardent Indian politicians poured contempt on him and charged him with harbouring anti-democratic, anti-nationalist and pro-imperialist sentiments. But he persevered and continued to preach according to his convictions. Slowly but steadily he gained converts to his cause, and before his death in 1898 he could, with satisfaction, look back along the lengthening track of life.

Muslim India was yet not a nation by herself. Nor did she claim such a title. But the Muslims had begun to look upon themselves as a separate entity, a different community, a group apart. This feeling of separateness from others and of oneness among themselves was the first foundation and the first symptom of Muslim nationalism in India. In future,

[1] Quoted in *The Times*, 12 November 1888.

whatever course the political developments took, there was only a remote possibility of a complete fusion of the Muslims and others.

The work of Sayyid Ahmad Khan was carried forward by his colleagues and junior partners at Aligarh. Their combined efforts produced what is commonly known as the Aligarh Movement. It was fundamentally a cultural movement aiming at a regeneration of liberal values in literature, social life, education and religion.

In literature it stood for simplicity of diction, purity of ideas and an imitation of nature. Hali, the poet and literary critic, occupies in this respect the position enjoyed by Wordsworth in the Romantic Revival of English poetry. In social matters the Aligarians strove for honesty in daily intercourse, communal sympathy and the cultivation of unaffected habits. In education, the Aligarh College aspired to be a university and, in the meantime, upheld Sayyid's ideal of a balance between the learning of the West and the mores of the East. In religion the movement represented a shift towards reason and anti-fanaticism. The unhealthy influence of the half-educated *mulla* (priest) was counteracted by explaining, in simple but elegant language, the fundamental principles of Islam and by relating them to the sanction of human reason.

The Aligarh Movement was not short of human resources, and distinguished writers like Hali, Shibli and Nazir Ahmad put their shoulders to its wheel. Sayyid Ameer Ali was, strictly speaking, not of the movement, but he shared its ideals and in his own way furthered them. His *Spirit of Islam* was a new interpretation of Islam and Islamic history written with erudition and enthusiasm. His biography of the Prophet wielded great influence on the new generation of Indian Muslims, while his advocacy of such matters as female emancipation and the reform of Muhammadan personal law affected the community's thinking.

The impact of this reformism was revolutionary. The Muslims developed a confidence in themselves and in their traditions. They came to respect themselves. The pessimism of the post-Mutiny days gave way to what was almost a feeling of buoyancy. No longer was their loyalty questioned in British quarters. No longer did the Hindu dismiss them with a shake of the head. They were catching up in education. The Aligarh College was producing graduates who could fill the vacancies in government offices reserved for Muslims. They had begun to take an interest in trade and commerce and industry. Sayyid's policy was bearing fruit. Hope sprang in the hearts of men and some leaders even began to think political thoughts.

THE INTERREGNUM

By the turn of the century the Muslim community was pulsating with new ideas. Much had been achieved, though much remained undone. The old generation, which had tasted the bitter fruit of defeat and disgrace, was succeeded by a new generation, young in heart, fresh to the opportunities of life, aware of its solidarity and hopeful of the future. For them the old injunction of aloofness from politics was losing its topical utility. Events no longer justified it. The Hindus had organized a Congress, formulated their demands and made the British aware of their existence and their aspirations. Seeds of representative institutions, sown by the Indian Councils Act of 1892, might at any moment sprout into more far-reaching reforms. It was unwise to depend entirely upon the good opinion of the rulers, though it was a cause of much gratification. The age of political action was dawning and those who did not see the signs of the time would be left behind. Muslims must organize themselves into a political movement, not only to consolidate what had been achieved but also to make further advances and win new concessions from the powers that were.

But traditions die hard. Some leaders, bred in the stable of Sayyid, still hesitated to take the plunge. The Sage of Aligarh had uttered a ban on politics, and the ban must stand. The Oracle had spoken, and his word was final. Events had yet to prove the invalidity of his admonition, and unless new portents appeared on the political horizon no rash decision should be taken.

Events in Bengal soon took the decision out of their hands. In October 1905 Lord Curzon, the masterful Viceroy, announced and implemented a partition of Bengal with the dividing line between the Hindu west and the Muslim east. This harmless-looking administrative act and its consequences made the decision for the Muslims.

Curzon's chief argument was that Bengal was too unwieldy to be administered efficiently by one Lieutenant-Governor. To those who wanted Bengal to be put under a Governor and an Executive Council he replied in a letter to the Secretary of State for India: 'Government by one man is infinitely better than Government by three men if it can be so managed. What we want in India is personal knowledge of localities and personal touch with the people. This can only be gained by the familiarity of the Head of the Administration with the places and people under his charge. With a triumvirate as a ruling power this is quite impossible, and Bombay and Madras are both, in my view, illustrations that the weak points are in excess of the merit of the system.'[1] His original plan had been to take away one or two districts of Bengal and put them into the charge of the Assam Chief Commissionership. Later he appreciated the force of the opposition to this scheme and, replying to the addresses presented to him during his Bengal tour of 1903–4, he clearly laid it down that he would consider the larger project of increasing the size of the territory to be cut away from Bengal and of creating a new province, large and important enough to have a Lieutenant-Governor with a Legislative Council.

The Secretary of State for India sanctioned this scheme in June 1905. Large territories were transferred from Bengal to the new province, which was given the official title of Eastern Bengal and Assam. It contained a population of 31 million, of whom 18 million were Muslims and 12 million Hindus. Bengal was now left with 54 million inhabitants, of whom 42 million were Hindus and 9 million Muslims. 'In short,' said the White Paper, 'the territories now comprising Bengal and Assam will be divided into two compact and self-contained provinces, the largest constituents of each of which will be homogeneous in character, and which will possess clearly defined boundaries and be equipped with the complete resources of an advanced administration'.[2] The Proclamation of the formation of the new province was issued in September and the province of

[1] Quoted in Ronaldshay, *The Life of Lord Curzon*, 1928, Vol. II, p. 324.

[2] *East India (Reconstruction of the Provinces of Bengal and Assam)*, 1905, Cd. 6258.

Eastern Bengal and Assam formally came into being on 16 October 1905.

The Hindus, particularly those of West Bengal, did not take kindly to this change. They charged the Government with having favoured the Muslims by giving them a province in which they formed a majority, having 'vivisected' the Bengali homeland, having disrupted the Bengali 'nationality' and having injured the 'nationalist' and 'patriotic' movement and spirit of the people of India. The Bengali-speaking people were cut asunder. A deadly blow had been struck at the culture of Bengal.

But contemporary evidence suggests that the Hindu opposition was not without ulterior motives. The partition was resented because the high caste Hindus desired to have the state of things which existed before the advent of the Muslims and of the low castes for jobs. The educated Hindu feared that the creation of a Muslim-majority province would tend to deprive him of his existing monopoly of influence and office. The new change had led to the development of Chittagong as a port, and the Hindus of Calcutta feared it as a possible rival.[1] In brief, the Hindus, first of Bengal and later also of other provinces, objected to the creation of a Muslim-majority province.

The Muslims, on the other hand, rejoiced at the partition. Six days after the partition was enforced, on 22 October 1905, a large Muslim meeting was held at Dacca at which the speaker impressed on the assembly the boon conferred on them by the change. On 24 October another big gathering offered thanks to God that the partition had been carried into effect. Speeches dwelt on the many advantages to the Muslims, who 'through the division of Bengal would be spared many oppressions which they had hitherto had to endure from the Hindus'. On the first anniversary of the partition in 1906, Muslims met throughout Eastern Bengal to adopt a memorial to the Secretary of State for India expressing gratification that he had declared the partition to be a 'settled fact'. The Muslim League, which had been formed in 1906, passed a resolution in Septem-

[1] See *Imperial and Asiatic Quarterly Review*, April 1907, pp. 293–4; *Quarterly Review*, July 1907, p. 215; H. E. M. James, 'Ambition and Sedition in India', *National Review*, June 1907, pp. 636–9; and *The Times*, 14 April 1906.

ber 1908, hoping that the Government would 'adhere to this settled fact'. The higher arose the crescendo of the anti-partition agitation the greater was the apprehension of the Muslims lest the British Government might surrender to the Hindu demand for a repeal of the partition. Therefore, not content with mere resolutions, the Muslim League sent a letter to the Under Secretary of State on 11 November 1908, in which it expressed the grateful acknowledgement of the Muslims for the Secretary of State's (Morley) intention not to interfere with the partition, and warned that any change would cause serious dissatisfaction among the Muslims.[1]

One of the most effective weapons in the agitators' hands was the *swadeshi* movement, or the boycott of all British-made goods. Hindus insisted that Muslims should also boycott foreign goods and refuse to sell them. This was distasteful and unacceptable to the Muslims, who had little sympathy with the agitation of which the boycott was one weapon and had no quarrel with the British or their textile manufacturers. Moreover, it was detrimental to their livelihood in so far as they lived on the trade in foreign cloth. When Hindus, in their zeal on behalf of the agitation, used physical coercion or intense social pressure on reluctant Muslim shopkeepers and traders, some sort of communal trouble was inevitable. As the *swadeshi*, or India-made, article was often inferior to the foreign article in quality, and higher in price, the poor Muslim naturally resented 'the sacrifice he has been compelled to make in the interests of an agitation that he has no sympathy with'.[2]

Further, the Muslims contended that, under the old régime when they were governed from Calcutta, they had no fair chance of progress. The Hindus, a minority in the total population, held ten times as many appointments as the Muslims. Five times as many Hindus held judicial posts and they practically monopolized the Bar. An unusually small proportion of European officials was appointed to the eastern districts, with the result that Hindu officials ruled over overwhelmingly

[1] See Reuter's messages, *Manchester Guardian*, 25 and 27 October 1905; *The Times*, 6 November 1906; ibid., 7 September 1908; ibid., 26 December 1908.

[2] India correspondent's dispatch of 16 May 1907 from Calcutta, *Manchester Guardian*, 3 June 1907.

Muslim areas.[1] Thus the Muslims interpreted the Hindu agitation against the partition as nothing less than an attempt to maintain Hindu superiority over them in, among other things, public services.

To the Hindu assertion that the partition cut at the root of Bengali 'nationality', it was pointed out that the word 'Bengal' had no definite historical or geographical meaning before it was adopted by the British as a designation for a large administrative unit. The partition still kept 'Anga Banga' together and segregated from them the trans-Gangetic Divisions of Bengal.[2]

Then there were precedents for divisions and mergers of Indian provinces when the populations affected by them had registered no protest. In 1892 Sir Charles Elliott, as the Lieutenant-Governor of Bengal, had advocated the cession of a part of the province of Assam.[3] The Delhi Division had been transferred to the Punjab. The Saugar and Narbada territories had been taken away from the North-Western Provinces and added to the Central Provinces. Oudh had been abolished as a separate unit and merged with the North-Western Provinces. The small province of Khandesh had been twice partitioned between 1870 and 1899. In none of these cases had the people made any serious issue of the matter.

This convinced the Muslims that the Hindu agitation for the modification of the partition was in its aims as much anti-Muslim as anti-British. An innocuous administrative decision had been made into something connected with the revolting ideas of matricide and deicide. It appeared that the Hindus were not prepared to countenance the creation of a Muslim-majority province. This, in the Muslim eyes, was very significant, for it exposed the hollowness of the Congress claim that it stood for Hindu–Muslim unity and did not distinguish between a Hindu Indian and a Muslim Indian. It reinforced the Muslim feeling that their interests were not safe in Congress hands, that they would never be treated fairly and justly by the Indian 'nationalists', and that any broad-based Indian

[1] 'The "Partition" of Bengal: In the New Province I', *The Times*, 2 April 1906.

[2] Sir George Birdwood, letter to *The Times*, 17 August 1905.

[3] A. C. Elliott, 'The Unrest in India', *Empire Review*, June 1907, pp. 383–4.

nationalism was bound to be Hindu (or at least *not* Muslim) in character.

The era of politics had set in and it was no longer possible to shut one's eyes to political changes and keep travelling on the apolitical path mapped out by Sayyid Ahmad Khan. This led straight to the idea of the establishment of a Muslim political organization.

Another important factor contributed to this change in the climate of opinion. The principle of representation had been established in the provinces by the Indian Councils Act of 1892. Now rumour ran that this principle was to be extended to a wider field. Therefore to safeguard their future interests the Muslims drafted a plan of separate electorates and laid it before the Viceroy at Simla on 1 October 1906 through a representative deputation headed by the Aga Khan. The Simla Deputation, as it is generally called, argued for two points of policy. First, in all elections in the provinces and in local areas Muslims should be represented by Muslims alone, and these representatives should be elected by purely Muslim electorates. Secondly, Muslims must have more seats and greater representation than their numerical strength warranted because of their 'political importance' and their greater contribution to the 'defence of the Empire'. The Viceroy, in his reply, agreed with the substance of the Address and promised to recommend it to the India Office. The gulf between the Hindus and Muslims, already widened by the Bengali agitation and its Hindu undercurrents, was now to manifest itself on the constitutional plane. The communal rift was becoming irrevocable.

THE BEGINNING OF POLITICS

This long swing of events brought the Muslims face to face with the issue of political action. It was no longer possible to avoid politics, for the march of events had already pushed them into the arms of constitutional agitation. They could not join the Congress because, in the words of a Muslim leader of the time, 'tied to the wheels of the Juggernauth of majority they would in the end be crushed out of the semblance of nationality'.[1] They espied a new aggressive attitude among the

[1] Ameer Ali, 'India and the New Parliament', *Nineteenth Century*, August 1906, p. 257.

Hindus. A contemporary Hindu observer noted that it was from the end of 1906 that the Hindus became conscious of a new kind of hatred for the Muslims. 'We began to hear angry comment in the mouths of the elders that the Muslims were coming out quite openly in favour of partition and on the side of the English. . . . A cold dislike for the Muslim settled down in our hearts, putting an end to all real intimacy of relationship.'[1]

Between 1902 and 1905 Muslim leaders had made some attempts to negotiate with Hindu politicians. The Aga Khan had remonstrated with Sir Pherozeshah Mehta about the necessity of persuading the Congress to gain Muslim confidence. When these efforts failed, it was felt that the only hope lay in the establishment of a Muslim political body to secure 'independent political recognition from the British Government as a *nation within a nation*'.[2] The All India Muslim League was accordingly established in December 1906 at a meeting of Muslim leaders in Dacca.

The Muslim League was thus the child of four factors. First, the old belief uttered by Sayyid Ahmad Khan that the Muslims were somehow a separate entity. Secondly, the Hindu character of the Indian National Congress which did not allow the Muslims to associate themselves with other Indians. Thirdly, the agitation against the partition of Bengal which conveyed to the Muslims the Hindu designs of domination. And, finally, the Muslim desire to have their own exclusive electorates for all representative institutions.

The years 1906–11 constitute a period in which the Hindu–Muslim rift continued to widen and deepen almost beyond repair. On the Hindu side, these years were big with the anti-British and anti-Muslim agitation in Bengal and other parts of India. Tilak was the most prominent leader who, by his orthodox religious views and belligerent political action, alienated the Muslims from the mainstream of Indian nationalism and renewed their faith in the British. On the Muslim side, these years saw the foundation of the Muslim League, the

[1] Nirad C. Chaudhuri, *The Autobiography of an Unknown Indian*, 1951, pp. 233–7.

[2] *The Memoirs of Aga Khan: World Enough and Time*, 1954, p. 76. My italics.

establishment of separate Muslim electorates and the beginning of the feeling that Muslim interest lay in continued co-operation with the British and in severe aloofness from the Congress.

The pith of Muslim policy during these turbulent years is well delineated in the Aga Khan's letter of September 1908 addressed to the Deccan Provincial Muslim League. 'British rule—not only a titular sovereignty, but a vigorous force permeating every branch of the administration—is an absolute necessity. Therefore I put it to you that it is the duty of all true Indian patriots to make that rule strong. . . . This is a duty which lies not only upon Muslims, but equally upon the Parsees, the Sikhs, upon all who are convinced of the benevolence of British rule. . . . These are the patriotic ideals which, I think, should animate the Muslim community at the present juncture. . . . Ours must be not a lukewarm patriotism, no passive unemotional acquiesence in the established order. It must be a living, controlling, vitalizing force, guiding all our actions, shaping all our ideals. . . . Rather should it be our task to persuade by precept and example those Hindus who have strayed from the path of true progress to return to it.'[1]

By and large this advice was followed by Muslim India. Only a few Muslims joined the Congress and they did not represent the mainstream of Muslim feeling. British rule was stoutly defended and bravely supported. The continuance of the partition of Bengal and the grant of separate electorates were made the central issues on which the Muslims tested the British recognition of their loyalty. Muslim leadership of the time was of a high order and succeeded in influencing the British Government in Muslim favour. In Britain the Aga Khan and Ameer Ali did yeoman service to the Muslim cause and it was mostly due to their efforts that the partition of Bengal was allowed to stand and Muslim prayer for separate representation was answered by the Morley–Minto reforms of 1909. In India the Muslims were trusted and respected by the imperial rulers. It was a comforting thought that their aspirations were not disregarded and that their loyalty was appreciated. The Anglo–Muslim amity was as mutual as it was deep.

[1] Full text in *The Times,* 7 September 1908.

THE BREAK WITH THE BRITISH

These halcyon days were brought to an abrupt end by the repeal of the partition of Bengal. The new province of Eastern Bengal and Assam had been making good progress. Its administration was firmly established and its economy was showing steady improvement. The agitation was admitted by the Government to be dead. The general condition of law and order was gratifying. Political crime had greatly diminished, the vernacular press no longer reeked of sedition, and outrages were more infrequent than at any time during the previous five years.[1] The authorities were said to be too firmly convinced of the administrative value of the division to attempt any modification. Any reversal of policy was liable to bring dangerous results.[2] Nevertheless, in December 1911 the partition was annulled.

Lord Hardinge, who had succeeded Minto as Viceroy on 23 November 1910, wrote to the Secretary of State for India on 25 August 1911 that the partition was resented by the Bengalis, though he confessed that the Muslims had benefited by it and were loyal and contented. He suggested a 'modification' of the partition based on two conditions. First, it should duly safeguard the interests of eastern Bengal and generally conciliate Muslim sentiment. Secondly, it should be so clearly based on broad grounds of political and administrative expediency as to negative any presumption that it had been extorted by clamour or agitation. Muslim interests were to be safeguarded by the special representation they enjoyed in the Legislative Councils. His scheme was to reunite the five Bengali-speaking divisions (an administrative area into which provinces were divided) into a presidency administered by a Governor in Council; to create a Lieutenant-Governorship in Council of Behar, Chota Nagpur and Orissa; and to restore the Chief Commissionership of Assam. Simultaneously the capital of India was to be shifted from Calcutta to Delhi. Action on these lines, he claimed, would be a 'bold stroke of

[1] Asiaticus, 'India: Lord Minto's Viceroyalty', *National Review*, November 1910, p. 526.

[2] Special Correspondent's dispatch from India, *The Times*, 8 February 1909.

statesmanship' and would 'open a new era in the history of India'.

The Marquess of Crewe's reply was phrased in equally enthusiastic terms. Giving his immediate sanction to the Viceroy's scheme, he wrote on 1 November 1911, 'I cannot recall in history, nor can I picture in any portion of the civilized world as it exists, a series of administrative changes of so wide a scope. . . .'[1] The decision was announced by the King in person at the Coronation Durbar at Delhi on 12 December 1911

Muslim reaction to this change was dumbfounded astonishment and bitter soreness. It gave rise to a feeling of distrust in the future promises and actions of the Government. It irritated the Muslims, who believed that they had been sacrificed to appease the Hindus. It alienated them and weakened their trust in British stability of purpose. It was a lesson that loyalty paid no dividends, that the Government listened only to agitation and sedition, and that the Muslims had been foolishly wrong in believing in British sincerity. Bombs alone led to boons. The failure of the Muslim policy of loyalty was proved to be as signal as the triumph of the Hindu policy of contumacy.

Hardinge was right—though unwittingly—in telling Crewe that his scheme would open a new era in Indian history. For the Muslims it heralded a new age of intense political consciousness and activity. A marked change came over their politics. They began to feel deeply that the Government was unable or unprepared to protect their rights. Official promises could no longer be trusted. The policy of 'sturdy loyalty', practised in the face of Hindu jeers, had brought no reward. Their first gesture of challenge was a resolution, passed by the Muslim League at its annual session held in December 1912–January 1913, changing the League's aim from 'loyalty' to a 'form of self-government suitable to India'. *Suitable* is the operative word, for the Muslims still refused to identify themselves with the Congress demand for unqualified self-government. They retained the right to modify self-rule in accordance with their needs and aspirations.

[1] Text of letters in *Announcements by and on behalf of His Majesty the King–Emperor at the Coronation Durbar held at Delhi on the 12th December, 1911, with correspondence relating thereto,* 1911, Cd. 5979.

This amendment in the constitution of the League seems to have conveyed, at least to some minds in Britain, the impression that Muslims were no longer loyal. To answer such reflections cast on their attitude,[1] and to clarify the situation arising out of their new aims and ideals, a Muslim deputation went to England towards the end of 1913, to apprize the Ministers and other officials of the essential feeling of the community. But the Secretary of State refused to receive it on the ground that an interview would be misunderstood by other Muslims who claimed equally with the Muslim League to represent the political temper of Muslim India.[2] Obviously Crewe was thinking of such 'loyalists' as the Aga Khan, whose traditional loyalty to Britain did not permit them to co-operate with the League after 1911 and who shortly afterwards left its fold, giving place to others better equipped to lead the community in changed circumstances.

From 1858 to 1905 the Muslims had been cultivating the British. From 1906 to 1911 this amity blossomed into friendship. From 1911 to 1922 their relations may be described as ranging from an armed truce to open warfare. This evolution may also be expressed in another way. From 1858 to 1905 the Muslims stood outside the political arena; from 1906 to 1911 they were schooling themselves in constitutional politics; from 1911 onwards they, or at least most of them, were agitators preaching with full-throated ease the gospel of disorder and sedition. There is still another way of describing this development. From 1858 to 1905 the Muslims were in a state of neutrality *vis à vis* the Hindus; from 1906 to 1911 the Hindu–Muslim rift was first marked and later ominous; from 1911 to 1922 the two communities co-operated against what they considered a common enemy—Britain.

This *entente* produced quick results. The Muslim League and the Congress met in a joint session in 1916 at Lucknow and formulated common reform proposals to be put before the

[1] This is very significant. Even in the flush of their anti-British emotion they were careful to maintain at least the appearance of a loyal attitude. The concept and history of Muslim loyalty in Imperial India should form a fascinating subject of study for a modern psychologist.

[2] See Muhammad Ali's interview in the *Manchester Guardian*, 2 December 1913.

Government for immediate implementation. By the terms of this Lucknow Pact the League, besides endorsing the Congress demands, resolved to send a deputation to England immediately after the war to present the Indian claims in co-operation with a similar deputation from the Congress.[1] In its next session at Calcutta, on 31 December 1917, the League endorsed the Congress resolution urging the necessity of a Parliamentary Statute containing complete responsible government; but it stipulated three conditions: (a) adequate Muslim representation in Councils, public services and universities; (b) no displacement of Persian characters from the Urdu language; and (c) no interference with the Id-uz-Zuha and Muharram festivals.[2]

The Lucknow Pact is of outstanding importance in the development of Indian Muslim nationalism for two reasons. It was the first Hindu–Muslim compact in modern Indian history and, in the hopes of several leaders on both sides, was expected to lay the foundation of a permanent united action against the British. It was also the first and the only occasion when the Hindus not only conceded separate electorates to the Muslims but agreed to the quantum of Muslim representation in different provincial legislatures and at the centre. Though some prominent figures in both camps criticized the nature and terms of the *concordat*, yet there is no doubt that for the nascent Muslim nationalism it was for the moment a victory without qualifications—though, as will be seen later, a victory of doubtful ultimate advantage. To bring round the Congress, which had been bitterly condemning separate electorates since 1906, to their point of view was no mean achievement for the Muslims. But, as we will see in the next chapter, it was not so much the genius of Muslim leadership as a fortuitous constellation of circumstances which brought forth this unique turn of events.

The Congress–League scheme of reforms was, however, not only far ahead of the times but in fact did not aim at realizing responsible government. It contented itself with leaving an irremovable executive at the mercy of a legislature which could paralyse it without directing it. The official reply to the

[1] *Manchester Guardian*, 2 January 1917.

[2] Ibid., 8 January 1918.

Lucknow agreement was contained in the famous Montagu announcement of 20 August 1917, the pith and substance of which was the sentence: 'The policy of His Majesty's Government, with which the Government of India are in complete accord, is that of the increasing association of Indians in every branch of the administration, and the gradual development of self-governing institutions, with a view to the progressive realization of responsible government in India as an integral part of the British Empire.'

This sentiment was soon given a practical shape when Montagu visited India from November 1917 to April 1918 and, in co-operation with the Viceroy, Lord Chelmsford, held discussions with Indian leaders of all opinions. The result of these conversations and the Viceroy–Secretary of State deliberations was the Montagu–Chelmsford Report, which was published on 8 July 1918.[1] The proposals of the Report were supported by all the members of the Council of the Secretary of State and of the Viceroy's Executive Council, and were welcomed by the non-official members of the Imperial Legislative Council,[2] but were severely criticized by the Muslim League and the Congress. The Report's plan was so far removed from that of the Congress–League scheme that no attempt was made to arrange a compromise, and the official recommendations were drafted into a Government of India Bill, which passed through Parliament in 1919 and received the Royal Assent on 23 December. The Act gave separate representation to the Muslims and also extended it to one other minority, the Sikhs.

Here we must break our chronological order and go back a little to take notice of another important development. Besides the repeal of the partition of Bengal there was another factor equally, or perhaps even more deeply, responsible for the anti-British feeling of the Muslims from 1912 onwards. This was the Khilafat issue. It is studied in greater detail in the chapter on the religious factor, but here a short reference to it is in order to make the story clear.

Briefly, the Indian Khilafat movement was a purely Muslim campaign in favour of Turkey and her Sultan. The Muslims felt that the integrity of the Ottoman Empire, the only

[1] Cd. 9109 of 1918.

[2] V. Lovett, *India*, 1923, p. 194.

surviving Muslim independent country, must be maintained at all costs. This was predominantly a political feeling, though with a not inconsiderable religious basis. But added to this was a purely religious sentiment which looked at the Turkish Sultan as the Khalifa of the Muslims of the world, and which therefore interpreted any dimunition of his authority as an assault upon the sovereignty of the supreme Islamic personality. The Turco-Italian War of 1912, the Balkan Wars of 1912–14, the Turkish participation in the Great War on the side of the Central Powers, and the defeat of Turkey in 1918—these developments were acutely embarrassing to Muslim India. Circumstances seemed to conspire to doom the tradition of loyalty. The Muslims, on the strength of their friendship with Britain, expected in 1912 that Whitehall would help Turkey. When they were disappointed in this hope they related it to the Delhi Durbar decision, put two and two together, and concluded that Britain was deliberately trying to crush the Muslims in India as well as elsewhere. The Balkan and the Great Wars strengthened this belief, and at the end of the hostilities when the Allies forced the Treaty of Sèvres on the tottering Ottoman edifice Muslims got wild with anger. Treason was openly preached and the anti-British sentiment reached a pitch of extremity unmatched in the history of British rule in India (the Mutiny fell under the régime of the East India Company). The pressure was so intense that the British Government had to revise its attitude and to give in to Indian feeling. The Treaty of Lausanne, which replaced the severe and stern Treaty of Sèvres, satisfied the Indian Muslims, though this satisfaction was short-lived. When Mustafa Kamal abolished the institution of Khilafat and a little later the Sultanate (monarchy) itself, there was disappointment among the Indian Muslims and panic among the orthodox. But of this more later.

From our point of view the importance of the Khilafat lay in two things. It was anti-British and it was, at least temporarily and on the surface, a further bond between the Hindus and the Muslims. It had to be anti-British, for Turkey had fought Britain and Britain was on the dictating side in the peace negotiations. What is interesting is that the bulk of the Hindus, led by Gandhi, made a common cause with the Muslims and fully participated in the extremist agitation of

1919–21. The spirit of Lucknow was yet strong and the British rejection of the Congress–League scheme of reforms strengthened the strands of unity. Hindu–Muslim fraternity manifested itself on all levels. Politically, the two communities had practically coalesced and for the first time forged a united front against the British. Religiously, the Hindus had shown great tactical skill in espousing the alien and purely Islamic cause of Khilafat. Socially, the Hindus and Muslims were now 'brethren unto each other', and all sorrows and triumphs were equally shared. So solid and strong was the new friendship that some Hindu religious leaders, who had a little earlier been castigated as unpardonable enemies of Islam, were now invited by the Muslims to preach from the pulpit of the Royal Mosque of Delhi. Solidarity, born of expediency, could go no further. Moral: my enemy's enemy is my friend.

But those who had let themselves be dazzled by this show of unity and had predicted a long life for it were proved false prophets. Even when the Lucknow compact was yet quite fresh Hindu–Muslim riots reared their ugly head. Patna passed into the hands of Hindu mobs and heads were broken with lethal avidity. The Government resolution on these disturbances minced no words and declared that for the like of such bloodshed one had to go back to 1857. Innumerable minor riots followed, but the limit was reached in 1921 when there was a communal explosion in Malabar. The Moplas of that area, mostly primitive Muslims of mixed Arab descent, fell upon the Hindus who lived amongst them and tore them to pieces. So fierce and widespread was the onslaught that the army had to be called in and for many months Malabar lived under martial law. At one fell stroke the carefully nurtured unity was shot to ribbons. Never again were the two 'nations' to come together in any sphere of life. The spirit of Lucknow was irrevocably dead.

Was this orgy of religious strife connected with the 1919 reforms? Some thought so and their main argument was that the provision of separate electorates was responsible for the aggravation. But this provision was not new and had dated from 1909. It could also be argued that the abrogation of communal representation would provoke still more violent friction. On the larger question whether any future reforms were at all possible in view of Indian disunity, *The Times*' comment[1] was both wise and prescient. The next instalment of reforms should continue to safeguard the rights of the religious and political minorities and to maintain the reserved powers of the provincial governments. To those who took this to be a reactionary thought, the journal addressed the pertinent question: will Indian nationhood be advanced by presenting powerful minorities with potent grievances or by seeking to deprive the executive of the authority necessary to preserve Indian political unity until Indian national union became a plain and irrefutable fact?

[1] *The Times* (leader), 19 June 1926.

Chapter 2

THE HISTORICAL FACTOR: II

THE Montagu–Chelmsford reforms came into operation in 1921. In the provincial field they erected the system of 'Dyarchy', i.e., a division of powers between the responsible ministers and the irresponsible executive councillors. Some subjects were made popular and given into the charge of popularly elected ministers who were responsible to the provincial legislatures. And some subjects were reserved to the Governor, who administered them through appointed executive councillors who were not accountable to the provincial assemblies. The idea was to train Indian politicians in representative government before trusting them with full powers in all fields.

THE SIMON COMMISSION

The essentially transitional character of the 1919 reforms was so well known to the Indian leaders that they began to clamour for the next instalment of reforms even before Dyarchy had worked for a year. The 1919 constitution had stipulated that after ten years the Government would again go into the question of constitutional progress. The terms of reference of this inquiry were to be to investigate the working of the system of government, the growth of education and the development of representative institutions. It was finally to report on the extent to which it was desirable to establish the principle of representative government, or to extend, modify or restrict the degree of responsible government already in existence. But the Indian demand for a revision of the constitution became so insistent that in 1927 the Government of India Act of 1919 was amended so as to enable the Government to hold a fresh inquiry before the expiry of the ten-year period.

Accordingly, on 26 November 1927, the appointment of a Statutory Commission was announced. With Sir John (later

Lord) Simon as chairman the Commission was charged with the duty of investigating the Indian constitutional problem in all its implications and to draw up recommendations for future action. In India the appointment of this body was received with acute disappointment because it contained no Indian on its panel. Indian critics of its personnel took it as a slight on their ability that an all-British body would determine their future. What they forgot was that, in the first place, it was a parliamentary commission appointed by Parliament and required to report back to Parliament, and, in the second place, that Indian disunity practically excluded the possibility of any two Indians agreeing on their recommendations. Indian participation in the Commission would have created serious problems. Was it to contain some Indians or more Indians than British? Were all Indian parties to be represented on it or only the major ones? And, in what proportion? Would the Indian members reach unanimous conclusions? Would their recommendations be acceptable to Parliament or even to all Indians?

The Indian Legislative Assembly resolved by a majority of six votes to boycott the Commission, while the Indian Council of State (the upper chamber) decided to co-operate.[1] The Congress was uncompromisingly opposed to it and called for a complete boycott. Small minorities favoured co-operation. Muslims were split. One section, led by Sir Muhammad Shafi, proclaimed support, while the other, led by Jinnah, shared the Congress view. In spite of the *Manchester Guardian*'s appeal not to class the British investigators among the Untouchables but to admit them to society and to attend to their education, the Congress and the 'Jinnah League' persisted in their opposition.

The non-co-operating Muslims got a good press—as non-co-operators always did—but it is wrong to think that they represented a majority of the Muslims. Exact figures are not available, but it is safe to say that the Muslims were almost equally divided between the co-operators and the non-co-operators. The arguments of the non-co-operators were the same as the Congress's. India was not represented on the Commission; this was a deliberate insult. Britain had no right to impose a constitution on India through the recom-

[1] Resolutions of 18 and 23 February 1928, respectively.

mendations of an all-White investigating body. Britain had not heeded the Congress–League scheme of 1917 and would again disregard whatever the Indians proposed. Anyway, there was no point in negotiating with unsympathetic, arrogant, reactionary rulers.

The co-operators had different views. They pointed out that many Hindus had expressed their disapproval of the Lucknow Pact. The Congress now was in principle once again opposed to separate electorates, and was carrying on an energetic propaganda to this effect in Britain. It was therefore all the more important that they acquainted the Commission of their stand. Communal representation was essential to Indian order and progress. The Hindus could not be trusted to the extent of surrendering the safeguard of separate electorates. Hindu domination was the real danger and Muslim security could only be assured by co-operating with the British and putting their views before the Commission.

THE NEHRU REPORT

In his speech in the House of Lords announcing the appointment of the Statutory Commission, Lord Birkenhead, the Secretary of State for India, had explained why no Indian had been put on the panel and had asserted that no unanimous report could be expected from a body with Indian representation. A Hindu Report or a Muslim Report or a Sikh Report was possible, but not an Indian Report. This was resented by the Congress leaders, who immediately decided to draft a constitution to confound the India Office. An All Parties Conference had already been convened to bring together all the non-co-operating groups. Now this Conference appointed a committee to draw up a constitution for a free India. Motilal Nehru presided over these deliberations and gave his name to the Committee as well as to the Report. There were two Muslims among its seven members—Ali Imam and Shoaib Qureshi. Both were unrepresentative of their community and had long ago been repudiated by the great majority of the Muslims. Shortly afterwards the Sikh member of the Committee was disowned by the Sikh League. The Indian Christian Conference also dissociated itself from the principles adopted by the Report on the protection of minorities.

The Nehru Report, published in August 1928, made the Hindu–Muslim rift final and irrevocable. It recommended a fully responsible system of government in which the majority would be sovereign. Muslim electorates were to be immediately abolished.

Muslims were shocked into unity. Members of the Central and provincial Assemblies found it impossible to agree with the Report.[1] The Aga Khan doubted if any serious-minded person could imagine the Muslims accepting such 'degrading' proposals.[2] The United Provinces All Parties Muslim Conference repudiated the Muslim members of the Committee.[3] In March 1929 the two groups into which the Muslim League had been split came together in opposition to the Report. When, on 12 March 1929, the Report was debated in the Indian Legislative Assembly all the Muslim members, including Jinnah, who had sided with the Congress in boycotting the Simon Commission, rejected it in such strong terms that *The Times* correspondent reported: 'The solidity of Muslim feeling in the Assembly was not unexpected, but certainly disturbing to those trying to represent the Nehru Report as a demand of a united India. Henceforth such a claim must be manifestly absurd.'[4]

On the other side the Congress made the rift irrevocable by not only adopting the Report in its entirety and congratulating the Committee on 'their patriotism and their far-sightedness', but also by giving notice that if the British Government did not accept it by December 1929 the Congress would launch a non-co-operation movement.[5]

There is little doubt that the Nehru Report conferred the real power upon the Hindu majority and envisaged a Hindu *raj*. At least that was the impression it conveyed to the Muslim mind. The Lucknow Pact had been forgotten. The good old

[1] Resolutions of 7 and 10 September 1928, *The Times*, 8 and 11 September 1928.

[2] Aga Khan, 'A Constitution for India: The Nehru Scheme', ibid., 12 October 1928.

[3] *The Times*, 7 November 1928.

[4] Ibid., 13 March 1929.

[5] Resolutions of 3 November and 31 December 1928, respectively; texts in *The Times*, 5 November 1928 and 1 January 1929.

days of the Khilafat were fled, never to return. The unity of the Congress–League scheme was buried deep under the debris of communal riots. Gandhi's emphasis on Hindu–Muslim unity sounded unreal in juxtaposition to his ultimatum to Britain that the non-implementation of the Report would lead to chaos. The fundamental Muslim demand for separate representation—conceded in 1909 by the British and in 1916 by the Hindus—was rejected by the Report and by the Congress in unqualified terms. The Muslims were completely disillusioned, and from 1928 onwards the Congress became all but in name a Hindu body. The Muslims would henceforth look upon it as the arch-enemy of their claims and interests.

In retrospect it is now apparent that the Nehru Report was a blessing in disguise to Muslim nationalism. It united the Muslims as nothing else could have done at that time. All political differences and personal rivalries were hushed. From this moment onwards there was nothing that could be called 'Indian nationalism'. A separate Muslim national feeling had by now grown almost to maturity, though it was not given a name for another ten years.

THE COMING OF FEDERATION

In the meantime the Statutory Commission had finished its labours and the Simon Report was finally published in May 1930.[1] The first volume surveyed the entire Indian problem and the second, published after an interval of a fortnight, set forth the Commission's recommendations for constitutional advance. Historians have lavished much praise on Simon's handiwork and, though sometimes overrated, it is certainly an impressive treatment of an exceedingly complicated problem. In the fullness of its study, the depth of some of its observations, the lucidity of its argument, the realism and reasonableness of its approach, it is a commendable essay at constitution making. Few White Papers have surpassed it in comprehensiveness, authority and practicability. In the first volume may be found one of the most ably reasoned refutations of the claim that India was a 'nation' in the sense in which France or Sweden were nations.

The publication of the Simon Report was followed by three

[1] Cmd. 3568 and 3569 of 1930.

Round Table Conferences convened in London by the British Government to determine the contents of the future constitution on the basis of the Report's proposals. The first met in the winter of 1930–31. The Congress was absent because it insisted that the Conference must not discuss whether India should or should not receive responsible self-government but must shape a constitution on the assumed basis of a free India. All other parties attended and the Aga Khan was elected the head of the total Indian delegation. Most of the work was done through the Federal Structure Sub-Committee and gradually the federal plan took shape and substance.

Muslims went away from the first Conference with the impression that the British Government was more interested in Hindu aspirations than in Muslim apprehensions and that insufficient attention had been paid 'to their wishes and to their power to make these wishes effective'. Ramsay Macdonald's speech at the close of the session, delivered on 19 January 1931, was particularly resented by them as a tactless slight upon their community. They took exception to the Prime Minister's remark that the question of Muslim safeguards was the kind of thing which had better be settled by Hindus and Muslims together.[1] Such attempts had not taken anyone far in the last quarter of a century. In the last resort the British Government would have to intervene, 'to settle, and to stand by some allocation of power and representation' between the two peoples. Muslims were reluctant to make material reductions in their demands in order to support the Hindus in their demand of Home Rule, because they believed that the real aim of the 'old, orthodox Hinduism' was to gain full mastery of the new India. The absence of the Congress had given an air of unreality to the proceedings of the first Conference, and early in 1931 the Labour Secretary of State (Wedgwood Benn) asked the Viceroy, Lord Irwin (later Earl Halifax), to open peace negotiations with the Congress leaders. This was done in February and in March the so-called Gandhi–Irwin Pact was signed which smoothed the way to Congress entry in the second Conference.

[1] Resolutions of the All India Muslim Conference Working Committee of 7 February 1931, *The Times*, 9 February 1931. See also *Empire Review*, February 1931, pp. 83–84.

The second Conference opened in the autumn of 1931. The communal issue was seriously tackled and the Aga Khan, acting as the spokesman of all the minorities, negotiated with Gandhi. But Gandhi, the sole Congress delegate to the Conference, refused to consider any compromise until the Muslims accepted the Nehru Report in its totality. Upon this all the minorities except the Sikhs drafted a joint demand of claims and presented it to the British Government as their irreducible minimum. This was not only a 'Bill of Minority Rights' but also furnished the Prime Minister and his colleagues with an extremely valuable guidance for their own future procedure if the settlement of the outstanding principles between the Hindu minority and five out of six chief minorities was to be left in their hands.[1]

Muslim demands at the Conference were based on the resolutions passed by the All India Muslim Conference at Delhi on 4 and 5 April 1931. In summary they were: residual powers with the provinces; separation of Sind from Bombay; full autonomy for the North-West Frontier Province; reforms in Baluchistan; transfer of power direct to the provinces; separate electorates; special Muslim weightage in all political bodies; constitutional sanction for the enforcement of basic rights; safeguards against communal legislation; adequate Muslim representation in Ministries; proportionate representation in public services; and amendment of the constitution only with the concurrence of the provinces. The real significance of these demands must be realized. The aim was to gain complete control over north and north-west India and then to feel secure and confident that the Muslim's culture and religion would develop and expand and that 'he would protect the scattered minorities of his co-religionists in other parts of India'.[2] Read with Sir Muhammad Iqbal's address to the Muslim League in December 1930 (to which we will refer later) this interpretation of Muslim demands came very near the heart of the matter. Muslim nationalism was coming to the point of demanding a territory for its consummation.

However, the second Conference ended at a dismal note. No

[1] *The Times* (leader), 13 November 1931. Text of the joint claims in Cmd. 3997, pp. 68–73.

[2] *Round Table*, March 1932, pp. 287–8.

agreement was reached on the Hindu–Muslim issue and it was clear to all that the British Government would have to assume the difficult task of arbitration. There were three obvious reasons for the Government to give the final verdict. First, they were morally bound to attempt by unilateral action to resolve the deadlock. Secondly, they were politically committed to see that the process of transfer of power was not arrested by communal bitterness. Thirdly, they were bound by the explicit warning of the Prime Minister himself, given on 1 December 1931, that in case of a deadlock the Government would have to give its own award.[1] The fact was that it was impossible to make any progress in constitution making without first determining the proportion of Hindu and Muslim shares in the proposed legislatures.

The last, and the least important, Conference was held in November–December 1933. The Congress was again absent and most Indians had by now lost all interest in the London deliberations. The broad lines of the coming constitution were now common knowledge and only details remained to be filled in.

The results of the long labours of the three Conferences were collected, sifted and summarized in a White Paper issued in March 1933.[2] It faithfully translated the measure of agreement reached at the Conferences. But the chief Muslim objection was that it created a strong centre. The Muslims urged that the provinces should be granted maximum fiscal, administrative and legislative autonomy. Further, they demanded a slightly increased proportion of the British Indian seats in the federal upper chamber over the one-third they had originally asked for, as no effective means were available for securing the necessary seats among the States to make up the proportion. They also wanted the provincial governments to control the public services adequately.[3]

A Joint Committee of both houses of Parliament was appointed to consider the White Paper. Constitutionally this body was exclusively composed of members of Parliament, but twenty representative Indians from British India and

[1] See *Economist*, 26 March 1932.

[2] Cmd. 4268 of 1933.

[3] Resolutions of the All India Muslim Conference Executive Board of 26 March 1933, *The Times*, 27 March 1933.

seven from the States were appointed as assessors to the Committee. The five Muslim co-optees were the Aga Khan, Sir Zafrullah Khan, Sir Abdur Rahim, Sir Shafaat Ahmad Khan and Sir A. H. Ghuznavi. The Committee was at work from April 1933 to November 1934, and finally reported to Parliament on 22 November 1934.[1] The Report was debated in the House of Commons on 10–12 December 1934, and in the House of Lords on 18 December. The second reading took place in February 1935, and after the third reading the India Bill finally reached the statute book on 24 July 1935.

Never before had the British Parliament taken so long and worked so hard on a colonial constitution. Never before had India figured so prominently and so consistently in *Hansard.* Never again was Britain to lavish so much care and ability on India. For those who had a hand in the making of the 1935 reforms it must have been heart-rending to see in later years their handiwork torn to pieces in India and the pieces cruelly thrown into their faces. History provides no instance of a constitution prepared so studiously and tried so partially and perfunctorily.

The federation set up by the Act of 1935 was the closer rather than the looser type. Hindu unitarianism had prevailed, particularly in the composition of the federal legislature.[2] The Muslims objected to it because, to them, a strong centre meant an increase of Hindu strength. They were also opposed to the central government having the power of interference in the criminal administration of the provinces, as this would have enabled a Congress Cabinet in the centre to paralyse the administration of a Muslim province.[3]

The Muslim League found the federal scheme to be 'fundamentally bad', 'most reactionary, retrograde, injurious and fatal . . .', and rejected it. However, it undertook to work the provincial part of the constitution 'for what it is worth'.[4] The

[1] Parliamentary Paper, H.L.6 (I Part I) and H.C.5 (I Part I) of 1934.

[2] R. Coupland, *India: A Re-Statement,* 1945, p. 144.

[3] William Barton, 'The State and the White Paper', *Empire Review,* January 1934, p. 21.

[4] Resolution No. 8 of the All India Muslim League of 11–12 April 1936, *Resolutions of the All India Muslim League from May 1924 to December 1936*, Delhi, n.d., pp. 66–67.

Congress turned down both the parts of the Act, but decided to contest elections and to wreck the constitution from the inside.

THE CONGRESS RULE

Elections to provincial assemblies were held early in 1937 and the Congress won majorities in eight provinces. But it refused to form governments unless the safeguards incorporated in the Act were suspended and the Governors undertook not to interfere with provincial administrations. This started a controversy as to whether the Congress was or was not justified in making this demand, and as to how far the Governors were right in refusing to exercise a responsibility placed on them by the provisions of the constitution and by the Instrument of Instructions issued to them on their appointment. For our purpose this controversy, though one formally between the Congress and the Government, has much significance partly because the Muslims had accepted the 1935 Act only because it contained certain safeguards and partly because this demand made them suspicious that the Congress wanted to impose a Hindu *raj* on India without any constitutional restrictions on its freedom of action. Already, in March 1937, Edward Thompson, who knew the Congress mind well, had predicted that the Congress would work the constitution so that when, in the summer of 1939, Germany declared war and Britain withdrew her forces from India, it could take charge of the whole country.[1]

This demand was not received kindly by either the Muslims or the British. The Congress was repudiating the authority of the Parliament and jeopardizing the whole edifice of the constitution. Its demand amounted to the plea that the Governors should bargain away the powers with which they had been explicitly entrusted against the contingency of political defeat. The minorities, and especially the Muslims, had accepted the constitution only on the strength of these safeguards and to demand their scrapping at the very opening of the new régime would only increase their apprehensions. Pure democracy postulated that minorities bowed to the will of the majority

[1] Thomas Jones's letter to Lady Grigg of 19 March 1937, see Thomas Jones, *A Diary with Letters, 1931–1950*, 1954, pp. 325–6.

because they had faith in its moderation. As this postulate was absent in India, these powers had been given to the Governors to protect the minorities from oppressive majorities. As Hindus were in a majority in most provinces, it was natural that they disliked the safeguards. It was equally natural for the Muslims to insist on them as they formed a minority in most provinces. No Governor could lawfully contract himself out of statutory provisions: the demand was thus unconstitutional. The reserve powers were an integral part of the constitution and could not be abrogated except by Parliament itself. The Governors could not treat the Congress as a privileged body exempt from the provisions by which all other parties were bound. The precautions so carefully inserted were not meaningless formalities which could be tossed aside under pressure. The Muslim ministries of the Punjab and Bengal had not made any such demand. Why should the Congress be made an exception?

A little later, however, the controversy was silenced by a statement of the Viceroy, Lord Linlithgow, assuring the Congress that the Governors would not use their special powers unnecessarily. The Congress accepted this assurance and took office. But the fact that such a demand had been formulated and pressed by the Congress was, to the Muslims, full of omen. Already, at the Round Table Conference, they had been alarmed by Gandhi's insistence on the Nehru Report. The Congress attitude to the Communal Award was another straw in the wind. Now the demand for doing away with the safeguards was indicative of the Congress's growing ambition to rule India on the principle of majority rule without its essential ingredient of the voluntary acquiescence of minorities.

The advent of the Congress to power opened a new chapter in modern Indian history in more ways than one. For the first time responsible governments were installed in the provinces. For the first time the Congress tasted the heady wine of power. And for the first time the Muslims realized what this meant to them. Some salient features of Congress rule must be mentioned here.

One was that the Congress ministries were accountable, not to the legislatures which had elected them or to the electorates which had given them the mandate, but to the High Command of the party. Strict control was exercised and even in minor matters ministers were obliged to take orders from the Congress Committee. This rigid application of party discipline was aimed at maintaining at all costs the unity of the Hindu nationalist movement.[1] Some likened it to the Nazi machine in Germany[2] and noted how provincial assemblies wilted under local bosses as parliaments in Europe wilted before a Nazi protector.[3] Though the Congress leaders justified this innovation on the ground that the Congress was a nationalist movement fighting for freedom rather than an ordinary political party forming a government, yet this practice was certainly at variance with democratic principles. The 'first true attempt to apply British parliamentary democracy to India at once produced a system which was not recognizably British'.[4] What is even more important, this practice was not in accordance with the underlying assumptions of the 1935 constitution, which had envisaged provincial autonomy as a training ground for self-government rather than as a testing ground for nationalist totalitarianism.

Another feature was the Congress refusal to share power with the Muslims. The Muslim League and the Congress manifestoes issued for the 1936–7 elections were so close to each other that most observers looked forward to co-operative coalition ministries. But the Congress was not prepared to abandon its claim to speak for the whole of India and insisted that the handful of its Muslim members were the only authentic representatives of Muslim India.[5] When the Muslims asked for coalitions, the Congress refused unless the Muslim League merged itself in the Congress machine and ceased to exist as an independent body.

Muslims were quick to recognize the extent and depth of Hindu hostility, and each atrocity perpetrated by Congress

[1] L. F. Rushbrook Williams, 'The Indian Constitutional Problem', *Nineteenth Century*, March 1939, p. 285.

[2] T. K. Johnston (I.C.S. retired), letter to *Manchester Guardian*, 9 October 1938.

[3] George Schuster and Guy Wint, *India and Democracy*, 1941, p. 171.

[4] C. H. Philips, *India*, 1948, p. 133.

[5] R. Coupland, *Report on the Constitutional Problem in India*, Part II, 1943, p. 15.

administrations was recorded, verified and published.[1] Sir Reginald Coupland admitted that there was some truth in these charges, and in 1939 *The Times* India correspondent reported that authority in the United Provinces was disintegrating, that law and order were not being maintained, that administration of justice was being tampered with, that the services and police were losing confidence, that agrarian discontent was spreading widely and that communalism was more rampant than ever. Petty Congress officials were interfering with the police, and the Government had issued a circular asking the district authorities to consult local Congress leaders.[2] A shocking example of Hindu intolerance was given by Sir Michael O'Dwyer, when he quoted a directive issued by the Congress chairman of a Local Board in the Central Provinces to the headmasters of all Urdu schools, which were attended by Muslim boys, to order the students to *worship* (the words *puja ki jawe* were used) Gandhi's portrait.[3] In short, 'there was every sign that the new constitution signified a Hindu *raj*, pure and simple'.[4]

By now it is a commonplace to connect the Congress rule with the emergence of the idea of Pakistan. Such an authority as a former Secretary of State for India, L. S. Amery, believed that it was the conduct of the Congress ministries that had driven the Muslims to separation.[5] What the Congress rule had taught the Muslims without a shadow of doubt was that administrative guarantees, the Governors' Instruments of Instructions and constitutional safeguards were not effective

[1] See *Report of the Inquiry Committee appointed by the Council of the All India Muslim League to inquire into Muslim Grievances in Congress Provinces (Pirpur Report)*, Delhi, published at the end of 1938; *Report of the Inquiry Committee appointed by the Working Committee of the Bihar Provincial Muslim League to inquire into some Grievances of Muslims in Bihar (Shareef Report)*, Patna, March 1939; and A. K. Fazlul Huq, *Muslim Sufferings under Congress Rule*, Calcutta, 1939.

[2] *The Times*, 27 June 1939.

[3] M. F. O'Dwyer, 'India under the Congress', *National Review*, July 1939, p. 47.

[4] H. G. Rawlison, *The British Achievement in India: A Survey*, 1947, p. 214.

[5] L. S. Amery in *Asiatic Review*, January 1941, p. 85, and in *My Political Life*, Vol. III (1955), p. 109.

protection against the coming of a Hindu *raj* in which they would be relegated to the unenviable position of a permanent minority. One historian of Indian nationalism has concluded that the unexpected accession to power had warped the judgement of Hindu leaders.[1] But this observation does not take into account the fact that the Congress ambition to rule over India singlehanded was at least as old as the Nehru Report, if not older, and till his death Mr. Jawaharlal Nehru justified his 1937 decision to refuse coalition with the Muslim League. Anyway, the Congress rejection of the idea of co-operative living with the Muslims was a fatal mistake which wrecked all chances of a united India and practically ensured a partition on religious lines.

Muslim reaction to the end of Congress rule was indicative of their feeling of extreme disquiet. When the Congress ministries resigned *en bloc* in October 1939, Jinnah called upon his people to observe a Deliverance Day on 22 December to mark the end of tyranny and oppression. This day was widely celebrated, not only by the Muslims but also by those Hindus and Parsees who were displeased with the way the Congress had used its power.[2] Christians and hundreds of thousands of untouchables joined in the demonstrations.[3] This showed most clearly the depth of communal feeling, and even those[4] who termed it an 'unwise action' which postponed the hopes of India's attainment of full nationhood conceded that it was a retort invited by the action of the Congress itself.

The Congress had been voicing a new demand since 1934. This was for the establishment of a constituent assembly elected by Indians to determine and draft the future constitution of the country. Obviously such a body would be predominantly Hindu and therefore incapable of safeguarding Muslim interests. The Muslims were not prepared to see the communal problem solved on a simple majority basis, and the idea of an assembly amounted to just this. No such proposal could be

[1] Sir Verney Lovett in *Quarterly Review*, October 1941, pp. 264–5.

[2] *The Times*, 27 December 1939.

[3] S. Srinivasan, 'Communal Problem in India', *Empire Review*, January 1941, p. 25.

[4] For example, Sir Alfred Watson, *Asiatic Review*, January 1940, p. 65.

contemplated unless the Congress had rid itself of its Fascist aspiration to dominate India.[1] The significance of the Congress demand was that it would have given the Hindu majority the power to impose a constitution on the minorities. What the Hindu leaders did not realize was that any imposition of a constitution that was not voluntarily accepted by the Muslims would lead to disruption and an irretrievable split in the country. But such considerations did not weigh with the Congress which continued to pass a resolution pressing this demand at every annual session. Thus by the end of 1939 'it was widely believed that, if the Congress Government had lasted much longer, communal fighting would have broken out on an unprecedented scale. The idea of a "civil war" had been an almost inconceivable idea so long as British rule was still unquestioned, but now many Indians were saying that it was coming'.[2]

TOWARDS SEPARATION

As was said above, the Muslim reaction to Congress rule may be said to have led directly to the idea of Pakistan. The more the Congress insisted on a strong centre and a constituent assembly the more it raised Muslim apprehensions. In 1935–7 Jinnah had opposed the 1935 constitution because it did not concede responsible government at the centre. After the experience of Congress rule in the provinces he had to revise his views. Provincial autonomy was a substantial concession towards responsible government, and he had seen how the Congress had used this power. If similar responsibility was extended to the centre, Congress rule over the whole of India would be unavoidable. And a Congress-dominated central government would nullify the autonomy of Muslim provinces. What was the remedy? A very weak centre might have satisfied the Muslims, but the Congress was adamant on a strong federal government. In the face of these possibilities the Muslims refused to have any centre at all. If the Hindus wanted to have a strong centre, let them have it. But then let the Muslims have their own separate centre. This was partition: the Muslim reply to Hindu unitarianism. This was Pakistan: the Muslim retort to Hindu hegemony.

[1] *Observer*, 25 November 1939.

[2] R. Coupland, *India: A Re-Statement*, 1945, p. 187.

It was in December 1930 that Sir Muhammad Iqbal, the poet, delivered his presidential address to the Muslim League annual session at Allahabad. In this speech he said that the principle of European democracy could not be applied to India. Communalism was indispensable to the formation of a harmonious whole in a country like India. The Muslims of India were the only Indian people who could fitly be described as a nation in the modern sense of the word. And then he came to the famous sentence which has earned him the title of the father of the Pakistan idea: 'I would like to see the Punjab, North-West Frontier Province, Sind and Baluchistan amalgamated into a single state. Self-government within the British Empire, or without the British Empire, the formation of a consolidated North-West Indian Muslim state appears to me to be the final destiny of the Muslims at least of North-West India.'[1]

It must be remembered that Iqbal did not argue for a Muslim State, but only for a Muslim *bloc* in an Indian federation. Moreover, Bengal and Assam (the present East Pakistan) did not enter into his calculations. It is grossly misleading to call him the originator of the idea of Pakistan or the poet who dreamed of partition. He never talked of partition and his ideal was that of a getting together of the Muslim provinces in the north-west so as to bargain more advantageously with the projected Hindu centre. It is one of the myths of Pakistani nationalism to saddle Iqbal with the parentage of Pakistan.

In 1932–3, during the sittings of the Round Table Conferences and the Joint Committee on Indian Constitutional Reform, a group of Muslim students in England were evolving another scheme for India. Led by Chaudhari Rahmat Ali, a Punjabi studying at Cambridge, they formed the Pakistan National Movement, which issued its first pamphlet on 'Pakistan' in 1933, entitled *Now or Never*. The essence of the plan was the formation of an independent Muslim State comprising the Punjab, the North-West Frontier Province, Kashmir, Sind and Baluchistan, in complete independence of the rest of India and in close alliance with the Muslim States of the

[1] Long extracts from this address are available in M. Gwyer and A Appadorai (eds.), *Speeches and Documents on the Indian Constitution, 1921–1947*, 1957, Vol. II, pp. 435–40. This sentence is on p. 437.

Middle East. The word 'Pakistan', coined by Rahmat Ali himself, was formed from the initials of the component units—P for the Punjab, A for the Afghan Province (North-West Frontier Province), K for Kashmir, S for Sind, and TAN for Baluchistan—and meant literally, 'the land of the pure' (pak=pure+stan=land). Iqbal's idea of a Muslim federation within a larger Indian federation might or might not have inspired Rahmat Ali, but the latter was at pains to emphasize that his scheme was essentially different from Iqbal's, since it involved the creation of an entirely separate Muslim Indian federation. It is interesting to recall that when the Muslim League representatives appeared to give evidence before the Joint Committee, and were asked if any such scheme existed, they vehemently denied that any responsible Muslim had put forward such a plan and, in so far as the League had considered it, they thought the idea was 'chimerical and impracticable'.[1] In India itself the Pakistan idea did not make any progress at all until after the Muslims had gone through the crisis of Congress rule.

In 1938–9 three other schemes appeared, each trying in its own way to appease the demands of Muslim nationalism. Abdul Latif of Hyderabad presented his 'zonal' scheme; Sir Sikandar Hayat Khan, the Punjab premier, proposed the division of India into seven regional zones; and 'A Punjabi' advocated the formation of five regional federations. None of these favoured a complete separation between the Muslim and non-Muslim areas.

None of these plans, however, met the approval of the Muslim League or captured the imagination of the Muslim masses. The partition of India—clean and complete—was officially adopted for the first time in March 1940, when the Muslim League, fresh from its freedom from the Congress rule, met in its annual session at Lahore and passed the famous Lahore or Pakistan Resolution on 24 March. After reiterating that the scheme of federation embodied in the 1935 Act was 'totally unsuited to and unworkable in the peculiar conditions of this country and is altogether unacceptable to Muslim India', and that the constitutional plan should be reconsidered *de novo*, the

[1] *Joint Committee on Indian Constitutional Reform: Minutes of Evidence*, Vol. 2C, p. 1496.

following important paragraph summarized the Pakistan demand: 'Resolved that it is the considered view of this session of the All India Muslim League that no constitutional plan would be workable in this country or acceptable to the Muslims unless it is designed on the following basic principles, viz., that geographically contiguous units are demarcated into regions which should be so constituted, with such territorial readjustments as may be necessary, that the areas in which the Muslims are numerically in a majority, as in the North-Western and Eastern zones of India, should be grouped to constitute "Independent States" in which the constituent units shall be autonomous and sovereign.'[1]

At long last the Muslims had taken the final plunge and committed themselves to complete separation. Muslim nationalism had come to full maturity and now demanded a territory of its own.

But to imagine that Muslims had never thought—however vaguely—of having a State of their own before 1940 is to misread Indian history. For at least fifteen years prior to the Lahore Resolution the notion, however nebulous, of a separate Muslim *bloc* or alliance or federation had been present in the minds of men. A remarkably large number of British students of Indian affairs noticed these rumblings and recorded them for us. Starting from 1925 and working down to 1939, we find a long line of such observers pointing to the coming of Pakistan.

In July 1925, William Archbold, one-time Principal of the M.A.O. College, Aligarh, foresaw a 'powerful Muhammadan combination in the north-west in alliance with Afghanistan'.[2] In March 1928, *The Times* correspondent in India reported a vision of effective Muslim rule in north India and prophesied a division of the Punjab and the creation of a solid Muslim

[1] Full text of the resolution is included in most collections of documents on Indian constitutional development, but the authoritative original source, from which the above extract is taken, is the Resolution No. 1 passed at the twenty-seventh session of All India Muslim League held at Lahore on 22, 23 and 24 March 1940, *Resolutions of the All India Muslim League from December 1938 to March 1940* (published by the Hon. Secretary, All India Muslim League, Delhi, n.d.), pp. 47–48.

[2] W. A. J. Archbold, 'Some Indian Problems', *Contemporary Review*, July 1925, p. 46.

bloc from Peshawar to the mouth of the Indus. His own comments on this were: 'It does not seem logical, however, or compatible with our avowed intentions towards India to discountenance out of hand a plan which is constructive and contains many elements of a practicable structure.'[1] In December 1928, the *Empire Review* favourably considered the suggestion of breaking up Indian provinces into small units in accordance with ethnic and local sentiment, and thus to allay communal fears. The implication was that at some future date it might be practicable or necessary to merge the Muslim and Hindu areas into some sort of separate *blocs*.[2]

In March 1931, the *Round Table* thought it 'certainly possible' that India might break up, first into a Muslim and a Hindu India, and later into a number of national States, as Europe did after the Renaissance and the Reformation.[3] In June, Sir Theodore Morison, a former principal of the Aligarh College, declared that Hindus and Muslims were not two communities but two nationalities, and envisaged a Muslim national State in the north of India, though he felt that this could not make for peace.[4] In July, the Marquess of Zetland appreciated that a chain of predominantly Muslim provinces stretching across the north-west of India would be 'a basis of great strength and influence' to the Muslims generally.[5] In November, the *Economist* saw the Muslims manœuvring for an effective control of the entire Indus basin, Eastern Bengal and a corridor between the two. With these territories in their hands, it said, the Muslims would hold a large Hindu population in pawn as pledges for the safety of the scattered Muslim minority in other parts of India.[6] In December, similar sentiments were voiced in a debate in the House of Commons when Colonel Goodman thought that the mutual suspicion of Hindus and Muslims was so deeply rooted that it would be generations before either would have any confidence in the other; Sir

[1] *The Times*, 14 March 1928.

[2] *Empire Review*, December 1928, pp. 369–70.

[3] *Round Table*, March 1931, p. 346.

[4] T. Morison, 'The Hindu–Muslim Problem of India', *Contemporary Review*, June 1931, pp. 710–14.

[5] In *Asiatic Review*, July 1931, p. 428.

[6] *Economist*, 7 November 1931.

Alfred Knox saw no hope of the Hindus and Muslims coming into one organic whole; and Sir Henry Page Croft likened India to the whole of Europe, the Indian nation to a 'Russo–European nation' and an Indian mind to a 'Chinese–American mind'.[1]

In 1932 appeared two books by Englishmen of life-long Indian experience, both refuting the arguments of those who pleaded for the existence and future of an Indian nationalism. Sir Reginald Craddock asked that if Norway and Sweden could not keep together, if Ulster and the Irish Free State could not be got to unite, 'how can it be expected that the infinitely greater diversities and divergent racial elements to be found in India could be welded into one self-governing and democratic whole?'[2] John Coatman was even more dogmatic (and prophetic in the bargain): 'it may be that Muslim India in the north and north-west is destined to become a separate Muslim State or part of a Muslim Empire'.[3] In April of the same year, Sir Walter Lawrence acknowledged the existence of many great and well-defined nationalities in India and saw the only hope of natural and healthy growth in their recognition.[4] In August, even the *Manchester Guardian*, an enthusiastic supporter of the Congress creed, realized how utterly opposed to each other were the Hindu and Muslim attitudes to life and how useless were such remedies as Pax Britannica, education and self-government. 'What is there to hope for,' it asked despairingly, 'except that in time the sense of communal allegiance may be translated into a sense of allegiance to India as a whole and the growth of scepticism make democracy practicable?'[5]

In February 1933, G. T. Garratt, a retired Indian Civilian, foresaw as well as feared that within a short period the projected federal government would be faced with a 'strong separatist movement'.[6] In May, Sir Elliott Colvin, another Civilian,

[1] *H. C. 260, 5S*, 3 December 1931, Cols. 1354, 1370–71, 1380–81.

[2] R. Craddock, *The Dilemma in India* (1932), pp. 7–8.

[3] J. Coatman, *Years of Destiny: India 1926–1932*, 1932, p. 376.

[4] Speech at the opening of the Indian Durbar Hall at Hastings on 29 April 1932, *The Times*, 30 April 1932.

[5] *Manchester Guardian* (leader), 8 August 1932.

[6] G. T. Garratt, 'The Third Round Table Conference', *Nineteenth Century*, February 1933, p. 137.

opined that the creation of a feeling of national union between Hindus and Muslims was likely to be a 'matter of a century's duration'.[1] In 1937, when the results of provincial elections had been published, the *Economist* remarked that the provinces could be divided into two simple groups: Muslim India and Congress India.[2] And in 1938 *The Times* added that the differences between the Muslim and Hindu provinces were 'at least as great in fact though not in form as those between the Provinces and the States'.[3] In March 1939, Professor Rushbrook Williams realized the significance of the new Muslim opinion demanding a separate zone and said that it testified to the degree of alarm characteristic of Muslim uncertainty.[4] Simultaneously the *Round Table* recorded that a fresh impetus had been given to the movement for creating 'a so-called "Pakistan"' of the Muslim provinces in the north.[5] At the same time, Sir William Barton tried to scare the Hindus into co-operation with the idea that the alliance of north India with Afghanistan would recreate the old Muslim menace and that Britain alone stood between Hinduism and their present danger.[6] In June, the Marquess of Zetland, the Secretary of State for India, wrote to the Viceroy of the possibility that Muslim provinces might declare that the safeguards for their community in the federation were wholly unsatisfactory and that they were not prepared to enter the federation. 'I do not see,' he concluded, 'how we could force the Governments of the Punjab or of Bengal to enter the Federation if they were determined not to do so.'[7] Thus by 1939 a partitioned India had come 'into the realm of practical politics'.[8]

[1] E. G. Colvin, 'India—The Longer View', ibid., May 1933, pp. 545–6.

[2] *Economist*, 23 February 1937.

[3] *The Times* (leader), 20 December 1938.

[4] R. Williams, 'Indian Constitutional Problems', *Nineteenth Century*, March 1939, pp. 292–3.

[5] *Round Table*, March 1939, p. 362.

[6] W. Barton, *India's North-Western Frontier*, 1939, pp. 297–8; repeated in *Asiatic Review*, July 1942, page 257.

[7] Letter of 27 June 1939, '*Essayez*': *Memoirs of Lawrence, Second Marquess of Zetland*, 1956, p. 251.

[8] N. Mansergh, *Survey of British Commonwealth Affairs: Problems of External Policy, 1931–1939*, 1952, p. 356.

In India, as we have seen, Iqbal had broadcast in 1930 the germs of what could be developed into the idea of a Muslim block. In 1933 Rahmat Ali spoke from Cambridge and gave the world a new name to a State yet in the womb of time. In 1938–9 Latif, Sikandar Hayat and others were seriously talking of zones and regions.

This shows that public opinion, both in India and in Britain, was by 1939 acquainted with this widening schism in the Indian body politic and that the Lahore Resolution, when it came in March 1940, could not have been such an unexpected shock as it is generally made out to be.

Why did the Muslims demand Pakistan? And, why was the demand made in 1940? The Pakistan scheme was a proof of the desperate apprehension with which Muslims regarded the prospect of Hindu domination. Had the Congress formed coalitions in the provinces the already existing fissiparous tendencies might have been prevented from spreading. The policy of the Muslim League in asking for a division of the country was a direct answer to the Congress policy of persisting in a unitary nationalism and in the rule of the majority. All the assumptions on which the Muslim acceptance of the 1935 constitution had been based were destroyed by the working of provincial autonomy in the Hindu provinces. The Hindu demand for a constituent assembly to draw up a constitution for all India proved the last straw. If the Hindus wanted a strong centre and were not prepared to compromise on it, the Muslims did not want a centre at all. If the Hindus believed in the rule of the majority, the Muslims denied that they were a minority. We are a nation apart, they proclaimed, and therefore entitled to rule ourselves. To the objection that the creation of Pakistan would not solve the minority problem, as a substantial Muslim population would still be left in India, they replied that Pakistan would not only safeguard the Muslims left behind in India (on the principle of 'mutual retaliation') but also give self-respect to those who lived within the boundaries of Pakistan.

With the adoption of the Pakistan ideal by the Muslim League in 1940, Muslim nationalism had come into its own. It had taken the Muslims three-quarters of a century finally to decide what they wanted. They had tried everything: a revolt in 1857, friendship with Britain, opposition to the Congress, extremist agitation, co-operation with the Congress, belligerent neutrality, negotiations, appeals and threats. First, as dethroned rulers, they resented the overlordship of the British. Then, as a weak minority, they sought friendship with the governing power. Then, for a time, they made common cause with the Hindus and led the Khilafat agitation. Then, once again, their separatism came to the surface and they fought for communal safeguards. When these safeguards failed to give them the protection they needed or expected the latent nationalism triumphed. The march of history had made a nation of a community. No longer did they eat out their heart in sullen impotence, trusting in the beneficence of the British or the goodwill of the Hindus. To the Congress claim that India was a national State, that it was neither plural nor multi-national, the Muslims answered with the brand-new idea of a separate Muslim nationalism. It was difficult to stage a battle between a minority and a majority; the principle of democracy would ensure the victory of the big battallions. But it was possible to elevate the conflict to the plane of nationalism. India, said Jinnah, was not a national problem at all; it was an international problem and must be solved as such.

THE CRIPPS OFFER

The greatest victory—all the greater because the least expected—of Muslim nationalism came in 1942, when the British War Cabinet accepted in principle the idea of Pakistan. The Draft Declaration,[1] brought by Sir Stafford Cripps to India and published on 30 March 1942, contained a provision whereby any province could stay out of the proposed Indian Union with the right of forming its own independent government. This 'non-accession clause' was a major, if not a complete, concession to the Muslim demand for Pakistan. Though the Muslim League rejected the offer on the ground that the non-accession clause did not go far enough to produce the Pakistan of their dreams, and though Lord Hailey thought that this clause was designed not with a view to creating Pakistan but to impressing on the Hindus the necessity of coming to some

[1] Cmd. 6350 of 1942.

form of terms with the Muslims,[1] the fact remains that within two years of the Lahore Resolution the British Government had officially and publicly accepted the spirit of Muslim nationalism and agreed to its political manifestation—Pakistan. This must have gratified even Jinnah, who was generally a man of incredible optimism. To the Muslims it gave confidence and courage. If the Hindus and the British were cast in the role of enemies to be vanquished before the achievement of Pakistan was possible, one of them had surrendered or at least promised to lay down arms.

Why did the British Government concede the Muslim demand, though British public opinion was overwhelmingly opposed to the idea of partition and called it by such disagreeable terms as disruption, a breach in Indian unity, a barren folly, and so on? Many explanations come to mind. One is that in 1942 the British were fighting with their back to the wall and dared not alienate the Muslims who provided the flower of the Indian Army. Another is that, as Lord Hailey said, the concession was not meant seriously; it was aimed at threatening the Hindus into a compromise with the Muslims. Still another is that the Cabinet decision, which was genuine, was the result of influence exerted by a section of the Cabinet's India Committee which was sympathetic to the Muslim cause and consisted of such persons as Sir P. J. Grigg and Sir John Anderson. Churchill himself might have been favourable to the idea. Still another explanation may be that this clause was inserted to ensure that the Congress (which was violently opposed to Pakistan) would reject the entire plan, thus providing the British with the excuse that India's largest party had turned down their generous offer made in all sincerity in the middle of a grave war. All this, however, is pure conjecture, and we must wait the real reason till official papers are made public or one of the participants in the act is guilty of a revealing indiscretion.

THE MOVEMENT FOR PAKISTAN

One outstanding fact emerges from this uncertainty. Pakistan was now within the realm of possibility. It was no longer the dream of one 'stubborn' leader, but the declared goal of Mus-

[1] *H.L. 122. 5S*, 29 April 1942, Cols. 771–2.

lim India. It might still have been a bargaining counter, but at least people had begun to take serious notice of it. Its realization did not now depend on whether the British looked favourably on it or not. 'It depends solely on what military power the Muslims really possess. If they have enough to hold Pakistan against Hindu opposition, then, even should the British prevent its appearing in the paper constitution, it will be established by the Muslims as soon as the British are gone. On the other hand, if they have not enough military power to hold Pakistan against Hindu opposition, even should the British get it put into the constitution. it would be swept out of existence by the Hindus when the British are gone.'[1]

So the Muslims began to strengthen themselves. They could not have any military power because they were not free. But the Muslim League's organization was improved, its publicity streamlined, its discipline tightened, and its message carried to all parts of India. Gradually it built up its power, prestige and popularity. Jinnah was no longer a Muslim leader. He was now *the* leader, the symbol of Muslim nationalism. As the League grew in stature, Jinnah gained in authority. His name was now bracketed with Gandhi, even by the Hindus. The Viceroy, conscious of Jinnah's strength and his following, now consulted him in all important matters. No longer was Gandhi the sole spokesman for India. No longer was Congress the sole repository of patriotism and nationalism. In practical terms, though without confessing it in so many words, everyone knew that within the bosom of India pulsated two nationalisms— one Muslim, the other Hindu. Some even realized that a conflict between the two was coming and would rip the continent from top to bottom.

Jinnah's task of rallying the Muslims around him and strengthening the League was greatly facilitated by certain Congress miscalculations. After the failure of Cripps's mission the Congress was frustrated. Its bid at controlling India had come to naught, leaving it impatient and bitter. The result was the disturbances of August–September 1942 which Gandhi called an 'open rebellion'. Widespread riots ensued aimed at disorganizing the war effort. The revolt failed but it sent all the

[1] Edwyn Bevan, 'The Congress Enigma', *Spectator*, 21 August 1942, p. 168.

Congress leaders to prison, thus giving Jinnah a rare opportunity of consolidating the League. He stoutly opposed the 'Quit India' demand and considered it an attempt by the Congress to win India for the Hindus: the revolt was as much anti-Muslim as anti-British.[1] At this time some people charged Jinnah with being obsessed with the fear of Congress domination, but the Congress president himself has since confessed that his programme was that as soon as the Japanese invaders reached Bengal and the British withdrew towards Bihar, the 'Congress should step in and take over the control of the country'.[2]

For two years, from 1942 to 1944, when the Congress leadership was in prison, the Muslim League was building itself into a powerful party. An overwhelming majority of the Muslims had by now declared themselves for Pakistan, so that when Gandhi secured his release in the late summer of 1944 he saw no alternative to negotiating with the Muslim League. The way to these talks had been prepared by C. Rajagopalacharia, a front rank Congress leader who alone among the Hindus was advocating a *rapprochement* with the League on the basis of partition. He had argued in a pamphlet, entitled *The Way Out*, that the Cripps offer was a bona fide scheme and a genuine gesture, not a mere attempt at expediency or appeasement, and had made a plea for its revival. But he was ignored in the Congress circles. Later he argued with the leaders, and especially Gandhi, that they should accept the Pakistan proposal and try to reach some agreement with the Muslims. In furtherance of this he prepared a formula in July 1944, known as the C. R. Formula after his initials, which conceded the principle of Pakistan under two conditions: partition would come after the British withdrawal and it would be contingent upon the favourable outcome of a plebiscite of *all* inhabitants of the areas claimed by the Muslim League. The crucial Jinnah–Gandhi talks took place at Bombay in September 1944, but failed to reconcile the differences between the two leaders. The heart of the matter was that the Muslims did not

[1] See Jinnah's statement of 9 August 1942, J. D. Ahmad (ed.), *Some Recent Speeches and Writings of Mr. Jinnah* (1952 ed.), Vol. I, pp. 443–5.

[2] A. K. Azad, *India Wins Freedom: An Autobiographical Narrative*, 1959, p. 73.

trust the Hindus and refused to accept Gandhi's word that partition would be effected when the British had departed. Jinnah wanted his Pakistan then and there, before the British went, and had serious doubts if the Hindus would keep their word when once India was free and Congress sat in the seat of authority.

The talks failed but brought some solid advantages to the Muslims. By the simple fact of agreeing to meet Jinnah as the representative of the Muslims, the Congress had tacitly abandoned its claim to speak for all India. It now acknowledged the Muslim League as a power with which terms must be made. Further, the sharpness and depth of the differences between the two peoples were revealed. No longer could the Congress take shelter behind the pretence that no communal problem gnawed at India's vital parts and that all was well. Jinnah had won a clear victory by getting Gandhi to recognize Pakistan. This also gave wide publicity to his two-nation theory.

Next year another attempt at reconciliation was made, this time by the Government, when all political leaders were summoned to a conference at Simla by the Viceroy, Lord Wavell. The idea was to discuss the formation of an Executive Council (entirely Indian except for the Commander-in-Chief) from amongst the Indian parties 'in proportion which would give a balanced representation of the main communities, including equal proportion of Muslims and Caste Hindus'.[1] The attempt failed because Jinnah not only wanted parity between the Muslims and the Hindus (which was conceded) but also insisted on the Muslim League nominating all Muslim Councillors (which was not conceded).

Two significant features of the Simla Conference deserve emphasis. The Congress accepted the principle of parity between Hindus and Muslims. This was a remarkable development, for it implied Hindu acquiescence in the two-nation theory. Hindus and Muslims were two separate nations coming together for the time being in the Viceroy's Council. The Muslims were not a minority to be fobbed off with a meagre representation. They were a nation entitled to equality with the other nation, the Hindus. It may be, as the Congress later

[1] Cmd. 6652 of 1945.

argued, that it agreed to parity as a political expedient; but to Muslims as to many others the Congress gesture conveyed the impression that at last the Hindus had accepted the existence of a separate Muslim nationalism in India.

Jinnah's demand that all Muslims appointed to the Council should be from among the Muslim League was in logical consistency with his claim that he represented Muslim India. The Congress rejected this claim on the ground that its acceptance would reduce it to the position of a sectarian organization representing the Hindus alone. Though, as we will see later, the Congress then did not represent more than 1 or 2 per cent. of Indian Muslims, yet it was loath to give up its appearance of speaking for all communities and creeds.

Jinnah had another objection to the procedure adopted for the formation of the Council. He contended that the principle of Pakistan should be recognized first, because if the League once accepted the Wavell plan 'the Pakistan issue will be shelved and put in cold storage indefinitely'.

For the Muslims the all-important question was whether the acquisition of a few seats on the transitional Council would or would not bring them any nearer to their final goal—Pakistan. Jinnah did not think so and therefore attached more importance to the ultimate solution than to the quota of Councillors. And, even if all Muslim Councillors were his nominees, they would still be in a minority of one-third in the entire Council. For, in addition to the Congress, the Council would also contain the Sikhs, the Christians, the Parsees, and the Scheduled Castes. And all these non-Muslim minorities shared at least one common sentiment with the Hindus—independence with unity and not with partition. Fundamentally, therefore, the Muslims would always be in a minority, in spite of the parity. Thus mere parity was not enough. When once Hindu–Muslim parity had been conceded, Jinnah raised his price. He wanted, by implication, a parity not between Muslims and Hindus but between Muslims and all others put together.

On the face of it, this was an absurd claim; but not really so if we remember that he was claiming to speak for a nation, not for one of the many communities. If the first premiss of his argument was granted—that Muslims were a nation—the conclusion followed with the certainty of truth. And there is no doubt that the clash at the Simla Conference was essentially between the irreconcilable claims of two nationalisms. The quarrel over the number of seats to be allotted was a sham battle fought over phantom issues. The real point in question was: who would succeed Britain when foreign rule was gone. The issues were not really as small as they seemed. They turned fundamentally on two conflicting claims—'that of Congress to be a national party representing all Indians throughout the country, irrespective of sect, and that of the Muslim League, which demands Pakistan and the government of the predominantly Muslim regions by a Muslim Government. It is the difference between an India united, in spite of internal divisions, and partition.'[1]

The Simla parleys had failed, at least in part, because both the Congress and the Muslim League had made claims about their representative standing unsupported by electoral evidence. No general election had been held since 1934 to the central legislature and since 1937 to the provincial assemblies. The balance of political power had shifted so much in ten years that new elections were imperative. In August 1945, therefore, the Viceroy announced that elections to all legislatures would be held in the following winter.

These elections were fought on the simplest conceivable programmes. The Muslim League contested to vindicate two elementary points: that it represented all Indian Muslims and that Pakistan was the only solution of the Indian problem. The Congress was equally clear-headed and uncompromising. It stood for independence without partition and claimed to speak for all India, including Muslims. In short, the election was fought on the crystal-clear issue of Pakistan versus *Akhand* (united) Hindustan.

The outcome was illuminating as well as confusing. The Muslim League won every single Muslim seat in the central legislature and 428 out of the possible 492 in the provinces. The Congress had similar success in the 'general' (non-Muslim) constituencies. The voters had given their unmistakable verdict and this was illuminating. But the deadlock deepened. One party had stood for united India and received strong support. The other had called for a divided India and had also

[1] *Spectator*, 6 July 1945.

received strong support. The cleavage was as deep as ever, and this was confusing.

In a final effort to reconcile the irreconcilables the British Government sent a Cabinet Mission, headed by the Secretary of State himself, to India in March 1946. After a round of unfruitful conversations with politicians of all schools, the Mission set forth its own scheme on 16 May.[1] The Mission plan ruled out Pakistan as a practical possibility and instead suggested a loose Indian Union arranged in three tiers—provinces, sections and the federal centre.

The Mission was 'greatly impressed by the very genuine and keen anxiety of the Muslims lest they should find themselves subjected to a perpetual Hindu majority', and found this feeling too strong and widespread to be allayed by 'mere paper safeguards', yet proceeded to argue against the Pakistan plan. It would not solve the minority problem as it would include in the Punjab and Bengal large Hindu minorities, and to divide these provinces would be 'contrary to the wishes and interests of a very large proportion' of their populations. Transport, postal and telegraphic systems were established on the basis of a united India and to disintegrate them would 'gravely injure' both parts of India. The case for a united defence was even stronger. The Indian States would also find it difficult to associate themselves with a divided India. Finally, the geographical fact that the two halves of the proposed Pakistan State were separated by hundreds of miles was an additional factor, i.e., in favour of one India.[2]

Jinnah reacted sharply to these arguments and regretted that the Mission had rejected Pakistan which was 'the only solution of the constitutional problem'. He found it even more regrettable that it had thought fit to advance 'commonplace and exploded' arguments and to resort to special pleading couched in deplorable language, which was calculated to hurt

[1] Cmd. 6821 of 1946.

[2] Ibid. It was said that the decisive consideration that led the Mission to reject the Muslim claim was military, and that Field-Marshal Sir Claude Auchinleck had given his opinion that, from the point of view of strategy, Pakistan was an impossible conception; see *New Statesman*, 25 May 1946, p. 372. Sir Claude confirmed this in a conversation with the author in London in 1960.

the feelings of Muslim India. It seemed to him that this was done simply to placate the Hindus.[1]

Some of the arguments given by the Mission were sound; some were not. But the important thing to remember is that the Mission's plan fell short of the separate State which had become the main plank of the Muslim League platform and had secured 85 per cent. of Muslim votes in the elections. Perhaps, Cripps, the author of the plan, tended to over-rationalize problems and to underestimate emotional forces. In this he had much in common with the Congress leaders. The strength of Muslim nationalism was grossly underrated by both. Because Pakistan was logically indefensible, therefore the Muslim demand for it was not irresistible.

It is not a part of our story to narrate the complicated and bewildering events of 1946–7, when each of the parties first accepted, then rejected, then again accepted (with vital reservations) the Mission plan. Suffice it to say that the plan failed either to win honest acceptance in India or to solve the constitutional problem to the satisfaction of anyone.

With the coming of the year 1947 the turn of events reached a new tempo. In April and May the new Viceroy, Lord Mountbatten, seemed to have come to the conclusion that partition was unavoidable. Widespread Hindu–Muslim fighting, the Congress–League rift within the rickety interim Government, Hindu claims about the sovereignty of the Constituent Assembly, and Muslim insistence on Pakistan, combined to persuade him of the necessity of a surgical operation. Towards the end of May he conveyed to the British Government his opinion that some form of division was inevitable. Whitehall at once concurred. The partition plan[2] was finally made public on 3 June and was immediately accepted by all parties.

The British Government had now recognized the inevitability of partition. The Hindus were ready to accept it under protest. The Muslims were not displeased, though they did not like the consequent operation by which the two major provinces, the Punjab and Bengal, were divided. The Sikhs were resolutely opposed to the creation of Pakistan but found it politically wise to acquiesce.

[1] Quoted in Cmd. 6835 of 1946.

[2] Cmd. 7136 of 1947.

Chapter 3

THE POLITICAL FACTOR

In the last two chapters we saw how the idea of a Muslim nationalism in India took birth and gradually developed into a force which could only be appeased by a division of the subcontinent into two national States. This chapter is intended to put flesh on the dry bones of the narrative so that the story of the growth of a national spirit comes alive. The historical recital will become meaningful if we take up for analysis some of the factors which played a prominent part in this development.

LOYALTY

The role of Muslim loyalty to the British in the formative phase of nationalism cannot be over-emphasized. During the testing years which followed the Mutiny Muslims were convinced that their only salvation lay in practising loyalty. Sayyid Ahmed Khan foresaw that the Muslim minority was no match for the progressive Hindus and that if it also alienated the sympathies of the rulers its ruin would be complete. He brought forth many arguments from his religious study and social experience in justification of his pro-British attitude. Was Islam not nearer to Christianity than to any other religion? Did the Quran not call the Christians the 'people of the Book' and sanction marriage with them? Did the Muslims not have more in common with the monotheism of Christianity than with the polytheism of Hinduism? In the social field, too, the two God-worshipping creeds shared common ideals and practices. Both abhorred the caste system. Both preached the brotherhood of man. This might have been a conscious or unconscious rationalization of his political views, but there is no doubt that Sayyid Ahmad passionately believed in the desirability, the practicability and the necessity of a Muslim–British understanding. As a Muslim he defended it on religious grounds; as an Indian Muslim he advocated it as a political necessity.

In this mission of bringing the two peoples together Sayyid Ahmad was helped by certain British writers who shared his views without necessarily sharing his motives. Sir William Baker, for example, brought out the close affinity between the two religions. 'Believing in the same God, and yielding nothing in respect for Christ, the Muslim among all oriental races is the nearest to what a Protestant terms Christianity.' He went further and suggested a close alliance between the English and the head of the Muslim religion which would arouse the entire Muslim world to a pitch of enthusiasm that could hardly be understood by the English phlegmatic nature.[1] Similarly, an English journalist found the spectacle of an Englishwoman—she was referring to Mrs. Annie Besant—allying herself with Brahmanism as curiously unpleasant, and discovered in Hinduism much that was revolting to a refined and fastidious taste.[2] There were not many who held such strong views or expressed them in such virile language. But these sentiments strengthened the hands of those among the British who wanted to be kind to the Muslims and heartened the Muslims who were soliciting such attention.

With the foundation of the Congress in 1885 the Muslims redoubled their efforts to prove their loyalty in the fear lest the Congress might be accepted as representative of all educated Indian opinion. They were alarmed by the Congress and what it stood for, for any advance towards self-government would imply their relegation to the position of an insubstantial minority. During the Hindu unrest of 1905–11 they supported the Government unstintedly. Such deeds of faithfulness did not go unnoticed in Britain, and in 1906 *The Times* wrote a long leader commending their policy and sharing their apprehensions. 'If the forces of disaffection are active in India,' it said, 'then it would be folly to estrange a great people who are on many grounds our natural supporters. It would be dangerous

[1] W. Baker, 'Reflections on India, 1880–1888', *Fortnightly Review*, August 1888, p. 225.

[2] Lilian de Gruyther, 'An Important Indian Institution', *Empire Review*, November 1904, p. 369. See also Henry Crossfield, *England and Islam*, London, 1900.

to us, because of the hostile influence which may react on India from the outside world. . . . Our only course is to show them plainly that they have not lost our sympathy, and that we value their loyalty and intelligent co-operation as much as ever. . . . If the Indian Government does not retain the confidence of loyal minorities by a steady and consistent policy, then, in words recently quoted in our columns, we may expect to see the Muslims "either join the Congress or set up a second agitation of their own".'[1]

Printing House Square was not the only quarter where Muslim fidelity was appreciated. It was then generally realized that Muslim policy had obvious benefits for England and her future. Gertrude Bell, the famous 'Arab', reported from India that the loyalty of Islam had not wavered in spite of a tendency among the British, resulting from the indifference born of security, to regard it with less than favour; in spite, moreover, of a growing anti-foreign spirit which had been visible in other parts of the Muslim world.[2] Another writer was in favour of encouraging the Muslims 'who are loyal to us lest they should be disgusted at our partiality and also turn against us'. 'Minorities deserve honour, and loyal minorities deserve double honour.'[3]

The greatest test of Muslim constancy came in 1911 when the partition of Bengal was annulled. Muslim India was shocked and some leaders talked of extreme measures in retaliation. But even in this crisis the tradition of years prevailed and the leading Muslims, though irate and indignant, instructed their followers not to agitate against the decision.[4] The Aga Khan issued a similar appeal. It is true that shortly afterwards the entire course of Muslim politics was changed by circumstances, of which the 1911 decision was one, but prominent 'loyalists' like the Aga Khan and Ameer Ali continued to tread the path of co-operation.

[1] *The Times* (leader), 26 September 1906.

[2] G. Bell, 'Islam in India—A Study at Aligarh', *Nineteenth Century*, December 1906, pp. 900–901.

[3] J. A. Sharrock, 'Some Misconceptions about the Unrest in India', ibid., September 1909, p. 375.

[4] For example, Nawab Viqar-ul-Mulk in the *Aligarh Institute Gazette*, 20 December 1911.

After the 'disloyal' interlude of the Khilafat agitation the old habit reasserted itself and at the Round Table Conference Muslims were by and large so co-operative as to evoke from the Congress the charge of being reactionaries and toadies. In 1931, just before the opening of the second Conference, a striking article appeared in the *Empire Review* which, along with the Aga Khan's letter to the Deccan Muslim League quoted above,[1] stands as a faultless testament of Muslim loyalty. What made it even more remarkable than the Aga Khan's letter were the antecedents of the author. It was written by Maulana Shaukat Ali, one of the famous Ali brothers who had led the Indian Khilafatists into a most virulent campaign against the British. Now as a delegate to the Conference, he made a stirring appeal for Muslim–British friendship. 'We both need each other,' he said. 'We would grasp that hand and Islam would stand with Britain, a good and honourable friend, a brave fighter and a staunch ally. . . . Should Hindus and Muslims live together a thousand years, there is no chance of the two cultures merging into one. This is adamant, bedrock fact, which cannot be glossed over. No settlement that ignores this can be of any value. Wise administration requires knowledge of the psychology of races. . . . At the back of every Muslim mind, based on our experience of the last fifteen or twenty years, is the fear that Great Britain had lost something of her old virility, and that she may let us down. . . . We want no handicaps against anybody, including the British.'[2]

What lay behind such expressions of loyalty? What was the philosophy of loyalty, if there was at all a coherent thought behind it? In the preceding pages we have referred to some of the motives that underlay this line of action. To recapitulate and add some more:

Item. It was the safest course of action for a minority which was backward and helpless. Either it could co-operate with the Hindus, which it would not, or it could keep on good terms with the rulers. To alienate both the present and the future rulers would have been folly without any mitigation.

Item. It may be a paradox but the fact is that the Muslims,

[1] See *supra*, Chapter 1.

[2] Shaukat Ali, 'An Appeal from the Muslim World to the British People', *Empire Review*, November 1931, pp. 307–9.

universally characterized in the West as a militant body of persons, were the only constitutional-minded group in India. Without trying to resolve this paradox (which may have been a reaction to the unsuccessful Mutiny), we must notice that the Congress was, except in the first few years of its existence, an agitational organization. *Satyagraha* was often made out to be a peaceful movement, but to break the laws of a country is unconstitutional, whether the deed is done by making women volunteers lie down on the road or by leading a band of mutinous riflemen. In fact, *Satyagraha* is more deadly, for it is planned and cold-blooded, than open agitation which may be due to the heat of the moment. Muslims were not fond of agitating, first under the influence of Sayyid Ahmad Khan, and later under that of Jinnah, both of whom were, for different reasons, almost constitutional martinets.

Item. The Muslims were sceptical both of the genuineness of the Hindu agitation and of the likelihood of its successful outcome. The agitation was for greater democracy, which to the Muslims meant greater oppression. The agitation was also unlikely to achieve its end because the rulers were strong and because all India was not on the side of the agitators. It was thus both unwise and useless to stand with the agitators and incur the displeasure of the Government.

Item. Most Muslims appreciated the fairness with which they had been, or were being, treated by the British. Between the Hindus and the British they chose to trust the latter, and on the whole found that this policy paid dividends.

Item. In terms of religion, the Christian rulers were closer to the Muslims than were the idol-worshipping Hindus. As religion was a vital factor in the awakening of their nationalism, this affinity tended to throw the Muslims on the side of the British.

Item. In social matters, again, the Muslim found himself in more congenial company among the British. The two could, and did, intermarry, interdine and intermix in society without disagreeable taboos. With the Hindu one was always on one's guard against breaking some caste restriction or polluting a Brahmin household. Social mixing is as essential an ingredient of friendship as aloofness is a creator of misunderstanding.

Item. One ingenious explanation of Muslim loyalty has been suggested. The argument runs thus: The Muslims had an aloofness and a grave, stern dignity which safeguarded them against the insulting treatment of the British. Insults to them did not rankle as they did in other cases with effects which recoiled on British heads. They either retaliated or held aloof, and in any case they refused to be humiliated or to surrender their pride or self-respect. They were remarkably free from servility, in contrast with the Hindus; and they entered scarcely at all into rivalry with other Englishmen or Hindus. Their conservatism kept them from it, and it appeared that they regarded Englishmen and Hindus as fitted by Providence for the discharge of functions with which they themselves did not care to meddle while they pursued the even tenor of their own way.[1] Interesting and very intriguing indeed, but, alas, only partially true.

Item. The educated among the Muslim community were greatly influenced by English literature, history, philosophy and art. This intellectual and academic deference paved the way to political loyalty.

Item. The British ruled the country and held power and patronage in their hands. The Muslims, as a minority, wanted safeguards, and the British alone could grant them.

Item. The Islamic injunction of obeying the ruler of the time may have weighed with a section of the Muslims. Disobedience to those in authority is not permitted unless the ruler interferes with the religious rites of the Muslims.

Item. Britain was the greatest 'Muslim' Empire in the world and had intimate relations with all independent and semi-independent Muslim States. As the Indian Muslims formed a part of the world Muslim community it was in the fitness of things that they remained on good terms with Britain.

IMPERIAL PRIDE

The Muslims had come to India as conquerors and had established an empire which lasted for hundreds of years. This factor moulded their outlook in many ways.

If we compare the Muslim invaders of India with the British invaders we find one momentous difference. The Muslims came as alien conquerors but permanently settled down in

[1] W. B. Oldham, *Imperial and Asiatic Quarterly Review*, July 1911, pp. 64–65. He was a retired member of the Indian Civil Service.

India. Unlike the British, they did not come from a 'mother country' to which they could look back or return after doing their spell of duty. They made India their home and this revolutionized their outlook. They became a part of India just as India made them a part of herself. The interaction had good results as well as bad. It precluded the possibility of a Muslim withdrawal, and this distinguished Muslim rule in India from such recent phenomena as the behaviour of the British community in India or the French *colons* in Algeria or the Belgian miners in Congo. It also made the Hindus realize that they could not get rid of the Muslims, for by the passage of time the latter had ceased to be an alien element of the Indian population. But at the same time they remained a distinct group and refused to become a part of the Hindu tradition of the country.

Imperialism and pride go hand in hand. In India their imperial past produced among the Muslims a pride bordering on vainglory. Pride is not altogether a bad thing, but when it survives the actual loss of power it creates an unhappy state of mind both in the individual and in the community. When Muslim hegemony was gone and real power lay with the British, the Muslims would not, could not, forget that they had once ruled over the land. Their reaction was bitter and truculent. The bitterness led to the 1857 revolt which was an unsuccessful attempt at regaining the past glory. It failed and this added frustration and humiliation to the bitterness. The truculence gave birth to an anti-British and anti-Western feeling, which kept the Muslims away from everything associated with the mainstream of progress. They were reluctant to learn the English language, to send their children to Government schools and to prepare themselves for public services under the British. They clung to their old ways of life and lost a golden opportunity of advancement. The Hindus, on the contrary, made the best use of the chance offered and captured the public services which a little before had belonged to the Muslims.

During this period the Hindu and Muslim mentalities exhibit a strong contrast. The Hindus had been a subject race for centuries. They were trained in the art of honouring the rulers. When a Muslim sat on the throne of Delhi they learned Persian and cultivated the graces of a Mughul court life. When a British Viceroy governed the country they learned English with equal diligence and entered Government service with alacrity. For them the change was not revolution: one alien invader had succeeded another. For the Muslim the change was cataclysmic. He had been dethroned and he did not find it easy to reconcile himself with the new times. He retracted into his shell and brooded and brooded, and this did not help. It was perhaps a natural result of the disaster that had overtaken him, but it was also very stupid and played havoc with his future. He never made up for what he had lost in those years and later paid a terrible price for this shortsightedness.

The Muslim pride *vis à vis* the British thus led to insularity. This pride *vis à vis* the Hindus led to an anti-democratic movement. The Hindus were the subject race. The Muslims were, or had been, the ruling race. How could the quondam masters now allow themselves to be ruled by *ci-devant* slaves? The Hindus were in the majority, but that did not mean that they should be the sole rulers of the country. The principle of the rule by majority did not, could not, apply to India. Democracy was therefore rejected, completely, finally, irrevocably. No matter what happened the majority shall not rule the country. If a choice had to be made British imperialism was preferable to native 'democracy'. Gradually this line of thought led to the concept of nationalism. If democracy was a good thing—as all the world said it was—and if India also was one day going to get it, well! then, India was not a nation. It was a continent and contained many nations. Anyway, the Muslims were a nation by themselves and would rather live in a poor, small, Muslim country than in a rich, large, Hindu subcontinent.

Another result of the imperial pride was that Muslims refused to be absorbed by Hindu polity. Brahmanism had a magnificent record of accepting into its fold diverse races and creeds which had travelled to India in search of food or fame. Islam was the first foreign element which refused to be merged with the Brahmanical polity. It was too individualistic, too stern, too personal a religion to be so treated. It was a way of life, not a mere set of spiritual principles. Further, it had come to India primarily to spread its own creed, not to compromise with the heathen. This prevented a merger or even a concord.

It was the first failure of Hinduism and the first fundamental breach in the Indian spiritual tradition. Islam established itself as a distinct entity and retained this separateness till the end. A nation could not be born when two opposing forces of such magnitude confronted each other like desperate gladiators.

One by-product of Hinduism–Islam conflict was that the Brahmanical polity was saved from dissolution, or at least from adulteration.[1] Had the two religions come together and borrowed from each other, both would have lost something of their uncompromising purity. But the lack of such contact safeguarded Brahmanism from what the orthodox might have considered pollution.

EXTRA-TERRITORIAL ATTACHMENT

Though the Muslims had made India their home and had no intention of leaving it, yet they 'looked *out* of India to recover their Arab, Turkish or Persian roots and retain their pride as former conquerors'.[2] Their origin was alien and so were many of their associations and attachments. The future of the Ottoman Empire was an important determinant of Indian Muslim politics from the last quarter of the nineteenth century right up to 1923. European ambitions of controlling Muslim countries like Persia and Egypt agitated Muslim India and conditioned her attitude to Britain, the only European country they knew at first hand. As we will see in a later chapter, events in Turkey, Persia, Egypt, Morocco and Palestine have at times decisively influenced the course of Muslim politics in India.

Religion was the most obvious—in fact the only—bond between Muslim India and the outside Islamic world. After losing their hold over their own country, the Indian Muslims derived a vicarious satisfaction from the existence of other Muslim States in the world. It gave them confidence and a feeling of security. They felt that they were not alone and friendless in a hostile world. Every addition to the community of Islamic nations was an accretion to their strength. Every Muslim country which went under was a blow to their self-

[1] S. Dutt, *Problem of Indian Nationality*, 1926, pp. 72–73.

[2] A. de Reincourt, *The Soul of India*, 1960, p. 296.

respect. Though they could do little for their co-religionists outside India they never made a secret of their sympathy for them. On one occasion, at least, their sympathy went beyond formal expression and achieved a signal success. The Khilafat agitation in India and the endeavours of the Aga Khan and Ameer Ali (of course combined with the success of Turkish arms) forced the British Government to replace the Treaty of Sèvres with that of Lausanne.

In contrast to this extra-territorial affinity of the Muslims, the Hindus had no problem of divided loyalties. They had their roots in India. Their religion, their traditions, their history, their philosophy, their literature—all were Indian in origin, mould and character. There were no Hindu States outside India to divert their attention from their nationalist struggle. They did not derive their political sustenance from Hindu sovereignty in foreign lands. They never quarrelled with British foreign policy since no Hindu interests were involved in international diplomacy. And therefore they were justified in taunting the Muslims with extra-territorial loyalty, though there was only a modicum of truth in the charge that the Muslims' lukewarm interest in 'Indian nationalism' was traceable to their pre-occupation with Muslim interests outside India.

But the strength of Muslim concern for the welfare of the Islamic world community cannot be denied. It had serious repercussions on their political activities in India and was, at times, an additional reason for their alienation from the Hindus. Some Hindu leaders successfully persuaded their followers to believe that the Muslims of northern India might one day join forces with the Afghans in overrunning parts of India and founding another Muslim empire in the country. There is no evidence to show that this was ever contemplated, but it is apparent that some Hindus suspected the Muslims of harbouring such designs, and this misunderstanding did not encourage communal amity.

INDIAN NATIONALISM AND HINDUISM

Indian nationalism has long been a Hindu nationalism in essence. The Marhatta Empire, the earliest manifestation of this spirit, was 'a revival of Hindu nationalism against Muslim domination'.[1] The earliest political bodies were Hindu even in their designation, e.g. the Sarvajanik Sabha of Poona and the Mahajana Sabha of Madras. In 1882 Dyananda founded the Cow Protection Society which was an overt anti-Muslim gesture. In the beginning the Arya Samaj was more religious than political, and it was one of its foremost leaders, Lala Lajpat Rai, who frightened the Hindus of the Punjab with the bogey of an Afghan invasion to be staged in connivance with the Indian Muslims. *Swadeshi,* the chief instrument of the Indian National Congress, was essentially a Hindu concept.[2]

Bankim Chandra Chatterjee, the Bengali Hindu novelist, who is generally claimed as one of the fathers of Indian nationalism, assiduously propagated anti-Muslim ideas in his popular stories. He consistently treated the terms 'Hindu' and 'Indian' as synonymous; there is no 'context in which "Indians" can be interpreted to include "Muslims"'. Muslims were not Indians, they were aliens. They are always cast in the roles of oppressors and tyrants. The references made to them are 'frequently sneers of contempt'. And 'there are no grounds for supporting this attitude to be other than the result of a deliberate choice'. The nationalism founded and nurtured by such writers could only be Hindu in character and content. This brought a new unity and national pride to the Hindus, but it 'instilled in the minds of the Muslims suspicion and fear, which subsequent events did not eradicate'.[3]

Nothing illustrates the Hindu character of Indian nationalism more faithfully than the agitation carried on against the partition of Bengal between 1905 and 1911. Religion and politics were combined in a good measure. Surendranath Banerjea, the foremost Congress leader of the time, wrote to one of the leaders of the agitation to organize a religious ceremony, such as *shakti puja* (worship of the Hindu goddess *shakti*) and

[1] John Cumming (ed.), *Modern India,* 1931, p. 22.

[2] For a description of the religious meaning and implications of *swadeshi* see C. F. Andrews, *Mahatma Gandhi's Ideas* (1930 ed.), pp. 118–30.

[3] T. W. Clark, 'The Role of Bankim Chandra in the Development of Nationalism', in C. H. Philips (ed.), *Historians of India, Pakistan and Ceylon,* 1961, pp. 439–40.

kali puja (worship of the Hindu goddess of destruction, *kali*) and to have a *swadeshi katha* or *jatha* (a boycott meeting). 'Give a religious turn to the movement,' he said, 'and as for the Muslims, if you can get them to your side, why not have a *waz* (an Islamic sermon) followed by *swadeshi* preaching.'[1] A Bengali Hindu, who was a young man when Bengal was partitioned, confirms that *swadeshi* was essentially a movement of Hindu revival.[2]

Apart from the general trend of the age, the one person who was responsible for the inoculation of Hindu orthodoxy into the nationalist movement was B. G. Tilak. Very early in his career he discovered that a religious fervour must be induced into politics if a missionary enthusiasm was to be created. 'He knew that once the spiritual and religious springs of India's great past were revitalized the greatness and glory of her future were assured.'[3] He idolized Shivaji, the Marhatta chieftain who had murdered the Muslim general, Afzal Khan, through deceit. He established anti-cow killing societies to stop Muslims from sacrificing cows on Eid-uz-Zuha. He appealed to the people to turn out all foreigners from India, and he included the British as well as the Muslims in that category.[4] He certainly succeeded in making the nationalist movement strong and potent, but at the same time alienated all Muslims.

When the Dacca Anushilan Samiti was first proscribed in 1908 for its seditious activities, more than a dozen copies of the Gita (the Hindu Bible) were found among its effects, and it was found that regular Gita classes were held there. Members of the Society were required to take oaths with a sword and a copy of the Gita on the head.[5] At the height of the agitation Sir Valentine Chirol visited India and found, in every Government office and in every profession, that Hindus were banding themselves together against their few Muslim colleagues. On Muslim refusal to join the *swadeshi* movement, words had

[1] Quoted by V. Chirol, *Indian Unrest*, 1910, p. 341.

[2] Nirad C. Chaudhuri, *The Autobiography of an Unknown Indian*, 1951, p. 226.

[3] D. V. Thamankar, *Lokamanya Tilak*, 1956, pp. 315–16.

[4] G. T. Garratt, *An Indian Commentary*, 1928, p. 129.

[5] Lord Ronaldshay, *The Heart of Aryavarta*, 1925, pp. 125–126.

been passed round in all big cities among the Hindus not to deal with Muslim shops and not to trade with Muslim merchants. Where Muslims were excitable the Hindus challenged them so that intervention by British troops should lead to the shedding of Muslim blood and thus drive the Muslims themselves into the agitation.[1]

The Bande Mataram song was a Hindu revolutionary poem, occurring in Bankim Chandra Chatterjee's novel *Ananda Math* (*The Abbey of Bliss*), which invoked divine assistance against the Muslims and the British and roused the people to drive both out of India.[2] This song, obviously distasteful to the Muslims, was made a sort of a national anthem by the Congress and was sung not only at all its meetings but also at the opening of legislative assembly sessions in the Hindu provinces when the Congress was in power during 1937–9. Despite Muslim protests it continued to be the Congress song till 1947.

Many impartial observers can be quoted in evidence of the Hindu character of the Congress. A former Governor of the United Provinces called it the political organ of orthodox Hinduism.[3] It made its appeal to Hinduism and worked for a Hindu India.[4] Muslims rejected Gandhi's ideas because he based the development of India on the cultural background of Hinduism and Hindu ideology. He took some of the religious terms of Hinduism and gave them a political meaning, so that 'political doctrines were clothed in the phraseology of spiritual conceptions'. Nationalism was presented in a Hindu garb when the ultimate gaol was named *Ram Raj*, the golden age of Hinduism.[5] The hold of orthodox Hinduism over the Congress was brought out when Mrs. Besant and Gandhi were turned

[1] V. Chirol, *Indian Unrest*, 1910, p. 121.

[2] An ex-Civilian characterized it as 'an appeal to the lower instincts and ideals of Hinduism in its most demoralizing aspects', Sir J. D. Rees, *The Real India*, 1908, p. 175.

[3] Lord Meston, 'India Today and Tomorrow', *Nineteenth Century*, March 1932, p. 310.

[4] E. G. Colvin, 'Trial and Error in India', *Fortnightly Review*, February 1932, p. 214.

[5] L. S. S. O'Malley (ed.), *Modern India and the West*, 1941, pp. 97–98, 106.

out of the Congress the moment they insisted on social reform and the abolition of untouchability.[1]

Well-known Hindu writers have admitted that Hinduism was the bedrock of the nationalist movement. From the end of the nineteenth century onwards, says K. M. Panikkar, Indian nationalism had two aspects—the one political, the other religious.[2] The nationalist movement was 'religionized' and was treated as a 'transcendental philosophy' rather than a 'mere political programme'. The basis of this philosophy was that 'there is a great Power at work to help India' and that the nationalist leaders were only acting on its bidding. In the words of a historian of nationalism, this politico-religious philosophy was 'meant to give the nation clear ideas about the conception of freedom'.[3] It stressed Hinduism and defended it as 'the symbol of Indian nationality'.[4]

Evidently such a nationalism, because of its Hindu roots and Hindu outlook, could not appeal to the Muslims. Of course, there were a few Muslims in the Congress and, for a time, it also attracted large Muslim groups. But that was owing to peculiar circumstances, which we will discuss later. Most of the groups which acted in liaison with the Congress or shared its ideals took care to retain their individuality. For instance, the Red Shirts, the Ahrars, the Momins, and the Jamiat-ul-Ulama, were independent political parties, existing in their own right, and never merged with the Congress. It is necessary to emphasize that they shared only the Congress's political objective, i.e. independence from the British, and not the underlying nationalist philosophy. To the masses of the Muslims the Congress never presented a programme which could win their allegiance. The presence and influence of a handful of Hindu liberals did not suffice even to enable it to save appearances. Altogether Hinduism was far too deeply imbedded in the Congress either to be explained away by its leaders or to be ignored by the Muslims

[1] See Lord Meston, *Nationhood for India,* 1931, p. 80.

[2] K. M. Panikkar, *Indian Nationalism,* 1920, pp. 15–17.

[3] I. N. Topa, *The Growth and Development of National Thought in India,* 1930, pp. 160–61.

[4] Frederick Hertz, *Nationality in History and Politics,* 1944, p. 139.

Principally, there were three ways in which the Hindus, or the Congress, could have dealt with the Muslim problem: toleration, discrimination, coercion. The Congress might have treated the Muslims on an equal footing, tolerated their existence, acknowledged their separate status and honestly tried to meet their wishes. This is how Britain and, to some extent, the United States have dealt with their minorities. But the Congress refused to adopt this method. Again and again its leading figures denied the very existence of the Muslim problem, blamed the British for creating this rift, and right up to the end ignored or grossly underestimated the strength of Muslim feeling.

Discrimination is another method of dealing with minorities. They are tolerated, but only as an undesirable nuisance. They are permitted to carry on their functions, but only under handicaps. In political terms, they are not given full rights. Socially they are made to labour under serious disadvantages, like inferior schools, special institutions, separate working rights and segregated quarters. This is characteristic of the South African Government in relation to the black population. This was also characteristic of the Ottoman Empire in relation to its European and Arab minorities. The Congress practised discrimination, particularly when it was in office in the provinces.

The third method is plain coercion, whereby the will of the majority is imposed on the minority. The Congress used this method when, for example, it ordered the use of Hindi in place of Urdu, or opened the legislative proceedings by the singing of Bande Mataram, or obliged the Muslim students to worship Gandhi's portrait, or lay down the Wardha scheme of education. Politically, it tried to override the wishes of Muslim legislators by ignoring the opposition and by getting its will imposed on the provinces through laws passed on the strength of brute majority.

The Muslims feared that in a united India they would be confronted with discrimination and coercion, and this was the principal factor behind their demand for a separate State. They did not trust the Hindus, and where there is no trust there is no co-operation, and where there is no co-operation there is no national spirit. It is in this sense that the Congress is to be held responsible for the creation of Muslim nationalism and, ultimately, of Pakistan.

To express the same thing in a different way, we may say that the Congress was too Westernized. It was not true to the spirit of Indian culture which has always striven to absorb, rather than alienate, foreign elements. In the long course of Indian history many streams of race and sect have flown in from outside and gradually found a place in the waters of the Ganges and the Jumna. The Huns, the Sakas, the Parsees and many others became a part of India and lost their cultural and political identity. But not so the Muslims. One reason for this was their large number. Another was the nature of their creed —militant, stern and individualistic—of which India had no precedent. Still another was their membership of the world community of Islam. But above all the failure was due to the Hindu determination that the rule of the majority must prevail. The separate personality of the Muslim community was not respected. Nor was a *modus vivendi* fashioned whereby it could be led into co-operation and ultimately perhaps into absorption. Instead, the Congress altogether denied its existence and at times tried to destroy its individuality. But the result was the opposite of what was expected. The community became a nation and an affected nationalism burst into two opposing nationalisms. A policy of toleration, even of amiable neutrality, might have achieved different results.

HINDU-MUSLIM RIFT

Though the Congress and most Hindus denied the existence of the communal problem in India, the problem remained and, in the end, created an unbreakable deadlock. Unpleasant realities could not be wished away by verbal denials.

Hindus and Muslims were only kept together by the bayonets of the Pax Britannica. So deep-rooted and universal was the alienation that in Ludhiana, in the Punjab, Muslims petitioned the Lieutenant-Governor for Englishmen to replace the Hindu personnel of the administration, and in another town they erected an arch for His Honour with the inscription: 'For God's sake save us from the rule of our fellow-countrymen!'[1]

[1] J. D. Rees, *The Real India*, 1908, p. 193.

No more impartial witness can be called than Ramsay MacDonald, who was not only a friend of the Congress but was actually invited to preside over one of its annual sessions. He found Indian nationalism shot through and through with Hinduism. 'No Muslim can enter its Holy of Holies, where politics are transfigured by the presence of gods into religious faith, and where the struggle for civic-freedom is transformed into the worship of the Hindu genius.'[1] An American visitor of the same period found the Hindus and Muslims locked in a 'deathless antagonism', and the equilibrium maintained only by the virile, fighting qualities of the Muslims. 'It is a far distant day,' he wrote wistfully, 'that will witness the final unification of the jarring elements of the Indian population. India as a nation is as yet the most shadowy of dreams.'[2] It was, in fact, widely realized that the continuance of British rule in India was owing to the fact that the Hindus and Muslims were disunited.[3]

In 1908 G. K. Gokhale, the Congress leader, told Wilfred Scawen Blunt that Muslims were all against the Congress and would constitute a danger in any reconstruction of India on a national basis, because, though much less numerous and less rich, they were united. Blunt asked him if his (Blunt's) appealing to the Muslims to join the Congress would do any good, but was told that it would not.[4]

Sometimes it is said that the Hindu–Muslim problem was of late growth and that the two peoples had been peaceably living side by side for a thousand years. But this overlooks the fact that Muslims had come to India as conquerors and that as long as they occupied that position the Hindus dared not show their enmity. When they ceased to be the rulers the antagonism burst out. And with the passage of time, as the immortality of British rule came to be doubted and the prospects for self-government became brighter, the Hindu–Muslim rivalry increased. The greater the advance towards democracy the

[1] J. R. MacDonald, *The Awakening of India*, 1910, p. 105.

[2] Theodore H. Boggs, 'England's Problem in India', *Yale Review*, February 1909, p. 402.

[3] Edward Dicey, 'Islam in Fermentation', *Empire Review*, August 1906, pp. 22–23.

[4] W. S. Blunt, *My Diaries* (1932 ed.), p. 635.

brighter the hopes of the Hindus and the deeper the fears of the Muslims. The more sanguine became the hopes of the Hindus and the more freely they quoted the Hindu philosophy as the basis of *swaraj*, the greater the apprehension of the Muslims that independence would 'end in merely exalting the horn of Hinduism'.[1]

The distance which separated the Hindus and the Muslims from each other in politics came out in full gravity at the Round Table Conference. All delegates were united on one demand, that India be given her independence. But beyond that not a single item of agreement was visible. Each delegate had, as the *Manchester Guardian* nicely put it, a dual role. 'He is a Nationalist longing for the time when India has self-government, believing that the time has now come for her to have it; and he is a Hindu or a Muslim eager to do the best he can for his own religion. As Nationalists the delegates are at one; as Hindus and Muslims they are rivals, suspicious and afraid of one another.'[2] The Conference failed, not because the British were wicked imperialists who wanted to keep India always under the yoke, but because, as Lord Birkenhead once remarked, 'all the conferences in the world cannot bridge the unbridgeable'.[3]

The spirit of Muslim separateness was admitted by the Congress itself in a curious provision in its constitution which, while allocating the seats for the All India Congress Committee prescribed that 'as far as possible one-fifth of the total number of representatives shall be Muhammadans'.[4] In as late as 1946 a semi-official history of the Congress confessed that Hindu–Muslim unity was as yet a dream.[5]

It seems that the Hindus and Muslims of Indian origin carry their differences with them even after leaving their country behind. In South Africa, for example, even today

[1] V. Chirol, *India*, 1926, p. 293.

[2] *Manchester Guardian* (leader), 18 December 1930.

[3] Quoted in Birkenhead, *Frederick, The Earl of Birkenhead: The Last Phase*, 1935, p. 246.

[4] See R. Coupland, *Report on the Constitutional Problem in India,* Part I, 1942, p. 46.

[5] Satyapal and P. Chandra, *Sixty Years of Congress: India Lost, India Regained*, 1946, p. 381.

Hindus and Muslims do not belong to one party. Hindus belong to the Congress party (no relation to the Indian National Congress) and Muslims to the Indian Organization.[1] Similarly before 1947 in Britain there was the London Muslim League which was affiliated to the All India Muslim League, and there was the British Congress Committee which acted under the supervision of the Indian National Congress. In the United States also there used to be an India League which was materially a Congress organ in the new world.

WHO REPRESENTED THE MUSLIMS?

In logical consistency with their claim that there were no Hindu–Muslim differences the Congress leaders continued, almost to the end, to insist that the Muslim League did not represent the Muslims of India. The Congress, they said, was the spokesman of all that was vocal in India, and the few Muslims who opposed it were reactionaries and hangers-on of imperialism. Even in its early years, Allan Hume, the founder of the Congress, was severely critical of all those who doubted the all-inclusive character of the organization, and called them 'fossils', 'wanting in understanding' and 'time servers' who hoped to be paid for their opposition to the Congress. He did not believe that the Muslim opposition represented genuine feeling: it was inspired by mischievous bureaucrats who wanted to create an artificial counter-agitation.[2] This line of argument became the standard pattern of Congress reaction to Muslim politics.

But facts told a different tale. Only a handful of Muslims chose to join the Congress, and on the whole Sayyid Aḥmad Khan's advice was heeded.[3] Between 1885 (when the Congress was founded) and 1894 the number of Muslim delegates to its annual sessions indicated the extent of Muslim participation. In 1885 there were 2 Muslims among a total of 72; in 1886, 33 out of 436; in 1887, 81 out of 607; in 1888, 221 out of 1248; in 1889, 254 out of 1889; in 1892, 87 out of 625; in 1893, 63 out of 867; and in 1894, 20 out of 1163. In 1902 it was reported that Muslims were not only abstaining from countenancing the

[1] G. H. Calpin (ed.), *The South African Way of Life: Values and Ideals of a Multi-Racial Society*, 1953, p. 85.

[2] W. Wedderburn, *Allan Octavian Hume*, 1913, pp. 71–73.

[3] See, for example, *The Times*, 19 and 26 December 1887.

Congress, but were contemplating the formation of a Muslim organization which would, among other things, hold aloof from the Congress.[1] One contemporary observer noted that all Muslims stood contemptuously aloof from this Hindu organization.[2] Still another found that Muslims did not support the Congress but identified themselves with the British rather than the Hindus.[3] A large number of Muslim organizations, the chief among whom was the Central National Muhammadan Association, publicly denounced the Congress and refused its invitation to send delegates to its annual meetings.[4]

Some of these reports may have been biased or exaggerated. And some Muslims were undoubtedly with the Congress and even contributed their quota to its presidentship, viz., Badruddin Tyabji and M. R. Syani. In fairness it must be said that the Congress was not exclusively a Hindu body; and it certainly represented a vast majority of the politically minded educated Indians. But the point is that it was predominantly a Hindu body and therefore failed to win Muslim support. On purely democratic grounds, therefore, it could not be said to speak for India. Take India and Europe-less-Russia as close approximations, and then: 'Now, let us suppose that there came to Marseilles from various parts of Europe some hundreds of persons answering to the description the Indian delegates give of themselves, i.e., "appointed either by open public meetings or by a political or trade association". Let us suppose further that these people, though strongly opposed by large numbers of their countrymen, called themselves the representatives of various peoples of Europe and entitled themselves "European-National Congress", and then let us ask if the title would be considered a legitimate one. . . . Would not an assemblage so constituted be more properly termed a debating society than either a National Congress or a spontaneous Parliament?'[5]

1 'Current Events in India', *Empire Review*, February 1902, p. 54.

2 W. S. Lilly, *India and its Problems*, 1902, p. 242.

3 John Morrison, *New Ideas in India during the Nineteenth Century*, 1907, p. 144.

4 For a list of such bodies see Leslie Smith, 'The Congress and Modern India', *National Review*, April 1889, p. 207.

5 Robert H. Elliot, letter to *The Times*, 28 September 1888.

With the partition of Bengal and the ensuing agitation the Congress became even more unrepresentative of the Muslims, and it was not till the Khilafat period that it could, with justification, claim the allegiance of a majority of Muslims. But here we must recall the fact that during these years of violent anti-British feeling it was not a question of belonging to the Congress or to the Muslim League but of fighting out the Khilafat issue with Britain. Both the Congress and the League stood squarely for greater self-government and for Khilafat. But still the Indian Khilafat Committee was an independent body, though it was given full support by both the nationalist organizations. The Muslims were then with the Congress in the same sense in which the British were with the French in the Second World War. The Congress did not represent the Muslims; it supported them so completely that for a time all differences were sunk in united opposition to the British.

With the passing of the Khilafat agitation the brief honeymoon was over and antagonism burst out once again—this time with redoubled fury and with no prospects for another reunion. The Nehru Report put a seal on this unfortunate discord and peace never returned to India. The Congress civil disobedience movement of 1930–31 was a purely Hindu campaign, which the All India Muslim Conference declared to be an attempt by the Hindu majority to acquire dominance over the minority communities in India.[1] The Round Table Conference only deepened the gulf and the scene was set for the incubation of separatism.

In the 1937 elections, the first held under the 1935 constitution, the Muslim League won only 103 out of a total of 482 Muslim seats. But the remaining seats were not won by the Congress but by other Muslim parties or groups. Out of a grand total of 1,711 seats the Congress won only 762; which means that the Congress could speak for less than half the total number of voters. Further, out of a total of 1,289 non-Muslim or 'general' seats the Congress won only 736; in other words the Congress did not represent more than a bare majority of even the non-Muslims.[2]

[1] *India in 1930–1931*, 1931, p. 77.

[2] Figures taken from *Return Showing the Results of the Elections in India, 1937* (November 1937), Cmd. 5589.

The Muslim League had done poorly because of bad organization and lack of unity among the Muslims. But nearly all Muslim seats had gone to Muslim parties. The Congress had so little confidence in its appeal to the Muslims that it contested only 58 out of 482 Muslim seats and won only 26 of these.[1] It is hard to understand how, in light of these figures, the Congress still claimed to represent the Muslims.

The Congress was said to have polled about 15,000,000 out of a total of 35,000,000 votes, and thus was a minority party in India.[2] It had come up against difficulties in finding Muslim candidates. In the United Provinces, the home of the Congress and the Nehrus, only one Muslim was elected on the Congress ticket, and he was returned from the special university constituency under joint electorate. The Muslim president of the United Provinces provincial Congress Committee was defeated. With the exception of the North-West Frontier Province the Congress had performed badly in all Muslim provinces. The election results confirmed that the Congress 'held Hindustan only, with an unfortunate stress on the first two syllables'.[3]

The election result was a rude shock to the Muslim League. The satisfaction that the Congress had won only twenty-six Muslim seats was soured with the thought that the Muslim community was a house divided against itself. The League now concentrated on remedying this and on building up its strength. So successful was this determined effort that in February 1938 the *Manchester Guardian* correspondent in India was able to report that the Muslims 'have rallied round Mr. Jinnah in such numbers that the Congress has been compelled, much against its inclinations, to recognize the necessity of dealing with him as their accredited leader'.[4]

There was no looking back now and the League continued to win nearly every by-election with monotonous regularity. Between 1937 and 1945, there were 77 by-elections in the provinces, out of which the League won 55, Independent

[1] R. Coupland, *India: A Re-Statement*, 1945, p. 154.

[2] A. R. Barbour, letter to *Manchester Guardian*, 23 September 1942.

[3] P. Lacey, 'Deadlock in India', *Nineteenth Century*, July 1937, p. 105.

[4] *Manchester Guardian*, 19 February 1938.

Muslims 18, and the Congress only 4. Between 1934 and 1945, there were 18 by-elections in the centre, out of which the League won 11, Independent Muslims 5 and the Congress only 2. If in 1937 the Congress had, on its electoral reckoning, represented about 5 per cent Muslims, by 1945 it did not speak for more than 1 or 2 per cent of Muslim India.

In light of these figures it is difficult to sustain the assertion that the Congress represented the Muslims or that Pakistan was the demand of only a minority of Musalmans. Those who argued, under Congress pressure, that the Congress should be accepted as the mouth-piece of India and its demands should be conceded, were shutting their eyes to the situation that would have developed if Muslim opinion had been ignored. They mocked the two-nation theory, overlooking the fact that it was the declared belief of the Muslim League. They abused Jinnah, forgetting that he held a mandate from the largest Muslim party to act on its behalf. They protested against the Muslim veto on constitutional advance, without realizing that there were 90 million Muslims in India. They persisted in the demand that Muslims must accept democracy as understood in the West, without foreseeing that this would lead to political strife and civil war.[1]

By reiterating again and again that it represented all India the Congress made it harder for the Muslims to share its ideals. By declaring repeatedly that there was only one brand of nationalism in India, the Congress brand, it forced the Muslims to proclaim themselves as a separate nation. Such claims created fear and hatred in the Muslim mind. And hate and fear are potent ingredients of militant nationalism. To break the monopoly of the Congress the Muslim League proffered its own brand of nationalism. To start with, this might have been done to spite the Congress. But pretence becomes conviction as its roots go deeper.

'DIVIDE AND RULE'

One of the stock arguments used by the Congress and all other parties in support of their thesis that Hindu–Muslim rift was unimportant and superficial was that of 'divide-and-rule'. The argument was short and sharp. All Indians were like brothers

[1] See India correspondent's dispatch, *The Times*, 22 January 1941.

unto each other. There were no differences among them. In particular Hindus and Muslims were good to each other and had only occasional, minor tiffs. But a rift had been created between them. The British were the villains of the piece. To achieve their selfish, sordid end they had divided the Indians into religious groups and sided sometimes with the one and sometimes with the other. This helped to prolong the tenure of British rule and kept the Indians quarrelling among themselves rather than fighting for independence.

From this proposition flowed many lines of thought. One was that the British usually favoured the Muslims against the Hindus and instigated the former to oppose every advance towards self-government. An extension of this allegation was that the Simla Deputation had been inspired by the British and that the Muslim League had come into being through official machinations.

Another was that Hindu–Muslim rivalry could not cease unless the British withdrew. Gandhi was fond of tracing the origin of the communal problem to the presence of the 'third party' and of declaring that as soon as the British left peace would prevail and amity would return to this stricken land.

It was also said that the 'divide-and-rule' policy was useful to Britain in so far as it enabled her to plead, in the international field, for the necessity of her presence in India—not in British interest but in the interest of India. If the British left India would be riven by a deadly civil war. Therefore they must stay until the advance of education and the training in self government had created at least a semblance of unity.

All Hindu and several British writers and politicians argued in this fashion, and millions of words have been written and spoken to prove the validity of the argument. But some substantial facts were ignored in this partisan disputation. Britain did not put the Muslims into India, and therefore did not *create* the minority problem. And there is no evidence to prove that separate electorates were imposed upon the Muslims against their will or without their asking for them. Nor can anything be brought forth in support of the charge that Lord Minto or other British officials stage-managed the establishment of the Muslim League. It is true that the Hindus condemned separate electorates in unmistakable terms during 1906–12; but it is also true that they voluntarily agreed to them in 1916. It is true that the Congress was opposed to the Muslim League and its general policy; but it is also true that it parleyed, negotiated and co-operated with it when it suited it to do so.

There might have been—in fact, there were—some among the British bureaucracy in India who looked amiably at the Hindu–Muslim schism and saw in it an additional prop to their imperial position. It may also be that on some occasions the British official machinery was more kind to the Muslim League than to the Congress. But by no stretch of imagination does that prove the indictment of 'divide-and-rule'. We saw, when we were discussing the nature of Muslim loyalty, that it was in the Muslim interest to be in the good books of the rulers. The Muslims rarely made a nuisance of themselves. On the whole they were 'good' subjects—co-operative, loyal, law-abiding. On the contrary, the Congress thrived on non-co-operation and agitation. If, in these circumstances, the Government tended to lean a little towards those whom it could trust, this could hardly be called a calculated satanic scheme to divide the Indians.

Let us keep before our eyes the elementary fact that the British were in India as imperialists. Foreign rulers are not generally pleased with refractory subjects, and when their supremacy is in jeopardy they are apt to use a heavy hand. By the same logic, it heartens them to find that a section of the subjugated people is, so to say, on their side or at least not on the side of the rebels. The Muslims were in a minority, and minorities always find it wise to maintain good relations with the ruling power. Thus the Muslim was thrown into the arms of the British by circumstances, and the Hindu did not like it and attributed it to British devilry or to Muslim reaction or to both. He did not realize that it was at least in part his own fault if the Muslim chose to ally himself with the foreign ruler rather than with fellow-Indians.

Hindu–Muslim antagonism was not merely religious or political, but was a clash of two separate and distinct civilizations. The incompatibility of the two peoples was certainly not the creation of the British.[1] It may be that on occasions the British profited by this immense breach in Indian unity; they would have been more than human if they had not. But that does not amount to the assertion that they divided and ruled. Indians divided themselves and let the British rule over them.

[1] I have been able to find at least one Congress confession on this point; there may be more. Delivering his presidential address to the Calcutta Congress session on 29 December 1928, Pandit Motilal Nehru said, 'Nor is the Government solely accountable for all the communal differences which have contributed a dark chapter to the recent history of our times.' K. M. Panikkar and A. Pershad (eds.), *The Voice of Freedom: Selected Speeches of Pandit Motilal Nehru*, 1961, p. 52. Motilal Nehru was the chairman of the committee which drafted the Nehru Report, in which the immediate abolition of separate Muslim representation was strongly recommended.

Chapter 4

THE RELIGIOUS FACTOR

RELIGION has been, since time began, a powerful nexus between individuals and groups. Communal solidarity and national unity have often sprung from religious roots. There is no civilization today which does not bear the impress of some religion. The life of the modern 'secular' man is moulded by his religious beliefs in more ways than he consciously realizes. In the Orient religion plays a paramount role and the following pages will, after some general remarks, describe the impact of religion on the problem of nationalism in India.

RELIGION AND NATIONALISM

History proves that religion is an essential element of nationalism and exerts a decisive influence on the national life of a people. One student of nationalism has gone to the extent of laying down that national States are 'political church organizations', that national consciousness is a religious concept, and that one is a German or an Italian, just as one is a Catholic, a Protestant or a Jew.[1] This is obviously an extreme view and few political scientists will accept it, even if he is taken to have used the word 'religion' in its widest and most catholic sense of general belief or philosophy of life.

But it is no exaggeration to say that many a nascent nationalism has thriven on a religious background, just as many a religious struggle has won the day by clothing itself in national drapery. In Europe it was the Reformation, essentially a spiritual stirring of the mind, which ushered in the era of modern national States. One important way in which religion helps nationalism is the supernatural authority that it imparts to the necessity of solidarity. All people must come together, for God wills it and His mission cannot be accomplished without

[1] Rudolf Rocker, *Nationalism and Culture,* trans. R. E. Chase, 1937, p. 202

such unity. In many cases a reference to Divinity has been a potent instrument in welding a heterogeneous people into a nationality.

Religion is also serviceable as a symbol, apart from being a sanction, of unity.[1] It provides an additional source of pride to the national group. It vouchsafes confidence and courage, particularly when other national bonds lack strength.

Numerous examples can be given to illustrate how often religion has moulded nationalism and served as a foundation for a nation. Modern Greek nationalism is largely a product of the Greek Church. It was the Orthodox Church which saved the Greeks during the Middle Ages and the early part of the modern age, and finally enabled them to become an independent nation.[2] It was the Kirk which made Scotland a nationality and it is Calvinism which has 'made the genius and the character of Scottish nationality'.[3] The Roman Catholic Church played an important part in the Spanish Civil War. In Italy Mussolini could not have succeeded without the friendship of the Church. In the colonization of the New Hebrides Islands the missionaries of France and England have been potent rivals for the control of the islands. The close tie between religion and nationalism may also be seen in Japanese Shintoism, Jewish Zionism, Irish Catholicism, Indian Hinduism, and Burmese Buddhism.

National churches have frequently aroused nationalism, and in a country where different nationalities live side by side, the weaker national group often uses its religion as a 'defence mechanism',[4] like Islam in India, Buddhism in Ceylon and Catholicism in Prussian Poland.

Mazzini is a very good example of a leader arousing national fervour through a religious appeal. His soul was permeated with a mixture of religious ethics and national-political aspirations. 'God and the People' was his slogan, for to him the

[1] See Frederick Hertz, *Nationality in History and Politics,* 1944 (3rd imp. 1951), p. 122.

[2] Ernest Barker, *National Character and the Factors in Its Formation* (rev. ed. 1948), pp. 151–2.

[3] Ibid., p. 152

[4] The phrase is Hans Kohn's, see his *The Idea of Nationalism,* 1944, p. 15

nation was 'a religious concept which he strove to confine within the frame of a political church'.[1]

Religion also affects national character and habits. Catholic nations exhibit traits different from those of Protestant ones. The impact of Calvinism is different from that of Lutheranism. The Scottish Kirk united the Scots and separated them from the English. Similarly, religion can be a unifying or a dividing factor, depending upon a nations's historical development. Where the authority of the national State was firm and strong, as in Holland, England and Scotland, the religion of the majority of the people became a part of the Establishment, thus adding to the unity of the country. Where, on the contrary, political authority was weak and wavering, as in Germany, no religion attained the privileged position of a national institution, and this heterogeneity worked as a divisive force.

Religion also builds up civilizations and moulds cultures. French nationalists, like Charles Maurras, have emphasized and appreciated the role of the Catholic Church in giving to France the glory of which they are justly proud. Some Frenchmen regard only a Catholic as a true compatriot. Similarly, German nationalists extolled Protestantism and attributed to it the greatness of the German nation. Even England, the renowned home of toleration, has not been free of such discriminatory bias. Not many years ago, Dean Inge could write: 'It is impossible to converse long with a Catholic without being conscious of an insurmountable barrier; and if we consider what this barrier is, we find that we cannot confidently appeal to those instincts and moral traditions which are the common heritage of all English people.'[2] Fifteen years later H. G. Wells, that disappointed prophet of a new age, rendered this judgement: 'You can no more trust a devout Catholic in your household and in your confidence than you can risk frankness or association with a Nazi spy. Never will the devout Catholic be really frank with you. Always there will be a reservation; always the priest will be lurking in the background. . . . To marry a Catholic is only half a marriage, and your children will be only half your own. And manifestly if you do business

[1] Rudolf Rocker, op. cit., pp. 59–60.

[2] William Inge, *England*, 1926, p. 68.

with Catholic shops, if you subscribe to Catholic charities, if you entrust your children to Catholic teachers, you are helping to sustain a hostile campaign against the candid life.'[1]

Inge's ideas may be slurred over as the cynicism of the 'Gloomy Dean' and Wells's diatribe may be dismissed as misplaced orthodoxy. Anyway, it is open to doubt if such views really reflected English opinion. But what is important, in our context, is to remember that if such thoughts could be expressed, even by a small minority, in one of the most homogeneous and sophisticated countries of the world, it is naïve to be surprised by the acerbity existing between the Hindus and Muslims in India, particularly if we recall that Hinduism and Islam are, unlike Catholicism and Protestantism, not two species of the same religion but two distinct creeds with not a single attribute in common.

HINDUISM AND INDIAN NATIONALISM

The history of India is 'fundamentally the history of the Hindu people.'[2] The earliest Hindu chroniclers of Rajputana referred to their enemies as *Asuras*, the traditional foes of the Aryan gods, thus indicating the depth of their hatred.[3] The idea of Hindu patriotism was mystical in its conception. The fatherhood was not important. The mother-earth was deified. Patriotism was a duty towards God, and was subordinated to 'immutable spiritual laws and to the religious ideals'.[4]

Early Indian nationalism was both religious (Hindu) and racial (anti-British). It was made a religious personification and an incarnation of Krishna. 'The Lord Krishna,' wrote a nationalist paper, 'is our nationality. . . . Nationalism is a divinely appointed *shakti* (i.e. power) of the Eternal.'[5] Arya Samaj, one of the earliest modern movements in Hinduism,

[1] H. G. Wells, *Guide to the New World*, 1941, p. 35.

[2] Michael Edwardes, *A History of India from the Earliest Times to the Present Day*, 1961, p. 13.

[3] S. Dutt, *Problem of Indian Nationality*, 1926, p. 72.

[4] I. N. Topa, *The Growth and Development of National Thought in India*, 1930, p. 13.

[5] Quoted in L. S. S. O'Malley (ed.), *Modern India and the West*, 1941, p. 750.

which soon became a force in politics, 'opposed Islam with bitterness and Christianity with vigour'.[1]

The Bengali revolutionary movement of the first decade of the present century had a 'renascent Hindu ideology' as its motive and inspiration and held up a 'purified Hindu idealism as a shield against the steady flow of Western influence'.[2] It aimed at the expulsion of the British from India and the replacement of the British *raj* by a Hindu *raj*.[3] At Poona Tilak founded a 'Society for the Removal of Obstacles to the Hindu Religion',[4] and in his list of such obstacles the Muslims and the British came on top.

The entire outlook of the Congress was Hindu. *Swaraj*, the Hindu and Congress term for self-government, meant Hindu rule.[5] In a book which carried a foreword by Jawaharlal Nehru a Hindu author wrote, 'Because of this story [the Ramayana] the whole country has one idea, one inspiration, one personification of manly virtue.'[6] The Hindu character of Indian nationalism is well brought out in S. C. Bose's *My Mission of Life* (Calcutta, 1953), which is a collection of his writings and speeches for the period 1921 to 1929. Throughout this book he uses Hindu words, invokes Hindu gods, quotes Hindu *shiris* (saints) and thinkers, and in general appeals to Hindu instinct. And all the time he is discoursing on Indian politics, not on Hindu religion or philosophy.

But it is the father of Indian nationalism whose pronouncements and ideas conclusively prove the Hindu nature of Congress politics. Gandhi's greatest contribution to modern anti-colonial political technique was non-violence or *satyagraha*. He believed it to be an expression of the Hindu philosophy of life.[7] It was, in his own words, 'the only way to keep Hinduism

[1] T. G. P. Spear, *The Oxford History of India* (1958 ed.), p. 731.

[2] Hirendranath Mukerji, *India Struggles for Freedom*, 1946, p. 84.

[3] Sir Basil Blackett, 'The Economics of Indian Unrest', *Foreign Affairs*, October 1929, p. 44.

[4] R. P. Masani, *Britain in India*, 1960, p. 83.

[5] See J. E. Ellam, *Swaraj: The Problem of India*, 1930, pp. 246–52.

[6] R. S. Dinkar, 'Rama as a Figure in Synthesis', *Samskriti ke Char Aohyaya (Four Phases of Culture)*, Delhi, 1956, p. 70, quoted in Selig S. Harrison, *India: The Most Dangerous Decades*, 1960, p. 97.

[7] S. Abid Husain, *The National Culture of India* (1961 ed.), p. 183.

alive and India undivided'.[1] And he proceeded, 'mass singing of *Ramadhun* [a Hindu hymn] and the beating of *tal* [cymbal] . . . are as much a part of discipline in non-violence as physical drill and training in the use of the arms are that of military discipline'.[2] The theory of *satyagraha* is an old Hindu concept and was enunciated and elaborated long ago by Patanjali.[3] *Ahimsa,* which Gandhi made a potent political weapon, was such an integral part of Hinduism that he himself once declared that if it 'disappears, Hindu religion disappears'.[4]

Similarly, Gandhi described cow-protection as 'the dearest possession of the Hindu heart', the 'central fact of Hinduism' and the 'gift of Hinduism to the world'.[5] Bande Mataram was, as was said above, a rabidly anti-Muslim song which Indian nationalism had owned. To Gandhi it had 'wonderful associations' and expressed 'the one national wish' of India. 'And I should prefer Bande Mataram to *Bharat mata ki Jai,*' he said.[6]

In 1945, one Shriman Narayan Agarwal published his *Gandhian Constitution for Free India,* which urged that the Indian constitution should be framed with the background of Indian political thought and tradition, which were mainly contained in the *Ramayana,* the *Mahabharata,* Kautallya's *Artha Shasthra* and Shunkracharya's *Nitisara.* Drawing upon these purely Hindu sources Agarwal suggested an outline scheme of constitution. To this book Gandhi wrote a foreword saying, 'I regard Principal Agarwal's to be a thoughtful contribution to the many attempts at presenting India with constitutions. The merit of his attempt consists in the fact that he has done what for want of time I have failed to do.'

Nationalism and religion were thus allied in Gandhi's teachings. He found the substance of India's life in Hinduism. Like

[1] M. K. Gandhi, in *Harijan,* 6 October 1946, p. 338,

[2] Ibid., 3 March 1946, p. 26.

[3] Rajendra Prasad's 'Introduction' to Pyarelal, *Mahatma Gandhi: The Last Phase,* 1956, Vol. I, p. vii.

[4] Quoted in Pyarelal, *Mahatma Gandhi: The Last Phase,* 1956, Vol. I, p. 386.

[5] M. K. Gandhi in *Young India,* 8 June 1921, p. 182, and 6 October 1921, p. 318.

[6] Quoted in Hirendranath Mukerji, *India Struggles for Freedom,* 1946, p. 115.

Tilak before him he felt that nationalism needed a spiritual base and provided it from the Hindu dogma. Moral teaching of the Hindu variety went hand in hand with political propaganda, and nationalism was presented in religious raiment. In the political education of the masses he fully utilized his and their religious background, and therefore 'to the majority of Hindus Hinduism meant Gandhi'[1] By using Hindu terms, rather than their rough Western equivalents, he gave a religious colour to his political opinions. It was *swaraj*, not self-government, that he wanted for India. It was *satyagraha*, not non-co-operation, that he commended to the people. It was *ram rajya*, not a golden age, which he set as the goal of Indian nationalism. It was *Bharat-mata*, not the motherland, to which he bore obedience. It was *ahimsa*, not self-control, that he sought to popularize. So he 'sanctified politics',[2] but made it a social version of the Hindu faith. The masses followed him because he was a saint, not because he was a nationalist, 'though it may be that persistent Congress propaganda had indeed spread the first article of the Congress creed that an Indian is first a nationalist and only secondly a communalist'.[3] In the words of a Professor of Social Anthropology, Gandhi was a 'Hindu metaphysician'.[4]

And still it was the Congress claim that it stood for Hindu–Muslim unity and the Congress regret that Muslims neither joined its ranks nor shared its ideals. When the Muslims refused to have truck with such a nationalism, they were condemned for proclaiming their separateness on the basis of religion. They were said to be a backward, primitive people who still took religion seriously and refused to be modern and secular. Enough evidence has been given above to show that Indian nationalism was as much grounded in Hinduism as was Muslim nationalism in Islam. In fact, the latter was more honest, for it did not pretend to be what it was not. Jinnah made it plain that he was a Muslim leading only Muslims and that Islam was the basis of his nationalism. Gandhi said that he was

[1] T. G. P. Spear, *The Oxford History of India* (1958 ed.), p. 836.

[2] Sampurnanda, *Memories and Reflections*, 1962, p. 149.

[3] Sir Ivor Jennings, *Problems of the New Commonwealth*, 1958, p. 17.

[4] Professor T. C. Hodson, letter to *The Times*, 24 January 1941.

an 'Indian' leading other Indians (of all religions) and that secularism was the basis of his nationalism. Of the two, Jinnah might have been, in Western eyes, a 'sectarian', but he was true to his political creed and made no false claims. Gandhi, by claiming to lead all Indians[1] and by condemning the Muslim leadership for uniting religion with politics, exposed himself to the charge of insincerity. On the record of their writings and speeches, Jinnah comes out to be far more liberal and secular than Gandhi.

The religious basis of Muslim nationalism will be discussed later when we come to analyse the two-nation theory.

HINDUISM, ISLAM AND NATIONALISM

Both Hindu and Muslim nationalisms were avowedly based on religion. But it is interesting to find that both Hinduism and Islam are, in theory as well as in practice, incompatible with the philosophy of nationalism.

Hinduism, with its emphasis on caste, encouraged class consciousness rather than national unity. That explains why in Siam and other South-East Asian countries it served as a check against the growth of a national idea.[2] In fact, caste system not only deferred the creation of a national spirit but was so anti-national in essence that it could be justly said that the unity of India had not gone 'beyond that of the unity of caste'.[3]

A caste system does not make for that spiritual unity, liberty, equality and fraternity, which are prerequisites of a healthy national growth. To an orthodox Hindu the caste is (or at least was) far more than the nation is to other peoples. Under the system the Brahman enjoyed more privileges as a matter of course than had been arrogated to itself by any

[1] 'The Congress represents the whole of India', Gandhi's speech before the All India Congress Committee at Bombay on 7 August 1942, quoted in Sampurnanda, op. cit., p. 118. Cf. Jawaharlal Nehru's confession that Congress was in the main a Hindu body, *Glimpses of World History*, 1935, Vol. II, pp. 689–90.

[2] Htin Aung in Philip W. Thayer (ed.), *Nationalism and Progress in Free Asia*, 1956, p. 85.

[3] Bernard Joseph, *Nationality; Its Nature and Problems*, ?1929, pp. 226–7.

race of conquerors, feudal nobility or a dynasty ruling by Divine Right. It was not easy for the high-caste nationalist leaders to talk of liberty and equality without renouncing their own privileges defended by sacerdotal sanctions. It was difficult for the masses to appreciate or comprehend the concepts of freedom and independence without enjoying fraternity within their religious circle.

Hinduism was inconsistent with either national unity or political democracy. 'A ruling caste, retaining power by force or fraud, holding authority over the masses without consulting them, oppressing them without compunction, and treating them at best as mere means to its own ends, appears to be the political system which alone corresponds to the religion of Hinduism.'[1]

Historically Brahmanism had a germ out of which a nationality could take birth, but such hopes had been disappointed. Hindus failed to exploit this reservoir of spiritual leadership which might have, in the course of time, laid the foundations of a semblance of national unity. Muslim invasion was not successfully resisted and for many centuries the Hindus eked out a far from happy existence as a subject people. The rise of the Marhatta power in the eighteenth century was the last opportunity when the Hindu force might have assured the rise of a national spirit, but 'Brahmanism did not pass into patriotism' and Shivaji's movement remained as 'an organization of plunder.'[2] It was only in the beginning of the present century that Hinduism experienced a stirring in its body politic and began to dream the dreams of an Indian nation. By then, however, it was too late, for the Muslims too had awakened to their plight. In consequence when national regeneration finally came to India it produced two nationalisms, instead of one.

Curiously enough, Islam, too, is anti-national in theory. In the traditional Islamic view States are not based on nationhood. All the Muslims in the world are supposed to belong to one big society—call it nation or *millat* or what you will. Till the present century many 'national groups' lived in one State and, in modern parlance, we may say that most Muslim States were multi-national.

[1] Ramsay MacDonald, *The Awakening of India*, 1910, p. 101.

[2] J. R. Seeley, *The Expansion of England*, 1883, pp. 221–7.

For many years during the last quarter of the nineteenth century and the first of the twentieth the Hindus believed in territorial nationalism. They had their roots in India which was their own country. Nationalism, a Western concept, was borrowed and quickly made the basis of their struggle for independence. The Muslims, however, tenaciously clung to their traditional idea and refused to face the problem of nationalism posed by special Indian conditions. Iqbal still sang of *Hindustan hamara* (India is our land) and few Muslim leaders or thinkers referred to the Muslims as a national group. It was much later, during the 1930s, that territorial nationalism began to intrude into their political thinking. Geography entered into their political calculations for the first time and the idea of a separate State began to take shape in their mind.

Even then the orthodox or *ulama* class denied the validity of the concept of territorial nationalism. They said it was un-Islamic, and by the logic of traditional dogma they were right. Their opposition to the idea of an Indian Muslim nationalism was, and could be, interpreted as their alliance with the Congress and the Hindus. In political terms this interpretation was justified by the maxim that anyone who is not with 'us' is with 'them'. But it is quite possible that the 'nationalist' (or pro-Congress) Muslims decried the Pakistan idea, not because they were anti-Muslim, but because they were orthodox Muslims for whom the association of territory with nationalism went counter to Islamic beliefs and traditions.

Abul Ala Maudoodi's writings furnish the best modern argument against the concept of nationalism in Islam. His chief objection to the policy of the Muslim League and to the idea of Pakistan was that they were based on the theory of nationalism, which he held to be incompatible with Islam. He argued thus: Nationalism is not only a wrong way of thinking but is the real cause of all those disasters which have overwhelmed the world. Nationalism means selfishness, blind prejudice and cruel pride. To believe in modern nationalism is to turn our backs on the Quran. To demand a State on this basis is to rebel against the teachings of Islam. 'The spirit of Islam, which you profess to believe and from which you derive the name Muslim, is in conflict with the spirit of this dirty and rotten system.' 'Muslim nationalism is as contradictory a term as "chaste prostitute".'[1] Till 1947 he maintained that he would not fight for Pakistan, that he did not believe in Pakistan, and that the demand for it was un-Islamic.[2]

Maudoodi was not ploughing a lonely furrow. Most of the *ulama* and nearly all the orthodox Islamic parties were with him rather than with Jinnah. Appeal to Islam was an instrument of extraordinary potency, and this vastly increased the difficulties of the exponents of Muslim nationalism. They had to fight on three formidable fronts: to persuade the British of their separate entity, to convince the Hindus of their determination to live apart, and, above all, to nullify the efforts of the anti-nationalist forces within themselves.

So far we have been discussing the theoretical position. But in practice, too, there were strong factors which retarded the growth of nationalism and impeded the work of Muslim nationalists.

One was the lack of education among the Muslim community. It is a commonplace that democracy cannot work without education. But we are prone to underrate the importance of education in the growth of a national spirit. The national creed cannot be propagated without a minimal level of education among the people. Muslims lagged far behind the Hindus in this field. They lacked schools and universities. They had practically no journals and publishing houses. To preach nationalism is to put across facts and arguments—a process well-nigh impossible without well-informed leaders and educated masses. The fact of the rapid growth of Hindu nationalism is largely due to the advance made by Hindus in the sphere of education. Sayyid Ahmad Khan's emphasis on education appears, in retrospect, in a new light. Besides the

[1] This is a summary of his ideas propounded in *Musalman aur Maujooda Siasi Kashmakash* (*The Muslims and the Present Political Struggle*), Lahore, ?1937–8, 3 Vols; *Nationalism in India*, Pathankot, 1947; *The Process of Islamic Revolution*, Pathankot, 1947, and *The Message of Jamaat-i-Islami: A Contribution towards Islamic Constitution-Making*, Lahore, 1955 ed.

[2] Freeland Abbot, 'The Jamaat-i-Islami of Pakistan', *The Middle East Journal*, Winter 1957, pp. 40–41.

obvious and immediate need of preparing Muslims for public services his educational policy also helped to spread education among the masses and thus to facilitate the work of the leaders who came after him.

Another factor of equal consequence was the low status of women in Muslim society. The orthodox section appealed to Islam as an argument against female emancipation: Maudoodi still denies the franchise to women. The moderately educated section was also reluctant to raise the position of women. Most parents did not send their daughters to school. To let the women enter a profession was a revolutionary step which few dared to take. With nearly half the total population thus disqualified and immobilized the spread of the national message inevitably suffered.

One undesirable result of Hindu impact on Indian Islam was that many Muslims borrowed the caste system and practised it almost as severely as the Hindus. Islam which had brought the message of equality and fraternity to India became itself a divided house. Castes and sub-castes maintained their separate status. Inter-caste marriages were uncommon. In politics and in the pursuit of national unity this proved a crippling handicap.

Finally, the Muslim community in India was a very conservative body of opinion. The influence of orthodox Islamic teaching killed the spirit of free inquiry. The *ulama* did not hesitate to invoke the sanction of religion in favour of the *status quo*. In 1934, for example, opinion in Multan ruled that compulsory primary education was 'an interference with religion and contrary to *shariat*'.[1] Some of the most highly educated persons were biased against independent research and inquiry. Sir Muhammad Iqbal thought that Sir T. W. Arnold's *The Preaching of Islam* was not a reliable book, because Arnold had nothing to do with Islam and because all his scholarly work had been done in the interest of England. Similarly he believed that Professor Brown's *A Literary History of Persia* was written to advance the English interest, so that by emphasizing Persian nationalism the unity of Islamic

[1] Letter of Sir Fazl-i-Husain, a former Minister of Education in the Punjab, to Sayyid Rajan Bakhsh, of 12 September 1934, quoted in Azim Husain, *Fazl-i-Husain: A Political Biography*, 1946, p. 137.

millat could be broken.[1] Islam was interpreted in the narrowest possible terms, and religion was made a dogma and a ritual rather than a pathway to God. Free thinking was discouraged. Feudalism was rampant, and the landlord class provided the bulk of the leadership. Jinnah was the first front-rank leader who did not belong to the landed aristocracy.

Thus the spirit of conservatism was strong and those who spoke of a wind of change spoke in vain. Muslim India produced no philosopher and no social thinker who could, by sheer force of his ideas, change the course of Muslim thought. The society was static, intellectually and mentally, and the deadening hand of reaction held all progressive forces in check. This was hardly congenial soil for the seed of nationalism, and the seed, sown by earlier leaders, might probably never have sprouted had political events of the 1930s not shocked the Muslims into a realization that any further inaction would spell certain disaster.

THE KHILAFAT MOVEMENT

Nothing illustrates the play of religious feeling in politics better than the short-lived but fervent Indian Khilafat movement.

The Ottoman Empire has figured prominently in British foreign policy. On what has gone down in British history as the Eastern Question, English sympathies were first given to Turkey for two politico-strategic reasons. Russia posed a threat to British imperial stakes in Asia, and therefore a friendly Turkish Empire was a British interest. The safeguarding of the Indian Empire became another element in the formation of British attitude towards Turkey. Palmerston was notoriously pro-Turkish and anti-Russian, and the Crimean War was fought to protect the integrity of Turkey and to hedge in the expansion of Russia in the East. With Disraeli this policy did not change, for he too thought it to be in the British imperial interest that Turkey should be strong.

With the coming of Gladstone this policy was forsaken.

[1] Iqbal's conversation with Sayyid Nazir Niazi on 17 March 1933, S. Nazir Niazi *Maktubat-i-Iqbal (Letters of Iqbal)*, 1957, pp. 96–97. Iqbal is generally considered to be one of the fathers of Muslim nationalism in India.

Britain was now more interested in the future of Armenia. Turkey was no longer a country to be wooed and won but an Asiatic intruder in Europe to be kept in its place. How could a Muslim power maintain itself in Europe? The Ottoman Empire was an outdated theocracy which had no further use for British diplomacy. The earlier it was liquidated the better it would be for Europe and Christendom.

Here it is relevant to recall that this anti-Turkish feeling coincided with (and was aggravated by) the then current theory that the Indian Mutiny was the handiwork of the Muslims. This added a bitter edge to British opinion. Had Britain come to the defence of the Turks and saved them from the Russian invader so that their co-religionists in India could rise against the British in revolt? Was this the reward of her traditional pro-Turkish policy?

Still another complication arose in the already tangled web. The Sultan of Turkey was not only the head of the Ottoman Empire but also the Khalifa of the world community of Islam. It is true that Khilafat was a purely Sunni institution and the Shias did not acknowledge the supreme religious status of the Khalifa. But he was also the head of the only surviving Muslim Empire, and this aspect of his position appealed equally to the Sunnis and the Shias. On the Khilafat question, therefore, all the Indian Muslims were combined against the British. The Khalifa's powers must be maintained. The Ottoman Empire must be retained. European (and particularly British) designs aimed at the dismemberment of Turkish territories were resented in India and gave birth to what came to be called the Khilafat movement.

This movement had obvious religious basis. The Muslim concern for the Khalifa was apparently an Islamic sentiment. To this was added the general feeling that European powers were fastening upon Muslim States in North Africa and the Middle East. Russian advance in Turkestan, French control of northern Africa, British intervention in the Persian and Afghan affairs, Italian occupation of Tripoli—all this was in Muslim eyes an unmistakable and deliberate plan to destroy Islam in the world. Then came the Turco–Italian conflict and the Balkan Wars in which Britain did not come to the rescue of Turkey as Muslim India had expected it to do.

With the coming of the Great War matters were made infinitely worse by Turkey joining the Central Powers against Britain and her Allies. When Turkey fought against Britain, the Indian Army fought for Britain and therefore against Turkey. As the Indian Army counted a great number of Muslims in its ranks, the situation was indeed grave. But the old habit of loyalty reasserted itself. Confidence in the British sense of fairness overcame Muslim suspicions and doubts. And therefore Muslim India took her full share in the war effort. The explosion came at the end of the hostilities when a peace treaty with the vanquished Ottoman Empire was being negotiated.

Muslims were beginning to take a roseate view of the future of Turkey. They had close affinity with Turkey on religious grounds. They were also, mentally speaking, not far removed from Britain. They looked forward to an amicable settlement of the problem with matters turning out in favour of Turkey. Lloyd George's declaration that Britain was not fighting to deprive Turkey of its territorial integrity held out a hopeful chance.

But the Treaty of Sèvres, which the Allies signed with Turkey on 10 August 1920, dashed the hopes of Muslim India. The Treaty took away large slices of Ottoman territory—Eastern Thrace, Gallipoli, Smyrna, the Straits and the Dardanelles, the Aegean Islands—and distributed them among the victors of war. Muslims reminded Lloyd George of his promises and of Muslim loyalty, but to no effect. They were rapidly losing their patience as well as their trust in British pledges. They believed that the Peace Conference was bent on the destruction of Islam. Much excitement prevailed and a seething restlessness took hold of Muslim politics.

An All India Khilafat Committee had been formed a little earlier, and one of its first actions was a call to the people, issued on 23 November 1919 as a religious edict, to abstain from participation in victory celebrations, to boycott British goods and to non-co-operate with the Government.[1] On 24 June 1920 ninety prominent Muslims wrote to the Viceroy that they would refuse to co-operate with the Government from 1 August unless in the meantime the terms of the Peace Treaty with

[1] See *Manchester Guardian*, 20 December 1919.

Turkey were revised.[1] One Muslim leader bitterly remarked that Muslims now considered the British as the enemy of Islam since they had seen how, for the sake of Greek imperialism, Jewish capitalism and the oilfields of Mesopotamia, their cherished sentiments had been deliberately assaulted. This had shattered their faith in constitutional methods and created the danger of India becoming Ireland on a huge scale.[2]

Lord Northcliffe, while on a world tour in January 1922, was deeply struck by the depth of the anti-British sentiment among the Muslims of all countries he visited. He found the Indian situation much uglier than the British Press appeared to make out, and warned that peace could not be assured until the Muslim question was 'adjusted'.[3] His paper told the British to stop thinking of the Khilafat agitation as engineered and fictitious and to accept the fact that Indian Muslims suspected the Lloyd George administration of an anti-Islamic bias.[4] Lord Reading, the new Viceroy, was sympathetic to the Muslim feeling and early in 1922 he sent a telegram to Edwin Montagu, the Secretary of State for India, urging the Government to concede the basic Muslim demands. Montagu sanctioned the publication of this dispatch without consulting the Prime Minister, and for this was asked to resign. In India, of course, this enforced departure of a friendly Secretary of State was interpreted as another proof of Lloyd George's perfidy. Muslim leaders appreciated Montagu's friendliness and condemned the Prime Minister's action.[5] Twenty Muslim members of the Indian Legislative Assembly wired to Lloyd George their emphatic protest against his 'deplorable action', their appreciation of Montagu's efforts in the cause of Khilafat, and their conviction that he was 'sacrificed in the anti-Khilafat cause'.[6] The Muslim belief hardened that the Government of India was favourable to Turkish claims but it was the British

[1] 'Lord Chelmsford's Viceroyalty', *Quarterly Review*, July 1921, p. 57.

[2] M. H. Kidwai in *Manchester Guardian*, 27 August 1920.

[3] Statement at Bombay on 21 January 1922, *The Times*, 25 January 1922.

[4] *The Times*, 11 September 1922.

[5] See Ameer Ali, letter to *The Times*, 14 March 1922, and the Aga Khan's statement of 9 April 1922, at Bombay, ibid., 10 April 1922.

[6] *The Times*, 13 March 1922.

Government which was the protagonist of the anti-Turkish campaign.

In Turkey, in the meantime, important developments were taking place. By diplomatic skill supported by the might of arms Mustafa Kamal beat the Greeks out of Turkey, shot the unity of the Allies to ribbons, and forced Britain to draft a revised treaty. The Treaty of Lausanne was accordingly signed in July 1923.

In India the most remarkable development was the Hindu–Muslim entente on the question of the Khilafat. Gandhi, on behalf of the Hindus, had pledged his support to the Muslims in their anti-British and pro-Turkish movement. The formidable Hindu–Muslim alliance had two immediate results. One was the final victory of the Khilafat agitation, clinched by the signing of the Treaty of Lausanne. Another was the joint front formed by the Congress and the Muslim League during the making of the 1919 reforms. But, in the long run, as we will see, this marriage of convenience was unproductive of any permanent results. In 1921 a correspondent of *The Times* had lamented that Muslims were joining hands with the hereditary enemies of British *raj*, the Hindus, 'through the misdoings of our own Government'.[1] In 1923 the same journal was publishing gory details of widespread Hindu–Muslim riots.

Two final questions remain to be answered. What lay behind the Khilafat movement? What permanent impress did it leave on Indian politics and especially on the growth of Muslim nationalism?

The Muslims looked at the maintenance of the Sultan as a great honour to Islam and keenly resented the process of cutting up the only great Muslim power and dividing it into nations or petty republics. They felt that, by their sentimental sympathy with the Oriental Christians and the Greeks, the British were forgetting the history of Muslim loyalty in India. They pointed out that Turkey had been, unlike Germany and Austria–Hungary, denied the right of self-determination. They looked unkindly at British encouragement to the Arabs to rise against Turkey and at British support to Zionism in Palestine. In their eyes the British, by their treatment of the Turks, had made it evident that they refused to Muslims a fair chance of

[1] *The Times* (Empire Day Number Supplement), 24 May 1921.

progress and would not let Islam revive. Islam was being looked upon as a dying religion and the agitation was being branded as a silly and insincere pretext. To prove that this was wrong, Muslims of all shades of opinion joined together in support of the movement.

The movement was fundamentally religious, though it had a strong political undercurrent. The Muslims were not prepared to see any diminution of the powers of the Khalifa, nor were they ready to countenance even the shade of a British or European control over the holy places in Arabia. Altogether, it was religion which determined the shape and content of the movement and which, for the first time, brought all the Muslims of India on one platform.

Whether the movement was a mere interlude—brief and pointless—in the history of Muslim India or an important milestone in the train of events is a moot question.

On the credit side several things can be mentioned. It trained the Muslims in political action and agitation. For the first time a definite plan of action was drawn up and executed. It also brought the extremists and the moderates on one platform, or at least brought a unity to their outlook and taught them how to work in unison. There was nothing in common between, say, the Aga Khan and Maulana Muhammad Ali or between Sayyid Ameer Ali and Dr. M. A. Ansari. But the 'loyalists' and the 'agitators' worked to the same end. Whether the 'rebels' were bringing out processions in India or the 'constitutionalists' were writing to *The Times* in Britain, the aim was identical. Never again was this synchronization of political action in India with publicity in Britain to be achieved.

The Khilafat movement also destroyed the myth of Muslim loyalty. The spectacle of the agitating Muslim was such a break with their traditional conduct that at first the British rubbed their eyes and refused to believe what they saw. The friends of yesterday had become the enemies of today. Whether this metamorphosis was caused by the exigencies of British foreign policy or by an inherent British enmity of Islam is irrelevant. The net result was that the mutual trust, carefully nurtured by the efforts of forty years, was gone and with it the old method of conducting politics. This change was also due to Hindu–Muslim unity, which lasted just as long as the Khilafat issue was in the forefront. Gandhi had thrown himself wholeheartedly into the fray because, as he confessed, it was an opportunity of uniting the two peoples which might never recur. The Muslims welcomed this reinforcement, for it swelled the ranks of the agitators and brightened the chances of success. This alliance was a new phenomenon in Indian history and created false hopes in countless breasts.

However, this unity did not last long. Even before the final battle was won cracks had begun to appear in the entente. For the discerning observer there were signs of the things to come in this rift. Many Muslims learnt one important lesson: that Hindu–Muslim differences were too deep to be bridged over by passionate professions of friendship and even by united action in the political field. The movement, in effect, underlined the basic Hindu–Muslim schism which nothing could heal. Never again were the two communities to combine forces against the British.

The movement also threw up some effective leaders among the Muslims. Effective, but not really of the first class. As the movement was highly emotional it was easier for the fire-eating demagogue to get himself lionized than for the cautious constitutionalist to catch the public eye. There was no Fazl-i-Husain or Jinnah among its leaders; only the Ali brothers, Azad and Ansari. By definition the movement was religious and anti-British. Therefore by definition it excluded the Westernized and co-operative public men from its ranks. The need of the moment was to rouse popular emotions to snapping point, to make fighting speeches to scare the British, to preach sedition even to the soldiers, to issue threatening statements promising dire consequences and, if necessary, to go to jail to prove one's love for Islam. Only a special kind of leadership was capable of this, and it ruled the roost.

Within these limitations and in their own province of activity, the Khilafat leaders were good tacticians and competent politicians. They rarely looked beyond the movement and had no vision of the future. But they were all sincere men, passionately attached to their religion and fanatically devoted to the welfare of Turkey. As long as the campaign lasted they rode on the crest of the wave of popular acclaim. There was no end to what the masses were ready to do at their bidding. But when the emergency passed away a calm resembling death settled upon Muslim India. New problems arose which the old leadership had not anticipated and for which they had no solution. For a time, in fact for the next eight years, politics were static and the masses confounded. It is in this sense that the Khilafat leadership was a failure and the movement itself a pointless interlude.

One would have thought that the success of the Khilafat movement would teach the Muslims one elementary lesson: that in unity lies strength. A joint effort had led them to victory and in future too they should seek their appointed goal in unity. But no sooner had the movement come to an end than the Muslims were once again divided into 'nationalists' and Leaguers, extremists and moderates, pro-separate electorate and anti-separate electorate. It seems that it is only in moments of dire danger that Muslims can stand shoulder to shoulder and defy the common foe. This has been proved again and again in Muslim political history all over the world.

Religion was the *raison d'être* of the Khilafat movement, and this had one important result for the subsequent growth of Muslim nationalism. By emphasizing Islam the movement made the Muslims conscious of their being Muslims. Of course, the feeling of being a separate religious group was at least as old as the time of Sayyid Ahmad Khan. Later the demand for separate representation was also based on the claim that their religion set them apart from other Indians. But it was only now that they felt, with unprecedented intensity, that they were Muslims first and Indians afterwards. This was a triumph for Muslim nationalism, for it provided a base on which other unities could be built. And this, as far as we can see, was the only permanent contribution of the Khilafat movement to the larger problem of nationalism. It was a contribution, however, which no historian can afford to underestimate or ignore.

PAN-ISLAMISM

It was Jamaluddin Afghani who first preached the doctrine of pan-Islamism. Broadly, the doctrine was that Muslims all over the world were brothers to one another and should unite in defence against the influences working against Islam. Later

Sultan Abdul Hamid of Turkey propagated the theory, partly out of genuine conviction, but largely out of the necessity of bolstering up his position as the Khalifa of the Islamic world. In his mouth it took the shape of an appeal (almost an injunction) to the faithful to rally round the Ottoman throne. Still later the Turkish Committee of Union and Progress took up the cause of pan-Islamism and spread its message to all Muslim lands.

Pan-Islamism was in the main a sentiment, a slogan, and it is extremely doubtful if it ever inspired the various Muslim countries or peoples to 'gang up' (to use a modern Americanism) against what they considered to be the enemies of Islam. Under its influence the Muslim League passed resolutions against the British policy of leaving Turkey to its fate during and after the Balkan Wars and of instigating the Arab revolt against Turkish rule. A modicum of pan-Islamic feeling was certainly behind the Khilafat movement. But it never became a plan of action. At the most it signified a desire to see the Muslims of the world standing shoulder to shoulder and sharing one another's adversities and triumphs.

In India the doctrine had a slightly stronger appeal than in other countries because the Muslims were in a minority. They insisted on the international aspect of Islam, but in this their motive force was a defensive attitude in the face of Hindu nationalism.[1] To them the need for unity was greater because their security was in greater danger. They needed help from their co-religionists in their flight from the peril of Hindu domination.

But many in Britain refused to see pan-Islamism in this light. They espied in it a potent danger to British world interests. Sir Ronald Storrs, who, with Sir Henry MacMahon, had played a major part in negotiations with the Arabs, lamented that the Treaty of Lausanne had been in part dictated by the British Foreign Office's fear of 'this well-known and discredited pan-Islamic bluff'.[2] Islam was a creed of narrow dogmatism and fanaticism, and pan-Islamism boded no good

[1] H. A. R. Gibb (ed.), *Whither Islam? A Survey of Modern Movements in the Muslim World*, 1932, p. 73. For a different view see W. W. Cash, *The Muslim World in Revolution*, 1925, pp. 25–29.

[2] Ronald Storrs, *Orientations* (1943 ed.), p. 192.

to humanity.[1] There was also the apprehension that, Islam being a conquering creed, a strong Muslim military power might make pan-Islamism a dangerous reality.[2] This misgiving was also behind the *Manchester Guardian*'s opposition to the entry of Turkey into Thrace, for it 'would mean the re-entry of the effective military power of Turkey into Europe'.[3]

On the other hand, it could be argued that pan-Islamism had been reawakened and regenerated from its long dormancy by the Christians themselves and not by Muslim thinkers and rulers. Egypt was held by Britain. Algiers and Tunis were ruled by France, Morocco was next on the French list of her colonial possessions, Tripoli had been earmarked for Italy, and the Ottoman Turks were being slowly but resolutely rolled out of Europe. It looked like a 'relentless Christian crusade against the Muslim world'. Was it then surprising if Muslims all over the world were closing their ranks for common defence against Christian aggression?[4]

Pan-Islamism might or might not have affected the Muslim nationalist movement in India, but on the whole it appeared to be more of a liability than an asset. It earned the Muslims considerable European hostility without receiving any succour from Muslim countries. It alienated many British commentators of weight and created an unnecessary barrier between them and their understanding of Muslim India's problems. It also frightened some Hindus and made them suspect the Muslims of imperialist designs. Many Hindus, who should have known better, sincerely believed that Muslims were planning, in co-operation with their co-religionists from across the border, to crush Hindu India and to re-found a Muslim Empire, at least in the north. The *Modern Review*, an influential Hindu journal ably edited by B. C. Chatterjee, propagated for many

[1] J. C. Hardwick, letter to *New Statesman*, 17 April 1920, pp. 37–38.

[2] J. Ellis Barker, 'The Future of Asiatic Turkey', *Nineteenth Century*, June 1916, p. 1227. For similar views see also H. A. Wilson, 'The Muslim Menace', ibid., September 1907: A. Vambery, 'Pan-Islamism', ibid., October 1906; and Henry Whitehead, *Indian Problems in Religion, Education, Politics*, 1924, pp. 291–2.

[3] *Manchester Guardian* (leader), 25 September 1922.

[4] See the remarkable article by Chedo Mijatovich, a Serbian diplomat, on 'The Problems of the Near East', *Fortnightly Review*, October 1906.

years the idea that a Muslim attack from the north was an inevitability in case of British withdrawal.[1] Even a liberal politician like Sir Albion Rajkumar Banerji gave currency to the idea that Indian Muslim nationalism would one day result in pan-Islamism and an Islamic Empire.[2] This fear was genuinely held in some responsible quarters and is said to have played a considerable part behind the scenes at the Round Table Conference.[3] In later years the Pakistan demand was opposed by the Hindus for, among other things, its alleged pan-Islamic tendencies. Once Pakistan came into being, the argument ran, India would be confronted with a hostile and aggressive Muslim *bloc* extending from Lahore to Constantinople.[4]

THE CHRISTIAN VIEW OF MUSLIM NATIONALISM

It must not be forgotten that some in Britain looked at British imperialism as a convenient instrument for advancing Christianity. This was particularly true of India, which some British administrators and their friends in England took to be a battleground for the rivalry of Christianity and Islam. Even Muslim loyalty could not, specially in the earlier years, drive out this impression.

Herbert Edwardes wanted to have nothing to do with Islam or Hinduism and to teach from the Bible in all schools. He was convinced that the only way to keep the Indian Empire and defer the danger of internal rebellion was to 'open the Bible wide' and teach the Indians the Christian view of life.[5] In 1860, 2,049 petitions were presented to Parliament for the admission of the Bible into all schools and colleges in India.[6] It was believed that, by refusing to proselytize in favour of

[1] See Renè Fulop-Miller, *Lenin and Gandhi* (1927 ed.), p. 290.

[2] A. R. Banerji, *The Indian Tangle*, ?1933, pp. 234–44.

[3] J. M. Kenworthy, *India: A Warning*, 1931. p. 57.

[4] See S. K. Ratcliffe, *The Resurgence of Asia*, 1946, p. 12, Stanley Rice, 'India: Partition or Unity', *Asiatic Review*, January 1943, p. 81, and Mrs. Middleton, *H.C. 431, 5S*, 13 December 1946, Cols. 1502–1504.

[5] H. B. Edwardes, *Our Indian Empire: Its Beginnings and End*, 1861, pp. 25–26.

[6] A. C. Lyall, *Asiatic Studies*, 1882, p. 277 fn.

Christianity and by imparting secular education, the Government was creating among the Indian students a 'tendency to general infidelity' and bringing about 'a negation of God in his practical life'. This was 'morally poisonous' and 'politically dangerous'. The British should teach 'dogmatically and firmly in all Government schools the great fact of God's existence, and his supreme moral government of the world, implying the ultimate and absolute responsibility of every human being to His omnipotent jurisdiction'.[1] The fact that Christianity had made no impression on Islam was regretted.[2]

Some British teachers and priests openly favoured Christianity and, when the conflict was between Hinduism and Islam, sided with Hinduism. Professor Monier Williams, for example, regarded Hinduism as 'the natural religion of humanity' and Islam as 'an illegitimate child of Judaism'. The teachings of the Quran tended to make the Muslims more intolerant, more sensual and inferior in moral tone to the Hindus. To him Christianity had more points of contact with Hinduism than with Jainism, Buddhism or even Islam.[3] Sir William Muir, the biographer of the Prophet, held that the sword of Muhammad and the Quran were the most stubborn enemies of civilization, liberty and truth which the world had yet known.[4] Islam was a 'strange travesty of Christianity'.[5] It was far more hostile to Britain than was Hinduism.[6] Keir Hardie warned the English people against the day when all the Muslims of the world 'take it into their heads to try once again to win supreme

[1] R. Machonacie, 'The Desirability of a Definite Recognition of the Religious Element in Government Education in India', *Imperial and Asiatic Quarterly Review*, October 1900, pp. 225–45.

[2] Dr. Congreve quoted in H. Cotton, *New India* (1907 ed.), p. 269.

[3] M. Williams, 'Progress of Indian Religious Thought', *Contemporary Review*, December 1878, p. 19, and his *Modern India and the Indians*, 1879, pp. 162, 165–6, 257.

[4] Quoted in S. M. Zwemer, *et. al.*, *The Muhammadan World of Today* (1906 ed.), p. 12.

[5] H. G. Keene, 'Women of Indian History', *National Review*, October 1886, p. 157.

[6] A. C. Lyall, quoted in Mortimer Durand, *Life of the Rt. Hon. Sir Alfred Comyn Lyall*, 1913, pp. 68–86. Another bitter critic was the Rev. Malcolm MacColl, Canon of Ripon. See his articles in *Contemporary Review*, April 1888, February 1897 and October 1897.

power for Allah in the East'.[1] It was unpardonable for Britain to allow the Turks to kill Greeks and Armenians to please the Muslims of India;[2] this only gained her a reputation among Christian nations for gerrymandering European frontiers in response to Asiatic Muslim opinion.[3]

It is a curious fact that, in the context of Indian politics, nearly all Christian missionaries and others in holy orders were partial to the Hindus and the Congress. Many names spring to mind: Malcolm MacColl, John Morison, Murray Titus, C. F. Andrews, J. Z. Hodge, W. W. Cash, G. E. Hickman Johnson, and others. Even the Quakers, actually professing a priestless religion, always sided with the Congress, *vide* Horace Alexander and Reginald Reynolds. What explains this? One answer may be that both Christianity and Islam were proselytizing religions, while Hinduism was not. So in the purely religious field the conflict was between the two imported creeds, not between Christianity and Hinduism. Another reason may have been, as has been described above, the usual Christian hostility to pan-Islamism which was sometimes made out to be the inspiration of all Indian Muslim political moves.

It was even suggested that the only effective remedy of the perennial Hindu–Muslim conflict was the Christian church.[4] If all India was converted to Christianity there would be no communal problem in the country.

This Christian attitude, which was by no means typical of British opinion, had three consequences for Muslim nationalism. First, this unsolicited hostility sometimes adversely affected the spirit of Muslim loyalty and came in handy to the extremists in enlisting fresh recruits to their ranks. Secondly, by sheer reaction, it consolidated the Muslim community; if some Englishmen were thinking of the problem in religious terms, Muslims must be Muslims and, in self-defence, even fanatics. Thirdly, it furnished a minor and vicarious example of divide-and-rule; Christians distinguished between Hindus and Muslims and supported one of the parties. This might have

[1] K. Hardie, *India: Impressions and Suggestions*, 1909, p. xvi.

[2] O'Connor, *H.C. 152, 5S*, 27 March 1922, Cols. 1018–19.

[3] Lord Eustace Percy, *H.C. 150, 5S*, 14 February 1922, Col. 944.

[4] W. W. Cash, *The Muslim World in Revolution*, 1925, pp. 73–77.

tended to throw the Muslims even farther apart from the Hindus than they actually were.

On the whole, the role of the missionaries and their friends at home put the Muslims on the defensive and made them more conservative than they ought to have been. It also quickened their nationalism by making them close their ranks.

Chapter 5

THE CULTURAL FACTOR

In the judgement of a well-known Muslim Congressman the partition of India was 'due mainly to the forces of cultural separatism'.[1] The theme of this chapter is to consider the role of culture in the making of Muslim nationalism and to see how far it contributed to the feeling of separatism among Indian Muslims.

CULTURE AND NATIONALISM

A culture, in the words of Sir Ernest Barker, is a 'mental construction'. It lives in the minds of men and moulds their way of thinking, their way of life and their character. It may not always be possible to define what a culture is or even to portray the lineaments of a particular culture. But we all know what it means to belong to a particular cultural group and how this 'belonging' distinguishes us from those who live in a different cultural milieu. In this sense, culture is probably the greatest determinant of a nation. A nation may have two or more religions. Many languages may be current within it. There may be no racial homogeneity in the national group. But sooner or later a nation is bound to evolve a culture of its own, which will be distinct and definite even if it is nothing but a mixture of cultural traits borrowed from other cultures. The United States and Canada are good examples of this.

Culture has a respectable antiquity and we find fully grown-up cultures at times when the concept of nation had entered neither the mind nor the vocabulary of man. In the fourth century B.C. Hellas was already a culture; at least Isocrates thought so. Within a hundred years a common Hellenistic culture flourished throughout Egypt and Western Asia, and the

[1] S. Abid Husain, *The National Culture of India* (1961 ed.), p. x.

Byzantine Empire later became its outward symbol. Rome too was a culture long before it was a nation, if a nation it ever was.

The point of the argument is that culture is a concept which belongs to the sphere of the mind. When a man thinks that he belongs to a culture-group, one cannot argue with him, as one can when religion or language or race is in question. When many people begin to feel that they have a common culture, they are already on their way to becoming a nation. Generally there is nothing which serves as a nation-nexus more effectively than culture. In India, however, religion had precedence over culture. But here, too, the culture itself was based on religion. The Indian Muslims claimed that their culture was different because it was a Muslim culture. This is no place to distinguish between Muslim culture and Islamic culture or to argue whether there ever has existed, or exists today, a thing called 'Islamic culture'. What is asserted here is that Indian Muslims had, broadly speaking, one culture and they chose to call it 'Muslim culture', because its distinctive character was based on Islam. One strong argument in favour of this is the fact that when an Indian changed his religion and was converted to Islam he immediately changed his cultural allegiance. Hindu or Christian converts to Islam then belonged to a distinct cultural group which they found to be as different from other cultures as was Islam from other religions.

In India there was no Christian culture or Sikh culture or Parsee culture. But there was definitely a Hindu culture—ancient and well established—with which the invading Muslims had clashed. As the background, content and contours of the two cultures were so different, their adherents never evolved a common society. The cultural differences were, in fact, at the root of separatism. The gulf was too deep to be bridged and too wide to be crossed. The two cultures stood side by side, adamant, exigent and inexorable. They met only on the field of battle. In the event, cultural separatism divided the country so that each of the two cultures, which could not live together in harmony, may flourish in its own dwelling-place. This is one way, the cultural way, of interpreting the genesis of Muslim nationalism. The following pages are meant to examine the validity or otherwise of this interpretation.

CULTURAL BODIES PRECEDE POLITICAL BODIES

In India cultural bodies were established long before political organizations came to life. In Muslim India the Muslim League was preceded by the Muhammadan Educational Conference. In Hindu India the National Congress came much later than the Brahmo Samaj.

This is a phenomenon common to many countries. In South Africa, the Broederbond was primarily a cultural organization and it was only in 1933 that it began to widen its sphere and gradually embraced the Nationalist Party's creed. In Ghana, the Convention People's Party was preceded by the West African National Congress. In Nigeria, the Action Group was the child of Egbe Omo Oduduwo, a Yoruba cultural organization; and the Northern People's Congress was an offspring of the Jamia, a Hausa cultural society.

One of the earliest actions of Sayyid Ahmad Khan in the way of educational regeneration was the establishment of a Translation Society and a Scientific Society. The former aimed at acquainting the non-English-knowing Muslims with works of European, and particularly English, literature and philosophy by translating them into Urdu. The latter was meant to encourage the study of pure science and other technical subjects. Later the Muhammadan Anglo–Oriental College was founded at Aligarh to impart enlightened education to the Muslims—enlightened because it was a nice balance of Eastern culture and Western learning.

The foundation of the Aligarh College turned out to be more than just the establishment of an educational institution. It gave birth to the famous Aligarh Movement, which was partly educational, partly literary, partly religious, and wholly cultural. It set new targets in education, new standards in literary composition and criticism, new ideals in social thinking, and new norms in Islamic exegesis. It was a social movement and preached the gospel of the 'good' life in the Aristotelian sense. It is impossible to exaggerate the role of this movement in the cultural regeneration of Muslim India. Sayyid Ahmad's sagacity saw that a strong cultural base must be built before an enduring political fabric could be erected upon it. Politics were for the time being forgotten and all energies were directed towards the development of education, language, literature and social uplift. The idea was that when once the Muslims had adequately advanced in the realm of mind a national feeling would follow as surely as day follows the night.

Subsequent history showed that this was the right course, and had the Muslim League been formed in, say, 1870 or 1880, it would have been built on sand, for political unity is but a delusive hope without prior cultural homogeneity. Moreover, the Aligarh Movement, in the sphere of education, not only produced public men who later took to politics but also inculcated some discipline in the mass of men.

LANGUAGE

It is not always possible to identify a nation with a language group. The examples of Canada, Switzerland and Belgium are well known. When the Peace Treaties of 1919 were being framed and the Wilsonian principle of self-determination was being translated into reality, it was generally taken for granted that language was sufficient basis for common nationality and several States were created on this premiss. But this assumption was proved false in some cases when plebiscites were held to ascertain the popular will. Some Slavs like the Masurians in East Prussia and some Slovenes in Carinthia were opposed to their inclusion in Slav States and wanted to be parts of the German-speaking Germany or Austria. The German-speaking people of Oedenburg, on the other hand, voted in favour of joining Hungary. In some cases the creators of the Peace Treaties themselves did not take language as their test of nationality: the German-speaking population of Austria and Northern Bohemia were not permitted to join Germany.

Language, therefore, is not a fundamental characteristic of a nation. It is not the essence of the nation, as some people claim it to be.

But language still remains one of the features by which a nation may be distinguished or one of the grounds on which nationalism may be founded. There is always an affinity between people speaking the same language. Language affects literature and literature affects national life. A language is made up of words, and words which we habitually use often mould our mode of thinking. Common words make for common thoughts and feelings. Language is primarily a vehicle of communication, and thoughts and feelings, when communicated through the same medium, tend to be stamped with a characteristitic unity. This affinity easily leads to national unity because a nation is a tradition of thought and sentiment.

India has traditionally been a paradise for philologists. Its several major languages, in addition to hundreds of dialects, have fascinated the foreigner as much as they have confused the native. In fact, one of the most potent arguments against there being one Indian nation was the bewildering variety of its languages.

Urdu was, by general consent, considered to be the language of the Muslims. Born under the Mughuls by a combination of Persian, the court language, and some indigenous Hindu dialects, it grew up in times of political and cultural stress. Many Hindus used it and some fine Urdu poetry has been written by them; but emotionally they always distrusted it. For this there was a simple reason. The Hindus had their own language, Hindi, which leaned heavily on Sanskrit for its vocabulary. Urdu, on the other hand, borrowed more freely from Persian and Arabic, though some of its sweetest phrases came from Hindi. As political and cultural rivalry increased the two languages began to fall apart. The supporters of Hindi claimed for it a national status; the Muslims hotly denied it. As the controversy spread, the two languages became more and more exclusive. Hindi was made 'pure' by the progressive incorporation of Sanskrit words. The Urdu enthusiasts went more often to Persian and Arabic for vocabulary as well as syntax. Though Urdu was in its origin neither the language of the Muslims nor a Muslim language, it gradually became so. Soon it assumed a place in their tradition 'second only to their religion'.[1] Thus linguistic conflict added to Indian disunity and helped the formation of more than one nationalism.

The more the Hindus laid stress on Hindi the greater emphasis the Muslims put on Urdu. The Hindi–Urdu controversy was by now an integral part of the Hindu–Muslim question.

[1] M. L. Ferrar, in H. A. R. Gibb (ed.), *Whither Islam? A Survey of Modern Movements in the Muslim World*, 1932, p. 182.

The Muslim League 'adopted' Urdu as its 'national' language, and among its demands for safeguards there always appeared a reference to the protection of this language. The Congress, on the other hand, attached itself to Hindi with equal resolution. Later, when the Hindus discovered that Hindi was not acceptable to all as the *lingua franca* of India, they 'tried to cut the knot' by avoiding the very names of Hindi and Urdu and by adopting the word 'Hindustani'.[1] But this was a very perfunctory way of dealing with the question.[2] Literally 'Hindustani' means 'the language of Hindustan (India)'. In fact there was no such language in existence. People either spoke and wrote Hindi or they spoke and wrote Urdu: none spoke or wrote 'Hindustani'. It was an imaginary language which did not exist and had never existed. But instead of saying so in clear terms they invented a new language which no one used. The name chosen for it was itself unfortunate, for it could also be translated as 'the language of the Hindus', and most Muslims chose to interpret it in this way.

When the Congress ministries were in power in the provinces one of the major Muslim accusations against them was that Hindi was patronized, promoted and extended at the expense of Urdu.[3] The association of the *Vidya Mandir* education scheme with the teaching of Hindi was one of the reasons for Muslim opposition to it. The Congress insistence on the use of Hindi was also behind the fierce controversy about textbooks in Bombay.[4] In Madras the Congress Chief Minister ordered that the teaching of Hindi should be made compulsory. This was bitterly opposed by the Tamil- and Telugu-speaking

[1] Sampurnananda, *Memories and Reflections*, 1960, p. 89.

[2] In fact the Congress policy was not at all clear on the language issue. In 1935, in his presidential address at the Nagpur session of the Hindi Sahitya Sammelan (Hindi literary conference), Rajendra Prasad, the well-known Congress leader and later the first President of the Indian Union, 'reiterated his faith in one language for the whole country, and this could only be Hindi'; Kewal L. Punjabi, *Rajendra Prasad*, 1960, p. 93. Gandhi himself many times pleaded the case for Hindi.

[3] See the *Report of the Inquiry Committee appointed by the Council of the All India Muslim League to inquire into Muslim Grievances in Congress Provinces (Pirpur Report)* (1938), p. 54.

[4] See *The Times of India*, 11 and 26 July, and 14 December 1939.

population who started a regular agitation leading to the arrest of nearly one thousand persons.[1]

The Congress policy of imposing Hindi on the whole of India was, however, not unprecedented in modern history. Europe provides some comparable examples. A similar attitude was adopted by the Germans in Schleswig, Prussian Poland and Alsace–Lorraine, and by the Magyars in Transylvania. After 1918 it was followed by some of the new Central European nations.

But this did not stop the Muslims from reacting adversely to the policy of the Congress. They now made the language issue paramount, and shortly afterwards, when the demand for Pakistan was formulated, it was categorically laid down that Urdu would be its national language. But even long before this they had made Urdu 'one of the elements of Muslim culture in India' and had called it 'the Muslim national language of India'.[2]

But this claim cannot be accepted uncritically. If we go by figures more people spoke Bengali than Urdu. As a mother tongue even fewer adherents could be claimed by Urdu. It was *not* the mother tongue, nor was it spoken generally, in the Punjab, the North-West Frontier Province, Sind and Baluchistan—in fact, in all the Muslim-majority areas which later formed Pakistan. Each of these areas had its own regional language which, though not so well developed as Urdu, had some impressive literary achievements to its credit. Languages which had produced poets of the rank of Khushhal Khan Khatak, Waris Shah and Shah Abdul Latif could not be dismissed as mere dialects. Nor was Urdu understood, let alone spoken, in the rural areas of the Punjab and Sind. Strictly, therefore, Urdu could not rightfully claim the status of the 'national language' of the Indian Muslims.

There seem to have been three factors which propelled Urdu to the forefront and made it, despite what was said above, the national language. One was a purely negative reason. The Hindus disliked Urdu and wanted to replace it

[1] R. Coupland, *Report on the Constitutional Problem in India,* Part II, 1943, p. 103.

[2] M. T. Titus, *Indian Islam: A Religious History of Islam in India,* 1930, pp. 192, 198.

with Hindi. This was enough for many Muslims to rally to the cause of Urdu. Positively, Urdu was the most developed language among all the tongues spoken in Muslim areas. It possessed a not inconsiderable literature; in poetry it was specially distinguished. Moreover, it was generally understood over vast areas. A Pathan or a Sindhi might not speak Urdu, but if there was a language other than his own which he could comprehend it was Urdu. It is not far from the truth to say that Urdu was at least understood in all towns and cities of Muslim India. Thus if a choice had to be made among the 'Muslim' languages, Urdu easily came first.

Finally, there was the national need for a separate language. The Muslims claimed to be a nation. A nation was usually supposed to have a language of its own. Therefore, the Muslims must have a language, too. Without it there would be no Muslim nationalism. In this sense Urdu was taken up, not only as a language but also as a sentiment, for cementing national unity and as a slogan with which to win a new country.

EDUCATION

Religion and education are the two most important parts of that spiritual superstructure which is the essence of nationalism. An integrated system of education influences social ideas and develops national character. It is trite but true to say that those who control the schools command the destinies of the people. In this respect, education is the mother of politics and precedes, or should precede, it. It is a proof of Sayyid Ahmad Khan's wisdom that he saw the truth of this principle and insisted on a sound educational foundation before entering the whirlpool of politics.

As in other fields so in education, Muslim ideals differed from those of the Hindus. Generalizations are notoriously fragile, but it can be affirmed that on the whole Muslims were less quick than the Hindus to pick up new ideas and more opposed to Western methods and content of education. During the post-Mutiny period Muslim conservatism kept them away from Government schools and colleges. Muslim parents distrusted the 'newfangled' theories of education and were content to send their children to the traditional *maktab* and *madrassah* where the curriculum was rigidly confined to religious teaching and, at some places, rudimentary arithmetic and history and geography. The Muslims did not take to the English language, and thus denied themselves opportunities of material as well as intellectual progress. Material, because Government jobs were open only to English-knowing persons; intellectual, because the entire corpus of Western knowledge and learning was shut out from them. It is usually said that Indian nationalism was brought up on the writings of Burke, Mill and Paine. But this was not true of Muslim nationalism in its earlier stages, and that is partly why the latter did not appear till quite late—not till the Western-oriented education imparted at Aligarh had permeated through the Muslim mind.

The role of what we may call 'educational nationalism' in Muslim India can best be studied in the history of the Aligarh University. One of the functions of a modern university is to raise the level of participation of the educated people in the creation and growth of the nationality. It aims at promoting the development of knowledge within its own national culture-society. These are the 'nationalistic' functions of a university, and historically they are exemplified by French and German universities at the beginning of the twentieth century. In India they are exemplified by the creation and functions of the Muslim university at Aligarh and the Hindu university at Benares. The former was a development of the Muhammadan Anglo–Oriental College founded by Sayyid Ahmad Khan, as the latter was an extension of the Central Hindu College promoted by Mrs. Annie Besant.

It took the Muslims nearly fifty years to get the Aligarh College elevated to the status of a university. The struggle was hard and long, partly because of monetary difficulties and partly because of a conflict with the Government on the issue of academic autonomy. This is not the place to describe the history of the growth of the university, but the point we want to make is that the Muslim community felt insecure, educationally naked, without a university of their own. They realized the importance of having their own educational centre, under their own control, which could enshrine their educational and spiritual ideals, and which could raise the level of their knowledge on their own lines. This Aligarh did for many years and the debt of Muslim nationalism to it is great and deep.

Aligarh was the symbol of Muslim nationalism in the fields of education and learning; but it was not the only symbol, though it was the most important. In Hyderabad Deccan was established the Osmania University, whose contribution to Muslim awakening was of a different kind. It was the only centre of higher learning in India which imparted knowledge in Urdu. Not only was the medium of instruction Urdu on all levels, but the university had also a large and well-staffed translation bureau which made available in Urdu a great number of Western classics in literature, philosophy, science, history, politics and economics. Many of the greatest European thinkers from Plato to T. H. Green were presented to the Urdu-knowing public in faithful translations. Philosophic and scientific technical terms current in the West were given Urdu equivalents, and thus an impressive scientific vocabulary was built up which enabled the teachers to teach the natural and physical sciences in their own language up to the highest level.

Besides the universities, all over India were found Muslim colleges, called varyingly Islamia colleges, Muslim colleges, M.A-O. colleges or Anglo–Arabic colleges. The Hindus had their own set of such institutions, named Dyanand Anglo–Vernacular colleges, Hindu colleges, Sanatan Dharam colleges, or colleges named after individual patrons. Basically these colleges had the same curricula and courses of study, for all of them were affiliated to undenominational universities. But their teaching staff and the student body were almost exclusively Muslim or Hindu.

In some cities Muslims formed societies or associations to establish and run schools and colleges, e.g. the Anjuman-i-Himayat-i-Islam in Lahore and the Anjuman-i-Islamia in Bombay. They ran chains of schools and colleges (sometimes also orphanages and women's homes).

As was said earlier, Muslims were slow in taking advantage of educational opportunities. This can be accounted for on three grounds. In the first place, there was the inertia of the post-Mutiny period when attachment to traditional modes had kept them away from the new enlightenment which came with Macaulay's theories and ideas. In the second place, they were a poor people and could neither afford to build their own schools nor bear the expense of sending their children to Government institutions. In the third place, their ideas of education, based on Islamic foundations, clashed with the then-prevailing conception of a secular system of instruction. This needs some elaboration.

British official policy in India was one of complete impartiality in religious matters. The Government gave full religious freedom to all creeds in consistence with public order. In the educational sphere this attitude excluded religious instruction in schools and colleges.[1] The Hindus did not much object to it, but the Muslims did. In consequence the Government schools were felt to be inadequate or downright unsuitable for the Muslim youth. They insisted on a course of Islamic teachings as one of the essential ingredients of the education of a Muslim boy. When this was not forthcoming they resented a foreign system of education which was secular and therefore un-Islamic.

Another source of dissatisfaction to the Muslims was that the British-imposed system of education did not make any concessions either to their traditional values of learning or to their cultural background. They felt a deep loyalty to Arabic, the language of their Holy Book, and to Persian, the language of their culture and the mother of Urdu. Oriental learning in general was also dear to them. But these were either ignored or given insufficient scope in the official scheme of public instruction. Oriental classics found no place in the curricula. Oriental faculties did not exist in any college or university in the earlier years. For some time Muslim colleges were ineligible for affiliation to universities.[2]

The tardy and sluggish growth of Muslim nationalism was in great part due to a lack of educational progress. Conservatism, poverty and attachment to traditional and partly out-moded values slowed down the tempo of advance. The results were unhappy. Literacy was slow. Higher education was of poor

[1] Though in Britain 'religious instruction is an integral part of the teaching given in our elementary schools, whether public or voluntary', Ernest Barker, *National Character and the Factors in its Formation* (1st ed. 1927, 4th ed. 1948), p. 225.

[2] L. S. S. O'Malley, op. cit., p. 648.

quality. Schools and colleges were neither adequate to the needs of the Muslims nor good enough for the standards demanded of them. Some Muslim areas suffered badly. When Pakistan was created there was no university in the Frontier Province or in Sind or in Baluchistan. Sind and Baluchistan had a negligible number of colleges. The University of Dacca was not established till after 1912. Such lack of opportunity as well as of interest was a stumbling block in the way of national solidarity. Political awakening follows educational awakening, and national unity is difficult, if not impossible, in the absence of a well-spread education.

This handicap was, however, partly compensated by one negative factor. Hindu opposition to Muslim educational aspirations and plans and Hindu insistence on implementing their own schemes throughout India were instrumental in uniting the Muslims to an extent unwarranted by their disunion and dissensions.

The Hindus were against the establishment of a Muslim university at Aligarh, professedly on the ground of national unity. If denominational educational institutions were permitted to exist and multiply, they said, Indian national unity would be jeopardized. They stood for secularism in education as well as in politics. To this the Muslim replied that the Hindu opposition was not innocent of vested interests: the Hindu did not want to see the Muslim progressing in the educational sphere and desired to suppress him culturally.[1] He supported this argument by pointing to the foundation of a Hindu university at Benares and to Hindu opposition to the creation of a university at Dacca (which was not to be a Muslim university but would detract from the importance of Calcutta).

In 1939, at its fifty-second session held at Calcutta, the All India Muhammadan Educational Conference (which was a completely non-political body and had no *liaison* with the Muslim League) appointed a committee to examine the entire educational field in India and to prepare a scheme for Muslim education with a view to 'the preservation of the distinctive features of their cultural and social order'. Nawab Kamal Yar

[1] For Gandhi's responsibility for creating sharp communal divisions through his educational theories see R. Fulop-Miller, *Lenin and Gandhi* (1927 ed.), p. 240.

Jung was the chairman of this committee, which consisted of some distinguished educationalists. The main work was done by a sub-committee headed by Sir Aziz-ul-Huq, then the Speaker of the Bengal Legislative Assembly and Vice-Chancellor of the University of Calcutta and later a member of the Viceroy's Executive Council and still later High Commissioner for India in London.

The Committee published its report[1] in the spring of 1942. The picture it depicted of the position and prospects of Muslim education was indeed dismal and gloomy. The proportion of Muslim students in all institutions was low. Muslim studies figured poorly in the courses of study. Higher research in Muslim history and culture was negligible. In primary and secondary education Muslim and Urdu schools were being closed down or strangled by niggardly grants in aid.

One full chapter (XIII) of the Report dealt with the Wardha Scheme of education which Gandhi had drawn up and which the Congress Governments had been implementing in the provinces. This, said the Report, was an essentially communal scheme shot through and through with Hindu ideals. The teaching of religion was completely ignored and this amounted to an attempt to disengage the Muslim child from his faith. Muslim children were obliged to honour the Congress flag, to sing the Bande Mataram, to wear home-spun cloth (*khadi*) and to do *puja* (worship) to Gandhi's portrait.

It was in the Central Provinces that the Wardha Scheme appeared in its most orthodox and (to the Muslims) obnoxious form. This was the Vidya Mandir, the creation of 'temples of learning'. In the provincial legislature and all over the province Muslims had bitterly opposed the introduction of this plan, but their resentment was unheeded. When the bill relating to the scheme came before the assembly it was opposed by every single Muslim member and also by a few Hindus, including the former Chief Minister, Dr. Khare, but it was carried through by the weight of Congress votes. Under this scheme, schools were to be managed by committees chosen by a joint electorate. No separate Muslim schools were provided, nor were arrangements made for training Urdu-speaking teachers. The very name Vidya Mandirs (*mandir*=Hindu

[1] *Report of the Kamal Yar Jung Education Committee*, Calcutta, 1942.

temple) was a challenge to the Muslims, for it smacked of Hindu idolatry.

In a brilliant note appended to the Report by Sir Aziz-ul-Huq occurred the following paragraph: 'Either the present system of school and university studies must have such syllabuses and themes that the Hindus, the Muslims and all other creeds and communities can meet on an essentially common platform with no influence, tendency or bias in favour of the one or the other. Or educational India must be a federation of two or more distinct types of educational organizations, each trying to develop its own culture and heredity, but in a spirit of catholicity and goodwill to others. I do hope and pray that wisdom and sense will still prevail and there will be a common and united plan and programme of education.'[1]

Thus in culture, too, as in politics, separatism was invading the Muslim mind.

LITERATURE

More than anything else it is literature which reflects the contours of cultural nationalism. That is so because it enshrines in itself the thoughts and ideals, the history and language, the art and character, of the people who have produced it. It is only by acquainting ourselves with their literature that we know so much about the cultures of past ages.

In India there was no dichotomy of Hindu and Muslim literature. There was an ancient Hindu literature, but no such thing existed in modern India. Similarly there was a body of literature in the world which could be called Islamic literature, but in India no such title could be given to the literature produced by Muslims. The distinction was more subtle. The Muslims' literary production was of a different nature, had a different background and was inspired by different sources.

Three sources of the literature of Muslim India may be identified. One was religion. Many writings were religious in character, without being theological; religious poetry (*na'ats*) is an example. The second was history. The Muslim past, in India or elsewhere, was the theme of innumerable poems, novels, essays and even plays. The third was the pervasive influence of Persian and Arabic cultures. A Muslim boy's education

[1] Ibid., p. 279.

was considered to be incomplete without a fair grounding in Persian literature. Old-style gentlemen could recite thousands of lines from poets like Saadi and Hafiz. In the traditional idea of culture Persian and Arabic had precisely the same position which was held by the classics in the education of a cultured Englishman in the nineteenth century. This inevitably left its mark on literature.

It was in this sense that what we may call for the lack of a proper name the literature of Muslim India differed from the literature of the rest of India. As most of this literature was produced in the Urdu language, we will here refer to it as Urdu literature, though we must bear in mind that several Hindus, a few of them eminent in their field, contributed to it.

The religious content of Urdu literature was not much. It contained a body of religious poems, mainly in praise of God and the Prophet, and one major item, the *Shahnama-i-Islam*, a long epic by Hafeez Jullundheri, soothing in its mellifluous and liquid rhythm and very moving for Muslim readers, but of no great poetic merit.

The historical content was considerable, both in poetry and in prose. Many poems, like several of Iqbal's, are incomprehensible without a good knowledge of Islamic history. Allusions to minor events and incidents of this history abounded, and the ability to understand them was taken for granted. In prose, too, historical works glorified the victors of Islam. Biographies of Muslim heroes were popular, with Shibli's six-volume biography of the Prophet as the crown of achievement in this genre. Historical fiction was not much in evidence, but the little that was was avidly read by the semi-educated, particularly by women. Literary skill was not their forte, but they appealed to the raw imagination of the newly-awakened masses and so accelerated the growth of national consciousness.

The most prominent characteristic of Urdu literature was the colour it took from Persian (and to much less extent from Arabic) literary and cultural heritage. Urdu poetry borrowed its scansion from Arabic and most of its metaphors from Persian. No poet worth his salt could be ignorant of these two languages, and some grounding in them was essential even for appreciating Urdu poetry. Furthermore, some Urdu poets wrote both in Urdu and Persian, and literary critics agree that in some cases the Persian work is superior to the Urdu. Iqbal is the outstanding example. Ghalib, too, wrote well in Persian. Even among minor poets it was not an uncommon practice to scatter Persian verses among their poems, which made their work unintelligible to those who knew no Persian.

This shows how deeply Urdu (Muslim Indian) literature was attached to and grounded in Islam, Islamic history and Persian and Arabic cultures. This made it essentially 'Muslim', and therefore essentially different from the literature of the rest of India.[1] The point is that Hindu and Muslim writers received their inspiration from different sources. The 'Hindu writer referred back to the time of glory under the Mauryas, Guptas and Marathas, the Muslim looked back to the glorious days under the Grand Mughuls and pinned his faith on pan-Islamism as a panacea for the ills of the present'.[2] Their memories of a golden past were as much at variance as their dreams of a future Utopia. Though there was a considerable body of Hindus *and* Muslims who enjoyed erotic Urdu poetry and whose hearts were deeply moved by the supple grace of a Momin or the naughty wit of a Dagh, yet the real spirit of Urdu literature remained alien to the Hindu mind, which did not, could not, share its cultural background. To expect a Hindu to understand and appreciate the bulk of Iqbal's work is like asking someone completely ignorant of Greek mythology and Christian lore to comprehend and enjoy Milton's *Paradise Lost.*

Literature can be a cruelly divisive agent in a multi-cultural society. And it is exceedingly difficult either to suppress it or to submerge it completely in a different literary tradition. It was after a century and a half of Germanization that the ideal of Bohemian independence reappeared through the deliberate recreation of Czech culture. The process of Lithuanian national independence did not begin until the Lithuanian literary culture was revived in the second half of the nineteenth century.

[1] Nothing has been said here of Bengali Muslim literature, because the author knows no Bengali and is not qualified to write about it. This is an unfortunate omission but does not invalidate his major hypotheses.

[2] B. G. Gokhale, *The Making of the Indian Nation* (1960 ed.), pp. 298–9.

Literary groups and associations play an important part in the regeneration and progress of literature. What would French literature be without the Académie francaise? Literary associations were formed in Canada for the purpose of promoting the growth of an 'original Canadian culture'. The United States considered it necessary in 1904 to found the American Academy of Arts and Letters. In India, the Hindus, under the inspiration of the Nobel Laureate Tagore, established the Shantiniketan, a sort of an academic centre for the protection and promotion of Indian (Hindu) culture and literature. The Muslims founded the Anjuman-i-Taraqqi-i-Urdu (Society for the Promotion of Urdu) at Hyderabad Deccan. Soon it had branches all over India and for a quarter of a century it did noble service to the cause of Urdu language and literature.

Men of letters play no small role in nation making. They develop the language out of either a rough dialect or a mixture of two or more regional tongues. They record and collect literary gleanings, relate them to current myths and legends, translate treasures of traditional (but linguistically foreign) literatures, and synthesize the various cultural streams by writing the hitherto unwritten folk-lore. They modernize the language and keep it alive by constant borrowings from other tongues. They point out the deep relationship between literature and its historical inspiration. They relate poetry to patriotism (at times even to parochialism) and prose to national pride. The grammarians among them prepare dictionaries and lexicons, thus legislating on the meanings, nuances and shades of words. They fix the usage of phrases, adopt new words and evolve new figures of speech.

All this was done in Muslim India by littérateurs of the calibre of Hali, Shibli, Sayyid Ahmad Khan, Nazir Ahmad, Abdul Huq, Niaz Fatehpuri and others. Great stress was laid on the development of the language. The '*Urdu bolo*' (speak Urdu) movement was initiated. Urdu literature was enriched by translations of Persian, Arabic and European classics. The language was extended by such efforts as the publication of glossaries, preparation of technical terminologies and coinage of new scientific terms. Even religion was 'nationalized' by translating the Quran, rendering Arabic prayers and writing sermons in Urdu. In short, the language was refined and polished by constant use and additions, and in the process literature was inevitably enriched.

Western parallels to this development are not hard to come by. French literature began in the eleventh century with the *Chansons de Geste* (epic stories recounting the achievements of military heroes) and later with lyric poetry. At the beginning of the fourteenth century Italian was accepted as the supreme common language of Italy because much creative writing—culminating in the works of Dante and Petrarch—was being done in it. But the classical example of a literary urge coming to the rescue of (or serving the cause of) national integrity and awakening is that of the Norwegian literature which instigated the Norwegian people to liberate themselves from the centuries-old cultural and social domination of the Danish national society.

Three literary figures of Muslim India must be given special mention for the powerful impetus they gave to national consciousness. Sayyid Ahmad Khan's essays on social-cum-religious topics were published in his own journal, *Tahzib-ul-Akhlaq* (which was modelled on Steel's *Tatler*), and their influence on social emancipation and religious liberalism cannot be exaggerated. Hali, a luminous star in the firmament of the Aligarh Movement, not only acted as the Wordsworth of Urdu poetry by simplifying diction and glorifying nature, but also gave the literary world one of its masterpieces, the *Musaddas*. Nothing like this had been written before. In sweet-melancholy rhythm he portrays the decline and fall of Islam in India and weeps over the misfortunes and miseries of his stricken compatriots. It is a dirge which moved the hearts and minds of men and did more than any other literary creation in opening their eyes to their perilous plight. This creative lamentation ranks with those few poems of the world which combine poetic merit of the highest order with far-reaching practical utility. The last among these giants was Iqbal, who sang of the storied past with a lyricism which was strong in accent but soft in tone. He had a message to give—the message of Islamic brotherhood and Islamic purity—and gave it well without letting his muse degenerate into dull didacticism. His *Complaint* (*Shakwa*) to God about the plight of the Muslim is at times impudent, at times supplicatory, yet ever sincere. The general effect is neither of a derisive howl nor of a cringing whimper, neither of gnashing of teeth in impotent rage nor of a maudlin emotion, but of a heart-breaking grief 'felt in the blood and felt all the way'.

What Sayyid had said in speech and prose Hali put in measured stanzas and Iqbal sang with the abandon of a Shelley. The combined assault on Muslim ignorance, apathy and conservatism was shattering. From a defeated and demoralized rabble Sayyid lifted his people and made them conscious of their identity. When Hali bemoaned their backwardness and offered a prayer for their salvation, he deepened their sense of guilt but also intensified their resolve to catch up with the times. Iqbal turned a minority, already half-conscious of its destiny (but only *half*), into a solid group. Mentally the soil had been well ploughed by these intellectual giants. It now waited for a statesman who had the vision to look into the future and the strength to make the people look with him. So when Jinnah arrived with his clarion call of a separate national State people welcomed him as the long-sought-for deliverer, the liberator of the oppressed, whom Divinity had sent in answer to their prayers.

PHILOSOPHY

Every nationality has its own philosophy, which may be a collection of certain definite philosophic teachings of the past or a body of philosophic ideas expounded by modern thinkers. Philosophy is not essential to nationalism in the sense in which, for example, language is. But it performs a necessary function. It gives ballast to the national idea, to the ideology.

In India the Hindus looked to their own ancient philosophy just as the Muslims traced their intellectual ancestry to Muslim thinkers like Avicenna and Al Ghazali. When the Hindu was contemplating his past, he thought of Kautallya (the author of *Artha-shastra*); when the Muslim looked back, he recalled Al Farabi. The philosophic past of the two peoples was so different as to obliterate any prevailing community of thought.

In the modern age, again, this dichotomy ran right through the country. To the Hindus inspiration came from Radhakrishnan, to the Muslims from Iqbal. Radhakrishnan's *Hindu View of Life* had as much in common with Iqbal's *Lectures on the Reconstruction of Religious Thought in Islam* as navigation has with play-writing. Even if India had, by the play of historical forces, continued to be politically one country, her Muslims would never have considered Radhakrishnan or Aurobindo as the mouthpiece of their ideas, just as her Hindus would never have looked to Iqbal or Shah Waliullah as the fount of their philosophy.

The influence of intellectual leaders on the history of nationalism should not be underestimated. Politicians come afterwards and build on the soil prepared by thinkers and writers. The emergence of Hindu (or 'Indian') nationalism was from the very first influenced by intellectuals who compared the history of Hindu civilization with the history of modern Western civilization and exalted the former. Gandhi was by no means the first to do so, but he is a more typical example because he lived in the twentieth century when the civilization of the West was known to the Orientals better than it was to their forefathers. In his opinion Hindu civilization represented the highest spiritual values in contrast to the West's stress on materialism. In the same way, though not to that uncompromising extent, the Muslims looked back to Islam's golden age with nostalgia and frowned upon both the Hindu and the Western ways of life.

Both Hindus and Muslims reacted unfavourably to the West, but there was one subtle and significant difference between the two approaches. The Hindu looked at the West not only with disapproval but also with hatred. Hatred always implies fear; we hate a man of whom we are secretly afraid, we have a contempt for a man whom we consider our inferior. To the Hindu the West was an unknown entity, a completely foreign element—foreign to his past, to his country and to his tradition. On the contrary, the Muslim looked with disfavour only at some aspects of the Western civilization. He did not reject everything Western, nor was his rejection so complete and thorough as the Hindu's. People like Sayyid Ahmad could go to the extent of comparing the English and the Indians and calling the latter animals and brutes. In their desire to borrow the best features of the West and to combine them with those of Islam, these makers of the Indian Muslim renaissance were reflecting the general opinion of Muslim India.

Ameer Ali, Cheragh Ali and others who came after them adopted the same line of thinking and did not allow their devotion to Islam to obliterate their wholesome respect (almost affection) for the virtues of the West. In political terms the same idea may be expressed by saying that while Gandhi was, by his own confession, an orthodox Hindu who was opposed even to such things as Western medicine and technology and who used *satyagraha* as his political weapon, Jinnah was a modern constitutionalist who fought the British with their own liberal weapons. This contrast is not merely a superficial way of bringing out the difference between the mentalities of the two leaders. It goes deeper and reflects the essential, though partial, affinity between Islam and the West. Muslim India never, not even in the heat of the political battle, called the British or their civilization 'satanic', as Gandhi did. The explanation lies in the fact that Islam had behind it a history of centuries of contact with the West; it was through the Arabs that Greek philosophy and science had passed into Europe. In meeting the West Islam had no fear of the unknown—that implacable enemy of confidence as well as courage.

ART

In the aesthetic sphere, too, different nationalities come to have an art of their own, or come to believe that the works of certain artists make up a national art. If art is an expression or manifestation of life and its values, its significance for the feeling of national solidarity needs no elaboration.

In India the Muslims looked to Mughul buildings as their artistic heritage. It was the Taj Mahal of Agra, or the Red Fort of Delhi or the Royal Mosque at Lahore, which stirred their imagination and excited their pride. It was the art of miniature painting, perfected in the court of Shah Jahan, which appealed to them. On the other hand, the Hindus were equally impressed and affected by the architecture of south Indian temples, the Rajput or Kangra schools of painting, or the Gandhara school which was definitely Hindu in origin and nature.

Every reader of Percy Brown's *Islamic Architecture in India* or Vincent Smith's *A History of Fine Arts in India and Ceylon* knows how different was the Hindu art from the Muslim's, and how rarely the two mixed or merged. To a Muslim a Hindu temple, with its naked goddesses and phallic images, was a positively distasteful sight; in fact, the anti-idolatry spirit of Islam was revolted by all kinds of Hindu architecture. The Hindu, on the other hand, saw most of Muslim architecture enshrined in mosques and domes and minarets and mausolea, which carried upon them the clear impress of Islam and therefore could not be a part of his artistic world. There were a few buildings here and there which were 'secular' in purpose or content and whose beauty was appreciated by both the peoples, but this rare coincidence could not make for a common artistic heritage.

CONCLUSION

Thus Hindu–Muslim conflict was not merely religious. It was the clash of two civilizations, of two peoples who had different languages, different literary roots, different ideas of education, different philosophical sources, and different concepts of art. Such a yawning cultural gulf was enough to destroy any affinity which the two peoples might have had and to bring to nought all efforts at unity. When this cultural variance was combined with diversity in social customs and modes of livelihood the emergence of a united Indian nationalism was doomed without redemption.

Chapter 6

THE PSYCHOLOGICAL FACTOR

'PATRIOTISM is in political life what faith is in religion, and it stands to the domestic feelings and to homesickness as faith to fanaticism and to superstition.'[1] Patriotism, like faith, is fundamentally a state of mind. There may be, and usually are, visible, material and tangible agents which create or promote patriotism. But in essence it remains a spiritual feeling. To pursue Lord Acton's analogy a little further, we may say that as faith is created and strengthened by the Book, the place of worship, the history of the creed and religious relics, so patriotism is born and fed upon the concepts of a territory, a human group, a literary or artistic inheritance, a language and political history. But by themselves these agents are not enough. They have to be sustained by a feeling that our faith is the true faith and that our patriotism is the right patriotism. There must be a conviction that our faith is not heresy, that our patriotism is not mere chauvinism. To create this belief people seek foundations for their faith or patriotism. These foundations or bases constitute the psychological factor in nationalism.

The importance of this factor is obvious. It is a very weighty factor—sometimes even more significant than the historical or cultural ingredients. History may all be wrong and culture may be a farce, but you cannot quarrel with the feeling of a people that they are a separate entity. You may not agree with them, but that would not affect their feeling of separatism.

In India the psychological factor gained even greater significance because Muslim nationalism (not unlike Hindu or Indian nationalism) did not receive strong support from either history or language or culture. By normal standards set by the theoreticians of nationalism neither India nor Muslim India

[1] Lord Acton, 'Nationality' in *Essays on Freedom and Power* (Boston, ed., 1948), p. 188.

could be called a nation. Several ingredients were missing. And so the final argument on which the claimants of nationalism took their stand was the argument from psychology. They felt that they were a nation: therefore they were a nation. No more effective definition of nationalism has yet been suggested than Renan's, and he based his theory on the simple but powerful fact that if a people feel strongly and passionately that they make up a nation, historical wisdom as well as political prudence dictate the acceptance of this claim. The clash of nationalisms in India was, as we will see in this chapter, basically a psychological conflict. The battle was fought not so much on the field of politics as in the minds of men—a battle ground where a different set of weapons is used, weapons like myths and symbols, images and legends, pride and hero worship.

MYTHS AND SYMBOLS

A myth is not a purely fictitious narrative or idea. In the political or psychological sense it has always an element of truth in it and an element of untruth. It is compounded of popular ideas, of which some have some reality and some are fabrications. The presence of both these elements in a myth must be kept in mind if what follows is to be understood.

One major myth in Imperial India was that she was one homogeneous country and therefore very nearly one nation. Geographically speaking India was one country; in fact, a glance at the map tells us that nature must have meant it to be one geographical entity. But sometimes it is nature which proposes and man who disposes. Because India was a convenient geographical concept, therefore it was also a national concept. This was a myth which was upheld by the Hindu as passionately as it was exploded by the Muslim. The Hindu deeply felt that his country was one, that his nation was one, and that the Muslim was a disruptionist who was bent upon undoing the work of centuries. The Muslim believed that the myth of an Indian country or nation was a figment of the Hindu imagination, that at least he did not subscribe to it, and that if such a thing as an Indian nation did exist he was not a part of it. The debate was peppery and pitiless. Both sides appealed to history for evidence and each found in it what it wanted to find. The bountiful and generous Clio shares its opulence with all. And so the two myths—that of the Indian nation and that of Indian disunity—grew up side by side, destined to run in parallel lines, never to meet or merge.

Another myth was that of an out-of-all-proportions emphasis on the martial qualities of the Indian Muslims. Its parentage must be equally shared by the British, the Hindus and the Muslims. First the British spread the news that Muslims were good fighters and therefore the backbone of the Indian Army. The Hindus resented this 'favour' to the Muslims and, politically, argued against its validity; but many of them believed in it and therefore feared a Muslim rising against other Indians. The Muslims accepted the myth like a woman accepting a compliment—without caring to verify its truth. Had they not conquered India by feat of arms and for centuries kept it by the sword? The Pathans, the Baluchis and the Punjabis were good fighting men, and this buttressed up the myth. What was forgotten in the flush of the tumult was that the Rajput had an even longer history of successful soldiering, that the Gurkha (for the purpose of the present argument an Indian) was a legend on the battlefield, that the Hindu of some areas had made a name among the sappers and miners, and that, above all, the Sikh was as good a soldier as anyone else. But the myth of the martial race flourished and the confusion it created was greater than the truth it contained.

Why was this myth invented? The British invented it partly out of a genuine conviction that the meat-eating Muslim was the hardiest and the bravest of all, partly because they wanted to frighten the Hindu into submission with the bogey of the fighting Musalman who would devour them as soon as imperial protection was withdrawn, and partly because they wanted to strike a communal balance in the Indian Army.

Still another myth was that India belonged to the Hindus and that Muslims were foreigners who had no business to be there. This was an exclusively Hindu myth given currency by Bankim Chandra Chatterjee and his fellow-Bengali novelists and by Bal Gangadher Tilak and his Maharashtra school of politics. They carried on a merciless propaganda aimed at bracketing together the Muslims and the British as aliens who, by conquering India, had committed an unpardonable sacrilege (incidentally, this helped to bring the Muslims and the

British closer). The Muslims were *melechchas*, lower than the untouchables, who must be driven out of mother India. The mythical part of this idea was that India was originally a Hindu land. In actual fact, if her parenthood had to be discovered it would probably be the present-day untouchables or the Dravidians who were the earliest known inhabitants of the country before the Aryan hordes came from the north and slowly pushed them to the south.

Another aspect of this myth was also historically untenable. The Muslims had come to India as conquerors, but they had settled down here and made a home. The point becomes clear by comparing them with the British. Both were alien to India in race, religion, language and culture. But Muslims became a part of India and disowned the lands of their origin. The British came as mere rulers, with no intention of living in India or even of mixing with the natives without careful discrimination. They sent relays of bureaucrats from the home country who took their turn at the imperial wheel and then returned to Britain laden with honours and sometimes also riches. They could be called foreigners who had to be turned out before India was free. But to make a similar demand upon the Muslims was mere sophism.

The last myth which we will consider here (every student of modern history can add his own to the list) is that of the glorious past. The Hindu harked back to the golden age of the Mauryas or the Guptas. The Muslim reverted to the Mughuls or to the past glories of Islam outside India. The idea was to demonstrate that the people, though now subject to a foreign rule, had once upon a time been great. This cheered them up and drew them together: people who believe in the same past tend to form a group apart.

This enshrinement of the past took many shapes. There was a new emphasis on the antiquity and merit of the Indus Valley civilization. There was a renewal of interest in ancient chronicles. The process of reinterpreting the past grew apace. Muslim historians had to prove how beneficial to India had been the advent of Islam or how great and pious was Aurungzeb. Praises were sung to the Mutiny which was now proclaimed to have been a 'war of independence' and a 'war of liberation'. All those who had resisted the British authority were deified

The remarkable thing is that these myths were taken seriously by the *élite* of the society and disseminated among the masses. Every Hindu and every Muslim took pride in the achievements—real or supposed—of his own particular past. Attachment to these myths produced two results. It separated the Hindu from the Muslim and aggrandized the nationalism of each.

A symbol may be defined as a thing regarded by general consent as naturally typifying or representing or recalling something which is common to a society or a people. It is the mark or character taken as the conventional sign of some object or idea or process. We say, for example, that white is the symbol of purity, the lion of courage, the dome or minaret of a mosque. It is a token or watchword which summarizes for us the association of some quality or object with another quality or object.

Symbols, like myths, have played a not inconspicuous part in the formation of nations. Of all the symbols it is the flag which is perhaps the most characteristic sign of nationalism. One historical instance will illustrate this. In France the revolutionary government of 1848 was confronted with a serious conflict between those who demanded the red flag and those who wanted the tricolour. Again in 1873 a fierce struggle raged over the question whether the white flag of the Bourbons or the tricolour should be adopted. In India both the Congress and the Muslim League had their own flags, and the reverence in which they were held was such as to convey an impression as if the two peoples were already free countries. During the Congress rule in the provinces the Congress tricolour was flown over public buildings, and this was taken by the Muslims as a sign of the coming of a Hindu *raj*.

Other symbols which cut the Muslim adrift from the Hindu may be mentioned. The Hindu (especially the Congressman) wore a *khadi* (homespun) cloth cap, which came to be called the Gandhi cap. The Muslim (in particular the Leaguer) adopted the *karakuli* (lamb fur) cap, which soon was given the label of Jinnah cap. Slogans also became symbols when the Hindu cried *Bharat mata ki jai* (long live the motherland) or *Jai Hind* (vive l'Inde), and the Muslim shouted *Allah o Akbar* (God is great) and *Pakistan zindabad* (long live Pakistan). Each party also boasted of a volunteer corps, a militia, which was integrated with the main political party. The R.S.S. and the Deval 'volunteers' among the Hindus and the Muslim League National Guards and the Khaksars among the Muslims symbolized militant nationalism.

Then there were symbols which were not political in nature. The Hindu began a letter or a book with the word 'Om', just as the Muslim inscribed the Arabic phrase meaning 'I begin in the name of Allah' on the head of every writing. The Hindu temple and the Muslim mosque were quite different in shape and aspect and the two emblems threw the two religions into a stark contrast.

Institutions, memories, traditions and ideals assume a symbolic shape by the process of historical forces and accidents. Many examples of this can be quoted. We used to associate the Swiss with the idea of neutrality, the Germans with the struggle for a place in the sun, the Italians with the effort to regain 'unredeemed' territory, the British with sea power, and France with the recovery of Alsace–Lorraine. In the world politics of today similar ideas are expressed by phrases like 'peaceful co-existence', Chinese 'expansionism', American defence of the 'free West', Japan's 'aggressive industrialism', and so on.

In India this kind of symbolism was expressed by the conception of a 'greater India' given currency by some Hindus, to which some Muslims replied with a plan to reconquer and Islamize the whole of India (*vide* F. K. Khan Durrani). Among the more responsible quarters, too, the picture of the future was expressed in two different words: 'Akhand Hindustan' (united India) and 'Pakistan'. In spite of, and during, all negotiations, discussions, compromises and agreements, these two symbols summarized the goals set before themselves by the two nationalisms.

To anyone acquainted with Indian history it will not come as a surprise that these myths and symbols appealed as much to the sophisticated intellectuals as to the simple masses. Emotionalism is always a powerful ingredient in that curious mixture of imponderables called nationalism. When it is allied to illiteracy and lack of education its impact on a people striving for independence can well be imagined. Countries which are worldly wise have cheerfully succumbed to these temptations. In India it was child's play to rouse the emotions of the people and to invent myths and create symbols. And one cannot say that they were completely useless. They might have been irrational (how little part does reason play in our life!), but they had immense psychological value in the nationalistic renaissance. They crystallized the issues at stake, hung out the signals of alarm and pinpointed the national objectives. It was unnecessary as well as undesirable to chop logic with the masses or to prepare them for subtle argument. The need of the hour was to persuade the people that their salvation lay in adopting a certain course of action and to make that course of action appear to be worth their while. If myths and symbols and emblems and signs achieved this object, they brought welcome grist to the political mill. In India the psychological factor was particularly useful not only in creating a new nationalism but also in sustaining a nascent nationalism. Its role on the national level may be likened to the impact of suggestion and auto-suggestion on the individual mind.

FEAR AND INSECURITY

It is a commonplace observation that the solidarity of a group becomes especially marked when it is threatened by other groups which do not share its particular beliefs and sentiments. One of the most powerful factors which nurtured Muslim nationalism was the Muslim feeling that they were not getting, and would not get, a fair deal at the hands of the Hindus.

Two pieces of evidence will suffice to demonstrate the validity of this feeling. Sir Fazl-i-Husain once wrote to one of his friends, 'An Indian Muslim in the Punjab may be intensely national, sincerely non-communal, not only in thought but in action, in all his dealings and none may point out a single incident to the contrary and yet when the occasion arises the non-Muslim leaders and the public would not prefer him especially if he happens to be capable and strong.'[1] The second piece of testimony is even more reliable, for it comes from one who was all his life a staunch Congressman and a leader of the

[1] Quoted in Azim Husain, *Fazl-i-Husain: A Political Biography*, 1946, p. 81.

Nationalist Muslims. 'The crux of the problem is,' said Shaukatullah Ansari in 1944, 'that the Hindus are small-minded in the social field, and that has touched the Muslims to the quick. Hindus have treated Muslims as untouchables. . . . You may be a *pucca* nationalist and four-square Gandhiite, yet you will be treated as untouchable as soon as you announce to a Hindu that you are a Muslim.'[1]

Such evidence can be multiplied a hundredfold. Everyone from Sayyid Ahmad Khan to the meanest leader felt and expressed this. Jinnah's speeches and writings are replete with this fear of insecurity, and so are the resolutions of the Muslim League and other Muslim organizations which did not share the optimism of the Congress that sometime, somehow, somewhere all will be well. In fact, it is no exaggeration, though it may be an over-simplification, to say that Pakistan is the child of this feeling of insecurity.

Lack of national unity is always productive of tension. In the case of India it was the Muslim community which was the victim of this tension. They felt that the majority community was imposing its views upon them, that this imposition of its will was leading to an oppression which became increasingly unbearable as the years passed. The Hindus—the majority community—themselves intensified this Muslim fear by adopting a muddle-headed attitude towards the Hindu–Muslim problem. The Congress leaders never took this issue seriously, and that was their greatest failure in politics. They always considered it as a problem which would solve itself with time. Jawaharlal Nehru underestimated the Muslim feeling to such an extent as to deny altogether the very existence of it. He harped upon the economic problem and explained away the communal rivalry as a sordid race for the loaves and fishes of jobs. Gandhi was equally convinced that it was the British presence in India that kept the problem alive, and that all would be well the moment the 'third party' was gone. This refusal to face the realities of the situation kept the Hindus away from understanding the Muslim point of view and in the end caused an explosion and a partition.

The Muslims were intensely suspicious of every Hindu move. Haunted by the fear of being dominated and then crushed by

[1] Shaukatullah Ansari, *Pakistan: The Problem of India*, 1944, p. 27.

the overwhelming Hindu majority, the entire course of their politics was coloured by a defensive attitude. These fears and suspicions may have been due to a sense of inferiority traceable to the post-Mutiny days when Muslims were the suppressed community—suppressed by the British in politics and by the Hindus in education and commerce. Or it might be accounted for by the simple fact that they were a minority in India, and minorities always suffer from a feeling of insecurity. Another reason may have been their backwardness in practically every department of modern life. They made a stupid mistake right at the beginning of their political career when they refused to take heed and continued to live in the cloister.

Economic nationalism was also active in this feeling of insecurity. Muslims resented the Hindu control of the economic field.[1] They were shut out from business, trade and commerce. They had no banks of their own, no insurance companies, no shipping lines. When a Muslim opened a shop or set up a production plant he ran a considerable risk by invading a sphere which was monopolized by the other community. There were no economic leaders among them, no capitalists, who had either the courage or the resources to stand up to the Hindu and break his stranglehold. It was only towards the end that one or two banks and insurance companies were opened.

It was in the political field that Muslim fears received the strongest confirmation. If the nineteenth century had been one of colonialism and imperialism, the twentieth was the century of democracy and self-determination. On both these principles the Muslim stood to lose in India. In a democratic government he would ever be a minority—and an unchangeable minority, to boot. He would never control the administration because he never could be a majority in the legislature. This was a chilling prospect which killed his interest in a future democratic Indian State. For this the Congress called him 'undemocratic' and 'reactionary', but political abuse could not alter the fact that in any popular system of government he must be satisfied with the status of a minority without hope

[1] This again is the testimony of a Nationalist Muslim leader who was a staunch opponent of the Muslim League, see Afzal Haq (Ahrar), *Pakistan and Untouchability*, 1941, pp. 89–90.

and without a future. This was the cardinal point which Jinnah drummed into Muslim ears and on which he built the campaign for a separate Muslim State.

The doctrine of self-determination, as originally applied to India, was equally deadly to the Muslim cause. The world knew India as one country and could, through propaganda and moral appeal, be made to constrain Britain to free it. But the world knew little of the Muslim nationalism within the larger 'Indian' nationalism, and the Congress saw to it that this gap in the world's information was not filled. When, therefore, the Muslims invoked the principle of self-determination, they were ridiculed as a small minority pretending to be a nation. This damaged their cause and also their reputation, but in the end acted as a spur to their determination to sever all links with India.

The real roots of the idea of Muslim separatism should therefore be sought in the minds of men rather than in political factors. The latter only reflected the struggle going on in the former. This explains the extraordinary strength of Muslim nationalism which was able to split India within seven years of the formulation of its demand for a separate State.

As a national minority three courses were open to Indian Muslims. They could seek help from their co-religionists in other States extending from Afghanistan to Turkey, as the Sudeten Germans did when, before the Second World War, they appealed to Germany for help. But this the Muslims never did, though they gave their own support to the pan-Islam and Khilafat movements. Or, they could secure privileges from the majority group within India, as did the Catalans in Spain before the time of Franco. This they had been doing since 1906 when they expressed a desire to have separate electorates. Safeguards and concessions were repeatedly demanded and mostly conceded—but by the British rulers, not by the Hindus. This was an important factor, for it convinced the Muslims that the Hindus were not prepared to safeguard their interests or meet their wishes. In actual working, moreover, even the safeguards proved to be futile. Gradually Muslim thoughts turned to the third course open to them, viz., complete separation from the major group. This the Muslims demanded for the first time in 1940 when the Muslim League passed the Lahore or Pakistan Resolution.

All safeguards, guarantees and promises of protection had failed to erode the foundations of suspicion and fear. Tension was not lessened. Insecurity had not decreased. Irritation had increased and with it the possibility of civil war. The spirit of compromise was absent. There was no point on which a bridge of understanding could be built. The psychological gulf finally proved to be too wide and too deep to be spanned by any known political device. So a separate State had to be created whose nationalism was psychologically well vested but politically yet untried.

PRIDE IN HEROES

The absence or otherwise of a spirit of nationality can be tested by observing whether all the people claiming one nationality adore the same heroes. Social solidarity will be as powerful and widespread as the attachment of the group to a body of heroes to whom it pays homage. A hero impersonates common values of a social group and the acceptance of him contributes to the maintenance of group solidarity.

The history of Western nationalism illustrates the connection between the spirit of nationality and the acceptance of common heroes. Heroes have been of several kinds. There were religious heroes or saints, like St. Patrick of Ireland, St. Denis of France and St. Stanislas of Poland. There were royal heroes, like Charlemagne and Louis XIV (the *Roi-soleil*) in France and Peter the Great in Russia. There were political heroes, like Napoleon in France, Bismarck in Germany and Garibaldi in Italy. There were 'national' heroes ('defenders of the country'), like Jeanne d'Arc of France, William Tell of Switzerland and Kossuth of Hungary.

Similarly in India Hindus and Muslims had different heroes. Hindu India looked to such figures as Shivaji, Tilak, Aurobindo, Gandhi and Nehru. Muslim India revered Shah Waliullah, Sayyid Ahmad Khan, Muhammad Ali and Jinnah. Going farther back, Hindu India extolled Asoka and Ghandargupta, for whom the Muslims could have no feeling of loyalty or even interest. Muslim India looked lovingly to Muhammad bin Qasim and Mahmud of Ghazna: the Hindus detested the memory of Qasim, who was the first Muslim to invade India, and cursed the name of Mahmud, who had despoiled their temples and shrines.

Hindu historians had a soft corner for Akbar, whom they regarded as a peacemaker and a monarch of great toleration. Muslim historians reserved their praises for Aurungzeb, whom they thought to have been a most pious and God-fearing king. The Hindus had no love for Aurungzeb on account of his orthodox Islamic views. The Muslims disliked Akbar for his renunciation of Islam. The Hindus idolized Shivaji as the liberator of South India and the founder of the Marhatta power. The Muslims frowned upon him as the inveterate foe of Muslim power and a crafty soldier who killed a Muslim general under deception.

HISTORY AS A DIVISIVE FACTOR

The philosophy of history is a part of the philosophy of nationalism. National bias is the most obvious trait of all historical work.[1] Battles, wars, territorial expansions, foreign invasions —all enter into the making of greater pride in national unity and feeling.

The growth of the nationalist sentiment in India affected the Hindu and Muslim chroniclers in different ways. 'The Hindus began to lay great stress on their heroic fights against Muslims. Tod's *Annals and Antiquities of Rajasthan* served as a model and a store-house of materials. Inspiring historical accounts were written of the long-drawn-out struggle between the Rajputs and the Muslims, in which the Rajputs almost always came out with flying colours.' In dealing with the Marhattas it was emphasized that they were inspired by the ideal of founding a Hindu Empire, but 'their treatment of the Rajputs and plundering raids against the Hindus were either forgotten or ignored'. Shivaji's faults were minimized or 'even explained away'.[2]

There is an interesting connection between Indian historical

[1] For the significance of history in the development of modern nationalism see R. W. Seton-Waston, *The Historian as a Political Force in Central Europe*, London, 1922.

[2] R. C. Majumdar, 'Nationalist Historians', in C. H. Philips (ed.), *Historians of India, Pakistan and Ceylon*, 1961, p. 423.

and political writings and the then prevailing state of Hindu–Muslim relations. The works written in the 1920's emphasized 'the community of interests and the cultural intercourse of Hindus and Muslims'; those of the 1930's underlined 'their polarity in religion and thought' but suggested that 'political co-operation had been and could be secured'; and those of the 1940's stressed 'the separate political achievements and destiny of the Muslims in South Asia'.[1] It is apparent that in the 1920's the Khilafat movement and the Amritsar shooting had brought the two peoples together and therefore the historians of the period spoke of their unity. In the next decade, however, this spirit of *camaraderie* was fast disappearing and an optimistic historian could at the most recall past unity and hope for the best. But in the 1940's even this hope was irretrievably gone and the rift was there for all to see, including the historians.

It is a pity that the Muslims, once renowned as the masters of the science of history, did little history-writing in India, particularly in the modern period. It has been pleaded on their behalf that they were so much engrossed in the developments occurring in other Muslim countries that they had little time to observe and asses their own history. But this is only an excuse. Their interest in world Islam was never so absorbing (except perhaps for four or five years during the Khilafat period) as to preclude all study of Indian past or present. Moreover, if Muslim historians were so greatly involved in the affairs of Turkey, Persia and the Arab world, why did they not produce some work on these areas?

The fact is that history-writing was not the Muslims' strong point in modern India. Historical works proper do not make an appearance in their literature. Apart from a few attempts in Urdu and Bengali, whose scholarly quality is doubtful, the only serious work was done by Ameer Ali, Yusuf Ali and Sir Shafaat Ahmad Khan. But Ameer Ali's interest was in world Islam rather than in India. Yusuf Ali was not a scholar, but the little he wrote on modern India at least spoke of promise. Shafaat Ahmad Khan's only work on the modern period was on the 1935 constitution and can hardly be classed as a piece of historical writing.

[1] P. Hardy, 'Modern Muslim Historical Writing on Medieval Muslim India', ibid., p. 308.

Historians play an important part in the formation of national spirit. They exalt the history of their own people. They seek to prove the supremacy of their civilization. In modern Europe, Italian scholars were probably the first to praise their history, culture and nationality.

In India, as we have seen, there was no mentionable work on the modern period, but some historians looked to the great Islamic past or to Muslim rule in India. The Mughuls and their Muslim predecessors attracted a few historians, like Abdul Aziz, but not much work was done, and it was not till after Independence that the importance of 're-writing' national history was emphasized.

Teachers of history can be no less effective agents of nationalism than the historians. The way history is taught is a good general help or hindrance to the inculcation of national loyalty. Glorification of one's own nationality becomes a part of the lesson. Biographies of great heroes are prescribed as aids to character formation. Only those historical events are treated in the classroom which add to national glory. Only such interpretations are given currency as agree with the prevailing national ideals. All this was done by Hindu and Muslim history teachers in schools and colleges. And it was here that the paucity of Muslim scholars and their works was keenly felt. Even the Muslim periods of Indian history were written up and taught by Hindu authors and lecturers.

NATIONAL CHARACTER

The idea of national character is highly deceptive because of the wide variety of individual characters and cultural traits in a national group. It has been suggested, therefore, that the term 'national character' should be replaced with 'national traditions', but traditions alone do not determine a group's way of life and thinking. Perhaps 'national mentality' is a better term to describe the impression that we want to convey about a group's communal thought and action.

Whatever words we use, the fact remains that nearly every national group has its own traditions, interests and ideals which distinguish it from other such groups and enable an observer to determine the lineaments of its national existence.

Applying this to India we see that though the Hindu and

the Muslim had many things in common and though a Punjabi Hindu looked and acted very much like a Punjabi Muslim, yet there was a manifest difference in their outlook on life. The Muslims had their own characteristics (in Frederick Hertz's words, a 'constellation of forces') which imparted to them a unity or fixity of character. These characteristics were so widespread and pervasive that, on the one hand, they transcended the features which the Muslims shared with the Hindus and, on the other, they moulded the image of the Muslim group both in the mind of the community itself and in that of the Hindus. However much the Hindus and the Muslims of one province appeared to have in common and however much a foreign observer might insist on refusing to distinguish between the two, their ways of living and thinking were certainly not the same.

An educated Hindu and an educated Muslim of the urban area were superficially alike. They lived and studied and dressed and enjoyed themselves in the same way. But there the affinity ended. At home their ways of eating were different. Food was not the same. They professed different religions. In the home most of them even dressed differently. They read different newspapers and had different views on politics. Their social institutions, in connection with marriage and death, were different. Apart from their social intercourse outside the home, which was both superficial and sophisticated, their lives had different values. The whole environment was different, for it was based on different traditions. In a word, they had different ideals, or, what is even more important, they felt that they had different ideals.

This feeling of being different, of not sharing the vital things of life, directed their political opinions. National character or mentality, or what you will, is predominantly a psychological sentiment. The Muslim thought that he had a mind different from that of a Hindu. When this feeling spread among the community and Muslims generally came to believe that they had a mentality which was not the same as the Hindus', the Muslim nation, or at least the spirit of it, was born. When time and assimilation confirmed this belief, it became a faith. And faith is a powerful, perhaps the most powerful, foundation of nationalism.

The grooves of a national character come to be fixed in perpetuity. The Muslims looked upon themselves as Muslims and not as anything else. The Hindus were Hindus, or non-Muslims, but not anything else. This feeling of separateness, which was in this sense purely a state of disposition, gnawed at the vitals of unity or the prospect for it. When two groups think that they do not belong together, it is impossible to make one nation of them. A multi-national political system could be devised, or perhaps a multi-national society concocted out of this disarray. But the first could only have been a rickety structure without the solid foundation of a united political impulse, and the second only a temporary expedient without the spiritual ballast of a shared view of life.

However poor the prospects for such a compromise, it cannot be said that no efforts were made to achieve at least minimal unity. There were several long-drawn-out negotiations between Hindus and Muslims and all of them cannot be dismissed as meaningless gestures. In 1916 and 1917, in 1928 and 1931 and again in 1944, there were conversations and exchanges of views. To pass judgement on the sincerity of the negotiating parties is neither possible nor desirable. But it is necessary to record the fact that the result was far from a success.

In another respect we may say that a continuous attempt at the creation of a national society was made by the political systems devised at various stages by the British. Local self-government institutions, separate electorates, increasingly representative legislatures, dyarchy, provincial autonomy, federalism, reservation of seats for minorities, weightages, safeguards—all these were tools and instruments shaped by the British to achieve Indian unity or at least to lay its foundations. The greatest experiment in this field was the 1935 constitution which had the dual merit of recognizing the lack of basic unity in India and at the same time of giving her a constitutional structure which, if worked in a spirit of goodwill and amity, could result in a coherent federal union. But the experiment, perhaps the greatest of its kind in the world, failed because one part of the constitution was not worked in the spirit in which it was intended to be worked and the other never came into operation by the intervention of the war.

Hypothetical questions are notoriously difficult to answer. But it was within the realm of possibility that a multi-national India might have maintained its unity had the Act of 1935 been given a fair and complete trial. But it can also be argued that the psychological rift between the Hindus and the Muslims had, by 1937, gone too far to be healed by political or constitutional devices. At what precise time did the Muslim feeling of nsecurity mature into a belief that they must part company with the Hindus? This leads us to the question of political consciousness.

NATIONAL CONSCIOUSNESS

Robert Michels was right when he said that the essence of nationality lies, above all, in the will of a people.[1] There are the usual components of a national spirit which we have mentioned in the preceding pages, but the common will to live and belong together transcends them all. If all these standard ingredients were absent, but the will was present, it would still be possible to have a national group.

As a 'pragmatic' or 'historical' factor, nationality has existed in history for a long time, but it is only through consciousness, or rather the awakening of it, that it becomes the 'absolute' factor. In the words of Hans Kohn, 'nationality is formed by the decision to form a nationality'.

Muslim nationalism conforms to this theory (or to part of it) to an extraordinary extent. It was the result, not of blood (race is a fiction), nor of a common language (the Bengalis did not speak Urdu), nor of pure religion (many Muslims were recent converts from Hinduism), nor even of a shared territory (not a single province was completely Muslim)—but of consciousness. It was the power of an idea which constituted and moulded it. Material facts, of course, helped the configuration, but the real driving impetus behind the movement was spiritual—'spiritual' in the broader rather than the religious sense. Without a sufficient measure of national consciousness there would have been no idea of separation, and therefore no nationalism.

National consciousness is an exceedingly complex process.

[1] Robert Michels, *Notes sur les Moyen de constater la Nationalité*, 1917, p. 1.

It is a sort of a group consciousness working on a larger canvas. It arises from, as well as causes, group solidarity. It aims at discovering, and then communicating to the people, the links which make for their unity. It points out the aims the pursuit of which becomes the duty of the group. It is not a uniform process, but contains many strands and variations ranging from definite ideology to feeble doubt.

The first indication that a national group has 'arrived' is the development of a consciousness of the fact that all the members of that group belong to one nationality. They must believe that they belong to one nationality. But that should not be taken to mean that each individual member of the group shares the will to live together. The Muslim League never claimed that it spoke for every single Indian Muslim. Nor was Pakistan the demand of all Muslims living in the sub-continent. There were some who were just indifferent to politics; there were others who did not agree with the League brand of politics; there were still others who did not care what befell their community. The national will must be shared by a great majority of the group. National consciousness does not have to spread to every nook and cranny to qualify as such.

The spirit of nationalism is actuated by three types of motives: traditions, interests and ideals. Traditions are 'patterns of behaviour which are regarded as values simply because they are a collective heritage regardless of any reasons of utility, beauty or supernatural sanction'. An interest is a 'claim regarded as useful to the existence and well-being of the group'. An ideal is an 'aim which is not a direct interest of individuals. It is regarded as possessing a high authority, and thereby has the power to command obedience and the sacrifice of individual interests'. The traditions connect a nation with its past, the interests with its present, the ideals with its future.[1]

It is not always possible to distinguish between these three motives. They form a part of a psychological sub-structure on which nationalism is built. National consciousness means the awareness of this sub-structure. Muslims were conscious of their being a nation when they became aware of their traditions and heritage, whether Indian or Islamic; when they came

[1] See the very interesting discussion on this point in Frederick Hertz, *Nationality in History and Politics*, 1944 (3rd. imp. 1951), pp. 18 et seq.

to know what their interests were and what was conducive to their safety, freedom and prestige; and when they came to have their own ideals of what they wanted to achieve.

National consciousness is another name for having national aspirations. These aspirations can relate to four things: unity, liberty, individuality and prestige. For Muslim India unity meant that all Muslims were one political body, with common social and economic ideas, professing the same religion and owing allegiance to the same cultural heritage. Liberty implied to them not the independence of India as a whole (though that was a part of their programme), but liberation from British as well as Hindu domination and from any external pressure or interference. Individuality was for them the assertion of their separateness and distinctness: they were *not* the same as other Indians, they were different. Prestige conveyed to them the idea of distinction; they wanted honour, dignity and influence, if possible in India, if not in a separate State of their own; they did not want to live as a helpless minority without self-respect.

The significance of these aspirations lies in the fact that they crystallized the psychological force behind Muslim nationalism. It was not enough to have a common religion, a common language or a common history. People must be conscious of their past and of their future. They must be aware of their individuality. They must believe that they are different from others. This belief was the hard core of their nationalism, and the most difficult to challenge or counteract. You can debate on historical antecedents, on linguistic unity, even on ideology. You cannot argue with faith.

Chapter 7

THE TWO-NATION THEORY

JINNAH was not the first to call the Muslims of India a nation. Before him Sayyid Ahmad Khan had addressed them as a *qaum*, an Urdu word which can be paraphrased as 'nation'. The Aga Khan, Ameer Ali and others often referred to their community as a 'nation' or a 'nationality'. But it was Jinnah who, for the first time, proclaimed that India was inhabited by two distinct nations—Hindus and Muslims—which could not live in one State. He expounded this two-nation theory in such detail and with such effect that most Muslims and even some Hindus came to believe in its truth. The Muslim League demand for Pakistan was based on this theory and, though generally neither the Hindus nor the British accepted it, India was partitioned on the premiss that Muslims constituted a separate nation and should therefore be given a separate State.

The real problem of India was national. The Hindus claimed that India was one nation and a united country and wanted independence. The Muslims replied with the counter-claim that India was neither a unity nor a nation, that the Muslims formed a separate nation, and that Muslim freedom from Hindu domination was as essential as Indian liberation from British rule.

THE THEORY ENUNCIATED

The most clear and emphatic exposition of the theory is to be found in Jinnah's statements and speeches. The substance of his argument can be put as follows.

Hinduism and Islam represented two distinct and separate civilizations and were in fact as distinct from one another in origin, tradition and manner of life as were the different European nations. In India there was a major and a minor nation, and it followed that a parliamentary system based on the principle of majority rule must inevitably mean the rule of the major nation. Therefore a constitution must be evolved that recognized the fact that there were in India two nations, both of whom must share the governance of their 'common motherland'.[1] One thing was now obvious, that 'we are by no means a minority but a solid and distinct nation by ourselves with a destiny of our own'.[2]

It was in his presidential address to the Muslim League session at Lahore, at which the partition Resolution was passed, that he explained the theory in detail. 'Notwithstanding a thousand years of close contact, nationalities, which are as divergent today as ever, cannot at any time be expected to transform themselves into one nation merely by means of subjecting them to democratic constitution and holding them forcibly together by unnatural and artificial methods of British Parliamentary Statute.' The problem in India was not 'of an inter-communal character but manifestly of an international one', and it must be treated as such. If Britain was really in earnest and sincerely wanted to secure the peace and happiness of India, it should 'allow the major nations separate homelands by dividing India into "autonomous national States"'. Hinduism and Islam were not religions in the strict sense of the word, but were, in fact, 'different and distinct social orders, and it is a dream that the Hindus and Muslims can ever evolve a common nationality, and this misconception of one Indian nation has gone far beyond the limits and is the cause of most of your troubles and will lead India to destruction if we fail to revise our notions in time. The Hindus and Muslims belong to two different religions, philosophies, social customs, literatures. They neither intermarry nor interdine together and, indeed, they belong to two different civilizations which are based mainly on conflicting ideas and conceptions. Their aspects on life and of life are different. It is quite clear that Hindus and Musalmans derive their inspiration from different sources of history. They have different epics, different heroes, and different episodes. Very often the hero of one is a foe of the other and, likewise, their victories and defeats overlap. To yoke together two such nations under a single State, one as a numerical minority and the other as a majority, must

[1] Jamiluddin Ahmad, op. cit., Vol. I, pp. 130–31, 138.
[2] Ibid., p. 154.

lead to growing discontent and final destruction of any fabric that may be so built up for the government of such a nation. . . . Musalmans are a nation according to any definition of a nation, and they must have their homelands, their territory and their State. We wish to live in peace and harmony with our neighbours as a free and independent people. We wish our people to develop to the fullest our spiritual, cultural, economic, social and political life in any way that we think best and in consonance with our own ideals and according to the genius of our people.'[1]

To the Hindu objection that Muslims were mere invaders and outsiders and had thus no territorial right to India, Jinnah's answer was rooted in the logic of Indian history. 'Surely India is not the sole property of the Congress, and if the real mother was to be discovered, it would be the Dravidians and still further the Aborigines. It would neither be the Aryan nor the Musalman. The Ayran claim to India is no better than that of the Musalmans, except that they were earlier arrivals in point of time.'[2]

Even a Nationalist Muslim, who was opposed to the two-nation theory, admitted that 'Muslims felt that they cannot withstand humiliating conditions and they would much rather live in the hell of Pakistan than serve in the heaven of Hindustan and its degrading economic and social treatment'.[3] The fact was that Muslims had maintained their separate entity in India for several centuries, first as victorious invaders and imperial rulers and later as fellow-subjects of the British. When the Hindus awoke to their position of strength vouchsafed by numerical majority, the Muslims realized their peril and reasserted their ancient superiority. Since it was no longer possible to rule over the whole of India as they had done in the past, they must consolidate what they had or could have and thus check the process which would certainly undermine the entire structure of their religion, culture and tradition. This was the central argument on which Muslim India reared the two-nation theory.

[1] Ibid., pp. 176–80.

[2] Statement of 1 April 1940, reproduced in *India's Problem of her Future Constitution*, ?1940, p. 31.

[3] Shaukatullah Ansari, op. cit., p. 28.

EXTERNAL EVIDENCE

Several Hindu and many British writers on India have admitted the deep rift between Hindus and Muslims in Indian society and politics. To take the Hindus first. In 1926, a Hindu emphasized the distinctiveness of the Muslim population and the fact that this distinctiveness had been maintained up to that time. The 'broadest division' of Indian population was between the Hindus and the Muslims.[1] In 1939, another student of the Indian minority problem, who wrote a doctoral thesis at Columbia to disprove the necessity and wisdom of communal representation, began his treatment of the subject by the bland statement that 'India is a land of nations'.[2] In 1943, another Hindu declared that the demand for Pakistan was the result of an acute and genuine Muslim apprehension that in case of a united India 'they would be submerged by the overwhelming majority of Hindus'. His picture of a future India was that of a number of autonomous States with a central government of a confederal type.[3]

A most perceptive explanation of the Hindu–Muslim discord is given by Nirad Chaudhuri. The Hindus, led by their scholarly *élite*, came to believe that there was a cultural heritage common to the Indian Muslims and Hindus. 'In reality, the so-called common heritage was hardly deeper than a veneer to begin with and found to be extremely fragile in the event. The relative quickness with which its hold weakened on the people of India leads one to conclude that it had some inherent weakness. So it had. The common heritage was not a homogeneous product. . . . As long as the Hindu masses of India remained the adherents of a primitive kind of Hinduism created by the break-up of the ancient Indian civilization, and the Muslim masses remained a horde of semi-Islamized converts, all was likely to go well with the common heritage. But were either of the two wings to rise to a higher plane, they were

[1] S. Dutt, *Problem of Indian Nationality*, 1926, p. 73.

[2] B. K. Krishna, *The Problem of Minorities or Communal Representation in India*, 1939, p. 20.

[3] A. K. Pillai, of the Radical Democratic Party and Indian Federation of Labour, in a discussion on Lord Erskine's paper on 26 October 1943, *Asiatic Review*, April 1944, p. 141.

sure to move in opposite directions. In that event the Hindus would become more Hinduized and the Muslims more Islamic. This was what actually happened. As a result of the resuscitation of the Hindu past, the nineteenth century witnessed a progressive de-Islamization of the non-Muslims of India and together with it a tremendous revival of Hindu traditions. On the Muslim side there was a continuous attempt to complete the Islamization of the Muslims of India, both qualitatively and quantitatively. . . . The process inevitably tended towards a waning loyalty to the common heritage. The common heritage was a pleasant *modus vivendi* for the Hindus and Muslims in certain conditions. But it could do nothing, nor did it do anything, either to modify the group consciousness of the members of the two societies or to make them forget that they were antithetical in all matters except a few inessentials.' The heart of the matter was that 'the Hindu, as a member of a closed society based on birth and blood', found it hard to understand 'the nature of an open society which can expand itself through proselytization and conversion'.[1]

This long passage has been reproduced because it touches the pith of the argument and uncovers the roots of Hindu–Muslim enmity.

During the same period several British observers with Indian experience had also underlined the essential disunity of India and her lack of national solidarity. Sir Sidney Low and Lord Meston enumerated the obstacles to the creation of a true national spirit;[2] while E. A. Horne saw, even when Hindu-Muslim amity was at its peak, a 'fundamental antagonism of thought and feeling'.[3] In India religions were a substitute for nationalities, and the Muslims in particular were 'to all intent a nation, and the Government has to regard them as such'.[4]

The pressure of British domination and the universal use of English as a language throughout the country were factors

[1] For this interesting discussion see Nirad C. Chaudhuri, *The Autobiography of an Unknown Indian*, 1951, pp. 480–83.

[2] See S. Low, *A Vision of India*, 1910, pp. 348–9, and whole of Meston, *India at the Crossroads*, London, 1920.

[3] E. A. Horne, *The Political System of British India*, 1922, pp. 23–24.

[4] C. H. V. Tyne, *India in Ferment*, 1923, pp. 216–17.

making for national unity, but these were artificial ingredients of nationalism and could not be expected to result in a group solidarity in a country with such wide diversity and variety.[1] The Muslims feared that in a united Indian democratic government they would be swamped and devoured by the Hindus. 'In the last resort, and this was freely acknowledged by leading Indian statesmen *in both camps*, the Muslims will fight rather than submit.'[2]

Indian unity was based on shallow and unhealthy foundations. 'After all, it is only the unifying bond of indifference, submission, or hostility to alien rule that has held India together.' As that bond was being removed the essential discord was being demonstrated. The Muslims did not seek supremacy over all India. They wanted to be sure that 'if harmonious co-operation with Hinduism proves finally impossible, they will not be denied on that account the next best thing in constitutional advance'.[3] By the beginning of 1942 there was 'not a single Muslim in India who would not resent any form of Constitution which put the Hindus into not only a permanent majority, but a permanent position of power'.[4]

A year before the creation of Pakistan the *Economist* traced the origin of Muslim nationalism in an article which showed a deep understanding of the situation. There had never been such a State as Pakistan, but then neither was there a Jugoslavia or a Czechoslovakia before 1919. 'The reality is the Muslim population of India—some 90 millions—with its own system of law and social organization, its own distinct variant of the Hindustani language, its historical traditions and its connections outside India. . . .' The Hindu-controlled Congress provincial governments of 1937–9 had behaved arrogantly and this caused the 'phenomenal growth' of Muslim nationalism. 'When the present tension in India is viewed in its historical setting, it cannot be denied that we are confronted by something more than a mere factional strife within a single nation.'[5]

[1] Lord Meston, *India and the Empire*, 1924, p. 21.

[2] J. M. Kenworthy, *India: A Warning*, 1931, p. 57.

[3] Patrick Lacey, letter to *Manchester Guardian*, 4 April 1940.

[4] Lord Hailey, *H.L. 121. 5S*, 3 February 1942, Col. 616.

[5] 'Black Flags in India', *Economist*, 7 September 1946, pp. 362–4.

INTERNAL EVIDENCE

The Usual Congress–Hindu answer to the danger of communalism was that with the development of economic ideas all Hindu–Muslim trouble would by itself come to an end. This, however, was no more than wishful thinking or shutting the eyes to unpleasant realities. The fact was that even among the Indian labour where, according to the Congress theory, there should have been complete solidarity, unity was missing. The Trade Union Congress and the Trade Union Federation were in their earlier stages purely labour organizations without communal bias. But as Muslim nationalism grew the Muslim working classes began to realize the danger of Hindu domination in trade unions. Gradually separate unions came to life which made a point of Muslim rights as strongly as the Muslim League was doing in the political field.[1] Just before partition the all India Trade Union Congress was as much representative of Muslim labour as was the Indian National Congress of Muslim masses.

The Hindus made no serious effort to reassure the Muslims or to allay their fear. On the other hand, several Hindu leaders and intellectuals of influence are on record as having glorified Hinduism and desired its supremacy over the entire sub-continent and even beyond her boundaries.

According to Rabindranath Tagore, the Hindu poet and Nobel prize-winner, the term 'Hindu' had an extended connotation. Islam denoted a particular religion, but the concept of a Hindu in the history of India was coeval with that of a nation in its social sense.[2] One Hindu writer, in a book which purported to be an academic study of communal riots, seriously suggested the following 'cures' for the removal of Hindu–Muslim rivalry: Islam should change its name to Nirakar Samaj; all Muslims should become Hindus; all communal educational institutions should be abolished; and

[1] See Sir Walter Citrine, Secretary of the British T.U.C., speaking on India, (British) *Trade Union Congress Annual Report of 1942*, p. 301; and H. G. Bottomley (who had visited India as a member of the British Parliamentary Delegation), 'Trade Unionism in India', *The Times*, 10 April 1946.

[2] Sachin Sen, *The Political Thought of Tagore*, 1947, p. 200.

all communal electorates should be immediately done away with.[1] A Hindu professor claimed that 'Hindu' was a territorial term rather than a badge of religion, and that therefore all Muslims were in fact Hindus. And therefore, by his logic, there was no communal problem and the Congress resolution on self-determination was silly.[2]

Lala Hardyal, the legendary figure of Hindu renaissance, was even more ambitious. He said that if Hindus wanted to protect themselves they must conquer Afghanistan and the 'frontiers' and convert them to Hinduism.[3] Another Hindu leader contented himself by saying that to force Muslims into an Indian national State would not be 'compulsion'.[4]

Such expressions of Hindu imperialism did not add to the Muslim feeling of security. Even Lord Mountbatten, no friend of the Muslims, had told Gandhi that 'if the partition had not been made during British occupation, the Hindus being the major party would have never allowed partition and held the Muslims by force under subjection'.[5] There can hardly be more impartial evidence to dispose of the Congress thesis that the moment the British withdrew communal peace would return to India and all Hindu–Muslim trouble would be forgotten in the glow of freedom.

SEPARATE ELECTORATES

Whether the Muslims demanded separate representation in legislatures because they considered themselves a separate nation, or the two-nation theory was advanced because the working of separate electorates for many years had made the Muslims conscious of their distinctiveness, is a pointless controversy. What is more important is to find out the connection between the two and to assess the influence of the electorate on the working out of the theory. We may say that the demand

[1] R. M. Agarwala, *The Hindu–Muslim Riots: Their Causes and Cures*, 1943, pp. 85, 93–96, 103, 106.

[2] See Radhakumud Mookerji, *Akhand Bharat*, Bombay, 1945.

[3] Quoted in Shaukatullah Ansari, *Pakistan: The Problem of India*, 1944, p. 37.

[4] C. P. Pillai, *Pakistan and its Implications*, n.d.

[5] Quoted in Pyarelal, *Mahatma Gandhi: The Last Phase*, Vol. II, 1958, p. 290.

for separate electorates was a manifestation of Muslim feeling of separateness; whether this feeling had by then matured into a full-fledged theory or not is difficult to see.

In the elections of 1892, out of the candidates recommended by the various electoral bodies for the Central Council the Muslims obtained only about half the number to which their numerical strength entitled them. For the Council of the United Provinces not a single Muslim had been recommended.[1] When, therefore, it was known that the British Government was contemplating reforms for India which would introduce a larger element of representation, the Muslims, in 1906, took a deputation to the Viceroy to argue their case for separate representation on all local and provincial elected bodies. This claim was based on three grounds. (*a*) In the existing state of tension between Hindus and Muslims, no Muslim who sincerely represented the opinions of his community could secure election in a general electorate, since in all but two provinces Muslims were a minority of the population. (*b*) If the two communities were not kept apart at the polls every contested election would result in communal riots, accompanied by bloodshed, and would leave bitter memories which would retard the political integration of the country. (*c*) Where the system of separate electorates had been established, as in municipalities and district boards, it had worked well and secured peace.

Simultaneously, the deputation also made a plea for weightage, i.e. the concession of more seats to the Muslims than their population figures warranted. This demand was supported by another set of three arguments: (a) Muslims still owned much of the landed property in India. (b) They constituted a very large proportion of the Indian Army. (c) They were, geographically speaking, the gatekeepers of India.[2]

The political principle behind this demand was underlined in an eloquent sentence by the *Economist*: 'Whatever may be

[1] R. Coupland, *India: A Re-Statement*, 1945, p. 105.

[2] Full text of the Deputation's address (which was drafted by Bilgrami) in *Addresses, Poems and other Writings of Nawab Imad-ul-Mulk Bahadur (Sayyid Husayn Bilgrami, C.S.I.)*, Hyderabad, 1925, pp. 139–44.

the political atom in India, it is certainly not the individual of Western democratic theory, but the community of some sort.'[1]

The significance of the Muslim demand was fully brought out in the debate which accompanied the making of the Morley–Minto reforms. The main point made by the Muslims was that the type of Muslim who secured Hindu support did so by virtue of his utility to Hindu rather than Muslim interests; yet this was the type most likely to be elected if separate electorates were not created. The expedient of a double register had proved very successful in the Austrian Empire as a means of preventing national conflicts. Where conflicting nationalities occupied the same territory experience proved that the most effective way of setting them by the ears was to let them fight out a contested election. To preserve harmony it was necessary to take away from them any such occasion for strife. This could only be done by separate representation.

One major argument against this system was that such admission of divided allegiance by the State was against the history of self-government. Another was that division by creeds and classes taught men to think as partisans, that the give-and-take which was the essence of political life was lacking, and that it stereotyped existing relations and perpetuated current splits.[2] To the objection that communal representation was opposed to the teaching of history, it could be answered that it was only the history of Western democracy that was being considered and that the teaching of Indian history exhibited an entirely different picture. Similarly the apprehension that it would stereotype existing relations presupposed that the Western pattern of popular government was suited to India—a presumption of doubtful validity.[3] There was another answer to this argument, too. The Muslims hoped that a time would come when the growth of full unity of sentiment and a complete consciousness of identity of interest

[1] *Economist*, 27 February 1909, p. 444.

[2] This is a summary of paras. 228–32 of the *Montagu–Chelmsford Report*, 1918, Cd. 9109.

[3] See E. G. Colvin, 'The Changing Scene in India', *Nineteenth Century*, May 1919, p. 1044.

would remove the necessity for special representation. Until then Muslim representation must continue.[1] (Incidentally, this line of thought goes counter to the idea that the demand for separate representation flowed out of a consciousness of separate Muslim nationalism). The Aga Khan gave still another reason for the extension of the principle of separate representation to other minorities—it would stimulate an interest in public affairs on the part of the backward classes.[2] In this he received firm support from Sir Valentine Chirol, who took exception to the inadequate allowance the Montagu–Chelmsford Report made for the deep lines of cleavage in Indian society. Theoretical objections to separate electorates had led the writers of the Report to restrict it within narrower limits than the actual circumstances showed. The report professed to be afraid of accepting existing divisions, but was there not a greater danger still in seeking to ignore their existence?—viz., the danger of doing a grave injustice to those who were most liable to suffer from their existence.[3]

The Simon Report shared all the objections raised by its predecessor, the Montagu–Chelmsford Report, against a separate Muslim electorate, but found it unavoidable in view of the general Muslim feeling of alarm if it were not conceded, the absence of a Hindu–Muslim settlement and the unanimity and firmness with which all Muslims demanded it.[4]

The issue of a Muslim electorate was thoroughly debated in British and Indian political circles on three major occasions, viz., the making of the 1909 reforms, the framing of the 1919 reforms and the Round Table Conference. On all of them the Hindus expressed their resentment against this 'concession' to Muslims, though on one occasion (1919) they had previously committed themselves to the principle by the Lucknow Pact of 1916. The Hindu argument that they were opposed to the

[1] Ameer Ali, letter to *The Times*, 14 August 1918.

[2] Aga Khan, *India in Transition: A Study in Political Evolution*, 1918, pp. 50–51.

[3] V. Chirol, 'The Indian Report', *The Times*, 10 July and 14 August 1918.

[4] See *Report of the Indian Statutory Commission*, 1930, Vol. II, Cmd. 3569, pp. 55–63.

system on purely national grounds is belied by the inconsistency they showed in applying this standard to India and to Ceylon. Whereas in India they objected to communal representation, in Ceylon they themselves asked for it.[1] The natural explanation is that in India they were a majority and did not approve of any diminution of their right to rule the country. In Ceylon they were in a minority and felt to be in need of safeguards. But what was politically practicable and wise in Ceylon was disruption and divide-and-rule in India. It was such show of blatant opportunism that alienated the Muslims and gradually led them to the conclusion that they could not live together with the Hindus under one political roof.

'NATIONALIST MUSLIMS' AND MUSLIM NATIONALISM

This alienation, however, was not total. There was, throughout the course of modern Indian politics, a section of Muslims which did not share the general Muslim view that a Hindu–Muslim entente was impossible or that separation was the only solution. This group may be called the Congress school of Muslims, as politically it always identified itself with the Congress; it may also be called the 'Nationalist Muslim' group, for that was the label given to it by the Congress and accepted by it. 'Nationalist Muslims' were Muslims who were opposed to Muslim separatism, to the two-nation theory, and later to the Pakistan demand, and who subscribed to the Congress view of the communal problem. They believed in one united Indian nationalism in which religious affiliations were both irrelevant and undesirable.

Some features of this group are noticeable. First, it was led by some men of exceptional ability and transparent sincerity. Their worst enemies cannot prove that they were men without deep convictions or without the courage to espouse an unpopular cause. Men of the stamp of Ansari and Ajmal Khan, Husain Ahmad Madani and Abul Kalam Azad, Mahmud Hasan and Muhamad Ali (one of them for a few years) could not be bought. Secondly, it was an *élite* of intellect rather than a band of mass leaders. It is true that Muhamad Ali was an

[1] Ivor Jennings, *The Approach to Self-Government*, 1956, p. 86.

idol of the people, that Ansari was respected by the whole country, and that Ajmal Khan enjoyed great popularity among the masses—but this was only true of the hectic Khilafat days when emotions ran high and anyone with Islam on his lips was treated as a celebrity. Once the sweep of the movement had weakened, their audience shrank and their following melted away. Others among them, like the Deoband *ulama*, were never the men of the public. On the whole, the group provided intellectual leadership to the non-Muslim League Muslims, thought out a philosophy to give backbone to their political activity and, quite unwittingly, emphasized the Muslim or Islamic strand of Indian nationalism.

A third characteristic of this group was the diverse backgrounds of its members. Their routes of entry into politics and their later careers and opinions were not the same. Azad started as a zealous Muslim, as an uncompromising upholder of pure Islam (*vide* his *al-Hilal*), as the man who, between 1912 and 1920, deepened and strengthened the foundations of Muslim nationalism; but after the demise of the Khilafat movement he shed his earlier ideas and almost overnight became an ardent supporter of a united Indian nationalism of the Congress variety, and remained steadfast to it till the end. Muhamad Ali was, by turns, a Muslim Leaguer, a Khilafatist, a Congressman and towards the end a virulent critic of the Congress. Both Ajmal Khan and Ansari were former presidents of the Muslim League who later turned to the Congress and never looked back.

The Nationalist Muslims were a small company and, outside the Khilafat period, their following among Muslims was insignificant. Their record in elections to legislative assemblies was inglorious. Their organization was weak, loose and sporadic. Their following was a motley crowd of disgruntled Muslim Leaguers, anti-British divines, Muslim Congressmen, and personal friends of Hindu leaders.

Before examining the role of this group in Indian politics let us briefly look at their opinions and beliefs. Maulana Abul Kalam Azad is, by common consent, the outstanding spokesman of this school. He is also an interesting study because of the sudden and sweeping change in his outlook which occurred in 1920 or immediately afterwards. He began his career under the inspiration of Sayyid Ahmad Khan's writings, which 'greatly impressed' him.[1] For him religion and politics were inseparable. When launching his weekly paper *al-Hilal* (the Crecent) in June 1912 he declared that its aim was 'to invite Muslims to follow the Book of Allah and the *sharia* of His Prophet. In cultural, political or other matters Muslims ought to be Muslims.' Asked if Muslims should join the Hindus in political matters, he answered, 'Islam is so exalted a religion that its followers are not constricted to ape the Hindus for the formulation of their political policy.' Distinguishing his theory of nationalism from the Hindu's, he wrote, 'Hindus can, like other nations, revive their self-awareness on the basis of secular nationalism, but it is indeed not possible for Muslims.'[2] He continued to profess and preach this brand of Muslim (or rather Islamic) nationalism from 1912 to about 1920.

After the failure of the Khilafat movement he took his followers by surprise by shifting his ground suddenly and unexpectedly. He renounced his Islamic nationalism and embraced Indian nationalism. The votary of Muslim nationalism had come under the spell of the new Turkish nationalism and the nascent Arab nationalism and forsaken all earlier beliefs and pronounced his faith in a joint (Hindu–Muslim) nationalism in India which, he said, was a prerequisite of winning independence from the British.[3]

From this time onwards he became a loyal and trusted member of the Congress and never deviated from its policies. He was first elected its president in 1923 and then every year from 1940 to 1946. His presidential address at Ramgarh delivered in March 1940 is worth a passing mention. When he

[1] A. K. Azad, *India Wins Freedom: An Autobiographical Narrative*, 1959, p. 3.

[2] A. K. Azad, *Mazameen-i-Abul Kalam Azad* (Essays of Abul Kalam Azad), 1944, pp. 17, 22, 25–26, 87, translated and quoted in Hafeez Malik, *Moslem Nationalism in India and Pakistan*, 1963, pp. 269–70.

[3] See his address to the All India Khilafat Conference at Cawnpur on 24 December 1925; summary in *The Indian Annual Register 1925, Vol. II: July–December 1925*, 1926, p. 343, the Urdu original reprinted in full in *Khutbat-i-Abul Kalam Azad* (Addresses by Abul Kalam Azad), Lahore, n.d.

spoke, Muslim plans for separation had matured and the Lahore Resolution was adopted in the same month. But oblivious of Muslim feelings and fears, he repeated the usual Hindu arguments and assured the Muslims that all would be well after the British had gone and freedom had come. There was no effort to understand the problem, to examine the foundations of Muslim apprehensions, to offer any alternatives to a united India or to Pakistan, to give any definite assurances to Muslims, or even to argue his own case with conviction.[1]

It was this blind identification with whatever the Congress laid down which was Azad's undoing. The more he merged himself with the Congress the more he estranged even his own following, until by about 1941 or 1942 it is doubtful if he represented anyone except the Hindus. The Muslims believed that he was being exploited by the Congress with a view to wearing the look of a 'national' party. How could the Congress be a Hindu party if its president was a Muslim divine and theologian? This was a clever idea, but failed to work. No one was taken in except a handful of British leftists who, anyway, were too partial to the Congress to be open to conviction. The Congress leaders themselves were well aware of Maulana's unpopularity among his own co-religionists. In a book planned and edited by one of his staunch admirers, a well-known Congress leader, while paying his tribute to Azad, wrote, 'If even Akbar was disappointed by his fellow Musalmans, why should we be surprised if Maulana Abul Kalam received no response from the organized Muslims of India today?'[2]

In consistency of opinion and originality of thinking the Deoband school and its political manifestation, the Jamiat-ul-Ulama-i-Hind, were more representative of the Nationalist Muslims than Azad (though he too was for a time in the

[1] A. K. Azad, *Musalman aur Congress* (Muslims and the Congress), Lahore, n.d.

[2] C. Rajagopalacharia, 'The Great Akbar of Today', in Abdullah Butt (ed.), *Aspects of Abul Kalam Azad*, 1942, p. 67. Comparison with Akbar is, in itself, significant. In Muslim eyes Akbar, in founding his Din-i-Ilahi, had definitely forsaken Islam and was no less than an apostate.

Jamiat). In 1867 a Dar-ul-Uloom (lit. 'House of Learning') was established in Deoband under the guidance of Maulana Muhamad Qasim Nanawtawi as a counterpoise to Sayyid Ahmad Khan's West-oriented movement. In religion it was sectarian, propounding the teachings of the Hanafi school of theology. In sphere of influence it was parochial, its reach confined to the United Provinces and Delhi. In politics it was rabidly anti-British, preaching disloyalty to the Government. In 1880 Nanawtawi died and was succeeded by Rashid Ahmad Gangohi, who gave a *fatwa* that in worldly matters co-operation with the Hindus was permissible provided that it did no violence to any basic principles of Islam.[1] This was done to allow the followers of Deoband to join the Indian National Congress. Gangohi was succeeded by Maulana Mahmud Hasan in 1905, and in 1920 the headship of the school devolved upon Husain Ahmad Madani.

Deoband was a centre of conservative Islam where young men of a religious turn of mind were trained in theology, Islamic history and other old-fashioned disciplines. Western learning was taboo, for it was one of the fundamental beliefs of the school that any truck with the infidel West was tantamount to a compromise with heresy. Inevitably, therefore, the Dar-ul-Uloom produced *mullas* who were skilful in theological hair-splitting, competent in expounding the orthodoxies of their particular sect, but completely ignorant of modern movements and developments even in Islam. When these graduates left the school and began the rounds of the countryside as peripatetic religious teachers, a 'great many' of them 'in the name of the spiritual guidance of the common man have lived on his blood and sweat. There they have also fought religious wars against their counterparts of other schools, like "Barelvis" and "Ahl-i-Hadith". Moreover, their purely religious training had kept them aloof and isolated and intellectually estranged from the people educated in secular schools and colleges.'[2]

The men of Deoband struck out a path for themselves which was different from Azad's, who was in the beginning an ardent

[1] Ziya-ul-Hasan Faruqi, *The Deoband School and the Demand for Pakistan*, 1963, p. 43.

[2] Ibid., p. 40 fn.

Islamic nationalist, and from Maudoodi's, who was anti-Muslim League but even more anti-Congress.

Partly to play a more important role in the Khilafat movement and partly to enter the political field in their own right, in 1919 the Deoband divines founded the Jamiat-ul-Ulama-i-Hind (Association of the Divines of India). For the first few years when party politics—within Muslims as well as between them and the Hindus—was silenced by the exigence of the Khilafat campaign the Jamiat contained all varieties of divines, but once the Khilafat issue was dead the Deobandis took it over and it became the political arm of the Deoband School. Among its aims and objects were 'to defend Islam . . . Islamic rituals and customs and Islamic nationalism against all odds injurious to them'; 'to achieve and protect the general religious and national rights of the Muslims'; 'to establish good and friendly relations with the non-Muslims of the country to the extent permitted by the *shariat-i-Islamiyah*'; and 'to fight for the freedom of the country and religion according to the *shari* objectives'.[1]

The Jamiat favoured 'unconditional co-operation' with the Congress 'so far as the cause of freedom was concerned'.[2] It believed that the Muslim minority in India need have no fear as, once the British were gone, the Hindus would come to terms with it. It was chiefly the British Government which was responsible for the Hindu–Muslim conflict. In 1928, however, the Jamiat surprised the Congress by rejecting the Nehru Report. Its criticism was based on two points. The safeguards provided for the Muslims were inadequate, and the plan for Dominion Status for India was inconsistent with the Jamiat's commitment to complete independence.[3] But this estrangement was temporary and peace was made in the following year when the Congress repudiated the Nehru Report. In the 1937 Muslim mass contact campaign organized by the Congress the Jamiat gave full support to the Congress.[4]

[1] Sayyid Muhammad Mian, *Jamiat-ul-Ulama Kia Hai* (What is Jamiat-ul-Ulama?), Part I, n.d., p. 10.

[2] Z. H. Faruqi, op. cit., p. 70.

[3] Waheed-uz-Zaman, *Towards Pakistan*, 1964, p. 177. The Jamiat had declared its goal as complete independence in as early as 1920, ibid.

[4] Z. H. Faruqi, op. cit., p. 89.

The Jamiat stood for a 'united Nationalism' ('*muthidda qaumiat*') for India, did not adhere to the two-nation theory, opposed the Pakistan plan, and argued for a territorial, as opposed to religious, nationalism. Its arguments against Muslim separation were: the Pakistan demand has British support and is nothing but an instrument forged by them to further their policy of divide-and-rule (no evidence was offered in support of this); Pakistan will split and therefore weaken the Muslims of India; our real enemy is British imperialism and our only duty to defeat it, only a united action can achieve this; Muslims left behind in India after separation will be at the mercy of the Hindus (no effort was made to reconcile this statement with the general stand of the Jamiat that there was no Hindu–Muslim problem); partition will hinder the missionary activities of the *ulama* (it was not made clear whether this would result from mere inconveniences of national barriers or from a possible lack of freedom of proselytizing in the free India); Muslim League leaders are ignorant of Islam, have no ideology, and are only exploiting the name of Islam for the worldly gain of Muslim vested interests; and Muslim League leaders are incapable of building up an Islamic State and their Pakistan will be no better than the Turkey of Mustafa Kamal (this provokes the question if the Jamiat would have agreed to support the Pakistan demand had the League leaders pledged that the new State would be Islamic; it also shows up a contradiction in the Jamiat reasoning: it was, in the same breath, upholding the secular nationalism of the Congress and condemning the non-orthodox nationalism of the League).[1]

Towards the end there was a split in the Jamiat on the issue of its attitude to the Pakistan plan. In 1946 a section defected and formed a Jamiat-ul-Ulama-i-Islam which worked in support of the Muslim League. Among the leaders of the

[1] This list of Jamiat's arguments is culled from the following sources: Husain Ahmad Madani, *Muslim League Kia Hai* (What is Muslim League?), Delhi, 1945; *Pakistan Kia Hai* (What is Pakistan?), Delhi, n.d.; *Makateeb-i-Shaikh-ul-Islam* (Letters of Shaikh-ul-Islam), Deoband, n.d., later enlarged ed. Azamgarh, 1952, 2 vols.; and Sayyid Muhammad Mian, *Ulama-i-Haqq aur un kay Mujahadana Karnamay* (The Truthful Divines and their Brave Deeds), Moradabad, 1946–8, 2 vols.

breakaway group there were two divines of admitted excellence and considerable influence: Maulanas Ashraf Ali Thanvi and Shabbir Ahmad Usmani.[1]

Let the final word on the Jamiat be said by one of them. 'The *ulama* were not prepared to follow the Western-oriented Muslim intelligentsia whom they suspected to be the representatives of a different culture. They were still medieval in their outlook. . . . They failed to understand the genesis of the Hindu Renaissance and never tried to comprehend the modern Islam which in the 1930's, under the poetic inspiration of Iqbal, became an ideological force. . . . The crux of its opposition [to the Pakistan plan] lay in its traditional conception of Islam and [the fear about] the future fate of its "Islam" in Pakistan. The *ulama* thought that it was only they who could give the right lead to the Muslims.'[2]

The Muslim League leaders were thus caught between two fires of exclusiveness—the Congress exclusiveness of nationalism and the Deoband exclusiveness of religion. For the Congress they were too reactionary to enter the mainstream of Indian nationalism; for the divines they were too secular to lead the Muslims aright. To escape from this cross-fire they created a different conception of nationalism which was partly religious (all Muslims are a nation), partly territorial (all Muslim-majority areas should form Pakistan) and wholly psychological (we feel that we are a nation).

In spite of their small size, their muddled thinking and other weaknesses the part played by the Nationalist Muslims in Indian politics was far from unimportant. How can this be explained? Several factors helped them to occupy an exaggerated place in the political field. Their most effective weapon was their alliance with the Congress. They were, so to say, adopted by the Congress and offered to the public as the only 'nationalists' among Muslims. They were happy to live in this borrowed glory, for it brought them status, stability and

[1] Husain Ahmad Madani's theory of a 'united nationalism' was not palatable even to his followers and, on the testimony of one of his colleagues, when he stood up to propound it 'hardly five hundred in a gathering of ten thousand would listen to him', Sayyid Muhammad Mian, *Ulama-i-Haqq*, Vol. I, 1946, p. 287.

[2] Z. H. Faruqi, op. cit., pp. 76, 85, 124.

immense monetary resources. This identification with a large Hindu organization had two other results. First, it made them indolent and intellectually sterile. If their political duty did not lie beyond endorsing the Congress policy, any further exertion was unnecessary. By becoming uncritical supporters of one party they lost their power of thinking, their independence of outlook, their former flexibility of manœuvre and even their former *penchant* for lively debate. Secondly, it made them even less agreeable to the Muslim masses. As the opponents of Muslim nationalism it was incumbent upon them to meet it with equal argument, to try to provide a platform for non-Muslim League politics, to evolve a creed which could at least compete with other ideas and offer an alternative to separation. By repeating the Congress dogma *ad infinitum* they confirmed that they had no wares of their own to put on the market. For this they paid the price of unpopularity and near political extinction.

This unwillingness to strike out a new path for themselves is astonishing because the Nationalist Muslims were men of wit and ability. Their learning was substantial, their scholarship exact, their intellectual achievements well known. When they spoke or wrote in defence of the Khilafat or in support of the Ottoman Empire their arguments were sharp and their knowledge deep. When Azad commented on the Quran his erudition was unrivalled and his understanding of Islam unerring. When the divines of Deoband expounded the orthodox Islam of which they were the modern torch-bearers, their vision was unclouded and their logic straight. Ajmal Khan was a poet of distinction in two languages and commanded a lively imagination. Ansari, though a surgeon by profession, was a very learned man. But in Indian (apart from Islamic) politics their contribution was slight and shallow. Habitual dependence on the Congress had dried up their fountainhead of thinking. And yet there were thousands of Muslims who, in spite of their politics, admired them for their writings, their achievements in the realm of mind and their reputation as *savants*.

The Nationalist Muslims were very vocal and their voice was amplified by the Congress Press. In the absence of a Muslim Press political propaganda in India was a Congress monopoly. This magnified their role and gave them publicity which was out of all proportion to their importance.

Alliance with the Congress brought them another advantage. They were, or at least claimed to be, anti-imperialists, and this made for popular appeal. Their public image was improved by their anti-British propaganda, by their participation in non-co-operation campaigns and by consequent imprisonment. For a great mass of people in India politics meant opposition to the British and the martyrdom of imprisonment. The Nationalist Muslims fulfilled these qualifications and so rose in public estimation. The Congress Muslim rank and file used to taunt the Muslim Leaguers by saying, 'What sort of leader is your Jinnah who has never been to prison!'

Another factor working to their advantage was their religious appeal to the masses. It is an irony of history that while the Congress always charged the Muslim League with bringing religion into politics and thus encouraging 'reaction', it was in fact the Congress Muslims whose entire popular support among the Muslim masses was rooted in religion. Azad's politics was not acceptable even to a small section of Muslims, but he was esteemed and admired for his religious works. Husain Ahmad Madani and his Deobandi colleagues had no position in politics (except as the hangers-on of Congress), but in some areas they commanded obedience as religious leaders of a certain school of thought. Ansari and Ajmal Khan had no political following among Muslims, but in the Khilafat days their star was in the ascendant. In Muslim societies it has always been easy to win popular acclaim by making religion an issue. This explains the hold of the Nationalist Muslims on certain Muslim circles; on the other hand, the fact that even this religious appeal failed to win them popular support explains the unshakable distrust of the great majority of Muslims in all those who allied themselves with the Congress.

CONGRESS AND THE TWO-NATION THEORY

In the preceding chapters we have tried to set Muslim nationalism against the background of Muslim thought and politics. But, how far was the Congress responsible for the emergence of national consciousness among the Muslims? This is an important question because Muslim nationalism did not grow in a vacuum. Two forces intermingled to give birth to it. One was the Muslim feeling of separatism; the other was the Hindu attitude to the Muslim problem as a whole. It is impossible to study the development of Muslim nationalism without closely examining the impress of both the factors. So far we have dealt only with the Muslim aspect of the question: how Muslim thinking and experience shaped their national growth. The rest of this chapter is intended to appraise the role of the Congress or the Hindus in its growth.

The question is complicated and therefore the temptation to over-simplify is great. It is commonly remarked that the Muslims owed the creation of Pakistan to the Congress, in the sense that had the Congress treated the Muslims differently there would have been no Muslim separatism and therefore no Pakistan. There is more than a modicum of truth in this popular generalization. But Congress thinking on the Muslim problem was so confused and confusing that it is difficult for an historian to portray the situation in straight, clean lines. There are too many curves and contours in the picture to lend themselves to a simple description or to an analysis in black and white.

The only stark fact is that the Congress never made a serious effort to *understand* the Muslim problem. It had no definite policy on the matter and tried to meet each crisis as it arose. But it is difficult to practise this typically British empiricism in politics without the British genius for compromise which goes with it.

When the Congress was founded in 1885 an attempt was made to woo the intelligentsia into joining it. But Sayyid Ahmad Khan in northern India and Ameer Ali in Bengal rejected these overtures, partly under the influence of the traditional post-Mutiny thinking, partly because of the Muslim policy of 'loyalty' which was then becoming fashionable among Muslim leaders, and partly because of the predominantly Hindu composition and tone of the Congress itself. This initial repudiation of the Congress was big with consequences and visibly reproduced itself on all important occasions during the following sixty years. And this rejection was not, as most Congressmen suggested, a mere figment of the Muslim and British political imagination. The Congress would not have chosen to castigate the Muslim demand for separate representation (which was made by the most representative Muslim deputation of modern history) had it really had a Muslim following. Pandit Madan Mohan Malaviya, a great Congressman–Mahasabhite, confessed that Muslims had kept aloof from the Congress.[1] By signing the Lucknow Pact the Congress supplied a statutory confirmation of its failure to speak for Muslim India: for a party does not enter into a pact of this nature with its own followers but only with a rival or enemy organization. Speaking as the president of the special Congress conference held at Lucknow on 10 August 1917, Pandit Motilal Nehru referred to the Congress and the Muslim League as 'those national bodies which represent the best intellect and culture of the country'.[2] Unfortunately this was the last occasion on which the Muslim League was acknowledged to be a national body by a Congress leader.

After the failure of the Khilafat movement the tide of events moved fast towards an irretrievable split between the two 'national bodies'. The Nehru Report, prepared under the chairmanship of Motilal Nehru, repudiated the status of the Muslim League as a representative body and challenged it to a show-down by recommending the immediate abolition of separate electorates without compensation. The flood of unrestrained democracy, against which Sayyid Ahmad Khan had warned his people, had overtaken the spirit of accommodation which the Congress had shown at Lucknow, and had in the process inundated all Muslim expectations of an honourable alliance with the Congress. The Round Table Conference and the making of the 1935 constitution did not mend matters. The divorce was signed, ratified and confirmed by the Communal Award and the Congress attitude towards it. The elections of 1937 registered this separation, and in 1938 two staunch Congressmen, writing a semi-official history of the organization, had to confess that the Muslims had generally kept away from it.[3]

[1] *Speeches and Writings of Madan Mohan Malaviya*, 1919, pp. 48–49.

[2] Quoted in K. M. Panikkar and A. Pershad (eds.), *The Voice of Freedom: Selected Speeches of Pandit Motilal Nehru*, 1961, p. 71.

[3] C. F. Andrews and G. Mukerji, *The Rise and Growth of the Congress in India*, 1938, pp. 170–75.

The part which the Congress provincial governments of 1937–9 played in alienating the Muslims, strengthening the roots of their separatism and laying the foundations of Pakistan, is too well-known to bear repetition.

Of all the Congress leaders Gandhi was the most vocal on the necessity of achieving Hindu–Muslim unity. He claimed that he had made it a part of the Congress programme and declared again and again that independence would not come till the demon of communalism was exorcized. But even he always spoke of Hindus as 'we' and of Muslims as 'they'.[1] He refused to distinguish between a Hindu Indian and a Muslim Indian, but said in November 1946, when Muslim fears were at the highest pitch, that when British troops were gone the majority would know how to behave towards the minority.[2] He repeatedly said that he had no objection if the central government was given into the control of the Muslim League and Jinnah was made the Prime Minister of the country, but when in November 1946 the Viceroy requested him to sign, along with Jinnah, a statement condemning violence and asking Indians to stop fighting among themselves, he refused with the remark that this was 'parity with a vengeance'.[3] A man who was ready to lay down his life for communal peace could not bear to see his name coupled with Jinnah's, with whom, in 1944, he had carried on negotiations on an equal footing. It was Gandhi who, in 1945, overruled Desai and ordered that the Congress should proceed to form a government in the Frontier Province, although the Congress was not allowed to take up power in any province under instructions from the High Command issued in November 1939.[4] Muslims were quick to see in this the Hindu determination to keep the Muslim League out of power in a Muslim province. In view of all this there was some justification for the Muslim inability to take Gandhi's protestations of his love for the Muslims as seriously as he himself took them.

Pandit Jawaharlal Nehru, after Gandhi the most important

[1] Hirendranath Mukerjee, *India Struggles for Freedom*, 1946, p. 162.

[2] Interview to the United Press of India on 6 November 1946, Pyarelal, *Mahatma Gandhi: The Last Phase*, Vol. I, p. 335.

[3] Ibid., p. 354.

[4] Ibid., p. 127.

Hindu leader, adopted a different attitude towards the Muslim problem. He denied its very existence. There was no such problem as the Muslim problem in India. Communalism was mere propaganda, and would 'not present the slightest difficulty'.[1] It was 'overrated and over-emphasized'. It did 'not fundamentally affect the masses'. As 'social issues' would come to the forefront, it 'is bound to recede into the background'.[2] Yet it was Nehru who started the ill-fated campaign of Muslim mass contact, thus not only admitting the existence of a Hindu–Muslim problem but also showing his true feelings in relation to the Muslim League. Subsequent events convinced Nehru that the communal problem could not be wished away by denying its existence. In early 1947, when the Hindus of the Punjab and Bengal urged him to demand a partition of their provinces in order to safeguard them against the rule of the majority, he immediately accepted the logic and the justice of their suggestion. This acceptance was a proof of the fact that 'in contrast to his earlier view of communalism, he now recognized it to be an abiding and centrifugal force in Indian politics'.[3] If he did not really believe in the two-nation theory he should have opposed the Bengali Hindus' desire to cut loose from the Muslim majority and, instead, should have supported the conception of a united Bengal which was then (March 1947) being propagated in earnest by some Hindu and Muslim Bengali leaders. Again, in his statement on 15 August 1947, he voiced the sadness of many Indians for 'our brothers and sisters who have been cut off from us by political boundaries and who unhappily cannot share at present in the freedom that had come'.[4] Obviously he was referring to the Hindus left in Pakistan who, in his opinion, were not free. The implication is apparent that the Hindus of India were one nation, that a part of this nation had been left in Pakistan, and that this part was yet not free because it was under the rule of another

[1] Interview to *News Chronicle*, 2 January 1937.

[2] Letter to Lord Lothian of 17 January 1936, Jawaharlal Nehru, *A Bunch of Old Letters* (1960 ed.), p. 148.

[3] Michael Brecher, *Jawaharlal Nehru: A Political Biography,* 1959, p. 377 fn.

[4] Quoted ibid., p. 358. Incidentally, the words 'at present' indicate his hope (or plan!) for a re-unity of India and Pakistan.

nation, the Muslims. It is difficult to put a different construction on his words.

The Congress responsibility for the creation and encouragement of Muslim separation lies in the fact that it did not evolve a policy to handle the Muslims. It made no effort to convince the Muslim masses of the goodness of its own brand of nationalism. It did not attempt to persuade the Muslim citizenry of the benefits of a non-communal democracy. It took a half-hearted stand on the Communal Award and did not counter the separatist tendencies of the Muslim voters which had unmistakably shown themselves in the elections of 1937. By refusing to contest Muslim seats in these elections it admitted its non-Muslim character. Out of a total of 482 Muslim seats in the provinces it had the courage (or the wisdom!) of contesting only fifty-eight and the ignominy of winning only twenty-six. By this performance, or the failure of it, it forfeited all title to speak for India. Yet it persisted in ignoring other parties and claiming for itself an all-inclusive status. The electoral verdict had gone against it and proved to all that it had no hold over the Muslim community. But that did not discourage it from accusing other parties of being unrepresentative of the people. It refused to acknowledge the credentials of any Muslim politicians other than its own Nationalist Muslims whom it duly paraded on all ceremonial occasions. This was a short-sighted policy and did great harm to its prospects as a nationalist party seeking independence for the whole of India. On the other hand, it incensed an overwhelming majority of the Muslims who looked at the handful of Congress Muslims as nothing less than renegades who had surrendered their self-respect for a ribbon to stick in their coat. This redoubled their resolve to consolidate their strength and to riposte the Congress nationalism with an equally resolute Muslim nationalism.

THE CONGRESS POLICY OF DIVIDE-AND-RULE

The Congress approach to the Muslim problem was complicated by yet another factor. Throughout its history there was an element of divide-and-rule in its policy *vis à vis* the Muslims. After its initial lack of success in recruiting Muslims to its fold, it practised in relation to Muslim India exactly what it accused the British of practising in relation to India as a whole.

A deliberate effort was made to break the political unity of the Muslims and to cajole, persuade and humour some of them into joining the Congress ranks. In its infancy it 'captured' a few Muslim public figures like Badruddin Tyabji and Rahmatullah Syani. During the debate on the Morley–Minto reforms it was able to enlist Sir Ali Imam, who was vocal in his opposition to the Muslim demand for separate representation. During the Khilafat period, of course, there was a sizeable group of Muslims who did not distinguish between the Congress and the Muslim League in so far as both were concentrating on the Turkish question. But after the disintegration of this unity a few Muslims still lingered on in the Congress—some out of genuine conviction that it represented the essence of nationalism, some out of blinding frustration which accompanied the fiasco of the Khilafat movement, and some because of the absence of a strong Muslim organization to which they could attach themselves.

There has been a long and at times distinguished line of Muslim leaders who at one time or another allied themselves with the Congress—Tyabji, Muhammad Ali, Shaukat Ali, M. A. Ansari, Ajmal Khan, Abul Kalam Azad, Zakir Husain and, above all, Jinnah. To recall their loyalty to the Congress is not to accuse them of insincerity in conviction or of treachery in politics. They were all men of intelligence and considerable political acumen, and their conversion cannot be explained away by Congress trickery. They were not bribed—though the Congress was not above dangling ministerial prizes before the lesser breed of Nationalist Muslims, particularly during its supremacy in the provincial field. The point is that the Congress made a consistent effort to breach the Muslim front and to take away from the Muslim League as many leaders as it could.

One important weapon in this one-sided war of nerves (one-sided because the Muslim League, by the definition of its creed, could not influence the non-Muslim membership of the Congress to forsake it) was the enthusiasm with which the Congress sought and forged alliances with some Muslim organizations which did not share the ideals of the Muslim League.

It allied itself with such miscellaneous bodies as the Red Shirts, the Ahrars, the Momins, the Shia Conference and the Jamiat-ul-Ulama. Sometimes it created an anti-Muslim League front, e.g., in 1940 it put up an Azad Muslim Conference to counteract the Muslim League and to oppose the Pakistan resolution. Sometimes this anxiety to keep the Muslim League isolated from other Muslim groups led it to acts of blatant opportunism and political folly. The best example of this was the Congress alliance with the Punjab Unionist Party in 1946 to form the Punjab provincial ministry. It must be recalled that in 1937 the Congress had flatly refused to share power with the Muslim League on the ground that it could not compromise its economic and social programme by forming a coalition with a conservative body like the League (though in fact the election manifestos of the two parties were almost identical even on economic and social matters). But in 1946 the same Congress party cheerfully agreed to form a coalition in the Punjab with the Unionist Party, which was notoriously reactionary in policy and feudal in composition, and which had won only a handful of seats in the legislature. It was even worse than a coalition because the leader of the tiny Unionist Party was accepted as Chief Minister. This unnatural alliance can be explained in political terms: it was a tactical move to keep the Muslim League out of office in a province where it had won an overwhelming majority of Muslim seats. This telling contrast between its proclaimed principles and its political action convinced the Muslims that the Congress had no policy or principle except to divide the Muslims with a view to maintaining its own hegemony.

Even the language used by the Congress to describe the Muslim League and its friends, on the one hand, and the Congress Muslims, on the other, was meant to divide the Muslims and to mislead the outside observers. Muslim politics was always referred to as 'communalism'—a dirty word in Indian politics. In all political debate the Muslim point of view was either airily dismissed or contemptuously sneered at as charlatanism. So persistent was this propaganda and so effectively done that all foreign writers on India adopted this phraseology without criticism. When the Congress made a demand, it was the voice of Indian nationalism. When the

Muslims asked for something, that was communalism. Even Pakistan was painted as a child of communal politics, rather than of nationalist urge.

In contrast to this, all Muslims who joined the Congress were given the honourable designation of 'Nationalist Muslims'. A Muslim was a communalist, and *ipso facto* an enemy of Indian freedom, if he was a Muslim Leaguer, but the same Muslim became a 'Nationalist', and therefore a valiant soldier in the cause of independence, as soon as he had filled in the Congress membership form. Here again Congress propaganda was so well done that to this day the phrase 'Nationalist Muslim' is reserved for one who sided with the Congress. Even the British rulers, who were alleged to be the perfect practitioners of the policy of divide-and-rule, did not create such phraseology or use it to such lethal effect.

Two interesting aspects of Congress policy must be noticed. The Congress encouraged and allied itself with only the weak and backward Muslim groups—the Jamiat-ul-Ulama, a reactionary, semi-theological body which looked askance at all efforts to liberalize Islam; the Ahrars, a Punjabi organization of middle-class Muslims whose militarism outran their intelligence; the Momins, a class of poor and illiterate weavers; the Shia Conference, a splinter group which wanted to fight the Sunnis with Congress help.[1] It is important to remember that none of these organizations contributed to the leadership of the Congress. The important 'Nationalist Muslims' were individuals who came to the Congress from other sources and not as leaders of these minor groups. On the whole, the so-called Muslim Nationalist Party was of no practical use to the Congress. On the testimony of a Hindu historian, it was 'so poor in numbers and so weak in influence that its voice remained almost unheard'.[2] Even in the Frontier Province, which the Congress always proffered as the most striking refutation of the League claim to speak for Muslim India, the

[1] This was the worst kind of divide-and-rule, for it fermented sectarian trouble between the two major sections of the Muslim people.

[2] M. B. L. Bhargava, *Political and National Movements in India,* 1936, p. 53. This was confirmed ten years later by such an orthodox Hindu leader as K. M. Munshi; see his *The Changing Shape of Indian Politics* (1946 ed.), p. 67.

Nationalist Muslim leaders did not have the courage to participate in the 1947 referendum which was held to ascertain whether the province wanted to join Pakistan or India.

This alliance with 'Nationalist' Muslim individuals and groups did not in the end pay the Congress. In practical politics they remained a drag on the Congress—for two reasons. They 'failed to convert any appreciable section of the Muslim community to Congress secularism', and they 'vitally influenced the Congress decisions relating to communal settlement'.[1] Not only that, but V. P. Menon, who had access to inside information, thinks that 'even the safeguard and protection demanded for their community by the Nationalist Muslims went so far that, if acceded to, they would have prevented for all time the growth of a united nation'.[2] It is not insignificant that in 1942, when C. Rajagopalacharia's resolution on recognizing the Pakistan scheme was voted upon in the All India Congress Committee, five prominent Muslim members of the Committee—Ghaffar Khan, Khan Sahib, Mian Iftakharuddin, Dr. Ansari (Secretary of the Azad Muslim Board), and the Muslim Minister of Education in Sind—supported the resolution. In addition, all the members from the Frontier Province remained neutral.[3]

In Bombay the Congress 'made a Muslim member of the Assembly sign the Congress pledge on one day and made him minister the next day. This was indeed a travesty of Muslim representation when that Muslim minister had not the confidence of the twenty-two Muslim League members of the Bombay Legislative Assembly.'[4]

The fact of the matter is that the Congress leaders were so obsessed with the Western principle of majority rule that they shut their eyes to the magnitude of the Muslim problem and thought that they would be able to deal with it effectively either by completely ignoring it or by weaning away Muslims from the Muslim League. They, and especially Gandhi, were

[1] Ram Gopal, *Indian Muslims: A Political History, 1858–1947*, 1959, p. 294.

[2] V. P. Menon, *The Transfer of Power in India*, 1954, p. 439.

[3] *Observer*, 17 May 1942.

[4] C. H. Setalvad, *Recollections and Reflections: An Autobiography*, 1946, pp. 414–15.

'anti-imperialist *vis à vis* Britain, but imperialist *vis à vis* Pakistan'.[1]

THE PARADOX OF THE CONGRESS APPROACH

The paradox of the situation lies in the fact that, in spite of this approach to Muslim nationalism, the Congress was at the same time conscious of the existence of Indian disunity and, in later stages, it in effect acknowledged the two-nation theory. That it did so reluctantly and under acute pressure of events does not affect the argument.

It is said that during the First World War the Hindus, particularly the Jats, showed great eagerness to join the Indian Army because they wanted to fight the Turks. The Muslims came forward to enlist in a spirit of loyal duty; the Sikhs for sheer love of fighting; but the Hindus 'rallied against their hereditary enemy as if to a crusade'.[2]

The Hindu masses looked upon Muslims as one big caste and as tresspassers in India,[3] and this underlying tension was noticed by many Congress leaders. Motilal Nehru, as president of the Congress, did not wish to make of India 'a cheap and slavish imitation' of the West, for Western democracy had not proved a panacea for all ills and had not solved the problems facing India.[4] In 1928, again as the Congress president, he confessed that 'there is no overlooking the fact that we are divided into a number of large and small communities, more or less disorganized and demoralized'.[5] This shows that in spite of the Congress insistence on the rule of the majority and on the supposed unity of India, it acknowledged the difficulties involved in erecting a political system which did not take notice of Indian divergences.

In 1947, soon after the All India Congress committee had

[1] Ralph Borsodi, *The Challenge of Asia: A Study of Conflicting Ideas and Ideals,* 1956, p. 25.

[2] Michael O'Dwyer, *India as I knew It, 1885–1925* (2nd. ed. 1925), p. 415.

[3] Harcourt Butler, *India Insistent,* 1931, p. 40.

[4] Presidential address at Amritsar on 27 December 1919, K. M. Panikkar and A. Pershed (eds.), *The Voice of Freedom: Selected Speeches of Pandit Motilal Nehru,* 1961, p. 40.

[5] Presidential address at Calcutta on 29 December 1928, ibid., p. 51.

ratified acceptance of the 3 June Plan (partition of India), the Chief Minister of one of the Hindu provinces declared in a public meeting that Muslims left in India 'could not expect to be treated otherwise than as aliens. They would have no citizenship rights.'[1] The Momins, who had always supported the Congress and were counted among the most ardent 'Nationalist Muslims,' were not spared the horrors of killing during the Bihar riots of 1946; in fact, they alleged that many leaders high up in the Congress had taken part in the riots directed against them.[2] India was not safe for any Muslim, 'Nationalist' or 'communalist'. The two-nation theory had annihilated all political values and distinctions created by the Congress. In the last analysis what alone mattered was whether an Indian was a Muslim or a Hindu. His political affiliations were swept away by the fact of his professing a particular religion. History was vindicating the two-nation theory, but at what human cost!

But the greatest refutation of the Congress logic is to be found in Indo–Pakistan relations after 1947. The Muslims left behind in India are still regarded by Pakistanis to be in some way related to them. Any communal riot in India sends a wave of resentment in Pakistan and the Government sends a note of protest to Delhi. Similarly in India, Hindus look to the future of the Hindu population of East Pakistan (there are no Hindus in West Pakistan) as their concern, and in 1950 the Prime Ministers of Pakistan and India actually signed a pact (Liaqat–Nehru Agreement) safeguarding the interests of Indian Muslims and Pakistan Hindus.

Pakistani interest in Indian Muslims can be explained by the two-nation theory. All the Muslims of the Indian sub-continent were one nation. It was an accident of history that a portion of them was left behind in the Indian Union, but that portion is still in some 'extra-political' way an extension of the Pakistani nation: because India was divided on the basis of the two-nation theory. But the interest of the Indian Government in the Hindus of Pakistan is impossible of any explanation except that the Congress also had at the end accepted the two-nation theory. How else can we justify or even explain

[1] Pyarelal, *Mahatma Gandhi: The Last Phase*, Vol. II, 1958, p. 318.
[2] Ibid., Vol. I, 1956, p. 624.

Jawaharlal Nehru's interest in East Pakistani Hindus? He looked at them as a part of the Indian nation—again in an 'extra-political' way—and therefore negotiated with the Government of Pakistan for their welfare and security. This should be answer enough to those Indian leaders who still declare that they accepted the partition of India under compulsion without accepting the two-nation theory which was the cause and the condition of the partition.

Chapter 8

EPILOGUE

IF the foregoing pages have painted a dark picture of incessant strife and unceasing warfare, it is necessary to emphasize that for a large number of people—both Hindus and Muslims—the normal, workaday life was one of indifference, though hardly of amity and harmony. In several fields of human endeavour and the daily grind people lived in peace. Certain bridges were made which served, albeit briefly and superficially, to bring the communities closer, to accentuate the common bonds, to magnify the links, to play down the diversities, and to create a spark of common sympathy. Sometimes these attempts bore fruit, sometimes they failed to compose the differences. The fact that such attempts were made is as significant as the fact that they ultimately failed.

Nothing illustrates the genuineness of these attempts so much as the fact that they were made even in a sphere where divergence was at the maximum, namely, religion. In the fifteenth century Kabir stands out as the paramount expositor of a *rapprochement* between Hinduism and Islam. Abandoned by her mother, a Brahmin widow of Benares, he was adopted and brought up by a poor Muslim weaver family. Goaded by an innate curiosity, bred with a mind torn by doubt and uncertainty, he wanted to ask questions, to seek the answers and to pursue the truth. Knowing that he was the son of a Hindu of the highest caste, living in and imbibing the influences of a Muslim household, breathing the air of the holy city of Benares, listening to religious and intellectual discussions, his natural intelligence awakened in him a desire to know more about the two religions. He listened and thought and absorbed the ideas of his friends, teachers and neighbours. What appealed to him, particularly under the inspiration of Ramananda, was the inherent significance of the spiritual side of religion. Spiritual attainments took precedence over being a

Hindu or a Muslim. A study of sufism strengthened this conviction. Forms and rituals were the husk of religion, spirituality its heart and core.

In both Hinduism and Islam he attacked the meaningless pursuit of external requirements and text-book formalities. But there was one difference. In Hinduism he criticized even the fundamentals: caste system, untouchability, taboos in food, idol worship, incarnation, polytheism, even metempsychosis. In Islam he was content to assault ritual and custom alone, never questioning its basic teachings. On the whole his ideas, his concepts, the contours of his thought, the turn of his phrase, the very edge of his argument, are Islamic, not Hindu. Formally he did not forsake Hinduism, but in all but name he became a Muslim and a sufi.

Yet his attitude to Hinduism differed from that of the Muslims. It was neither self-righteous nor superior. Both religions had weaknesses and it was futile to compare them in order to prove the primacy of either. All religious quest was virtuous. He made this not only the bed-rock of his belief but also the starting-point of his mission of creating and spreading Hindu–Muslim unity. If the followers of the two creeds were once united on the spiritual plane, social, cultural, perhaps even political unity would come of its own volition.

How were Kabir's teachings received by those for whose ultimate unity they were fashioned? They first startled and then enraged everyone. So great was the popular resentment that the case went to the Emperor himself, the orthodox Sultan Sikandar Lodhi. It is perhaps an indication of Kabir's acceptance (by the Muslims) as a Muslim that the royal eyes saw nothing improper in his teachings, and the controversy was dismissed by the suggestion that Kabir should betake himself to some distant and obscure place where his message would not disturb the peace of the realm. By the time he died a loyal body of disciples had gathered around him who propagated his word and did not let his name or effort die.

It is significant that the complainants against him came from both religions. Hindus and Muslims equally believed that their religion was being subverted, that Kabir, in following an *ignis fatuus*, was uprooting their beliefs, their traditions and their faith. To this day his following remains divided into a Hindu group and a Muslim group, each tenaciously holding that he belonged to its religion.

Kabir's place in the religious history of India remains high, 'because through him was articulated most forcefully and with great effect the belief that Hinduism and Islam could unite in a fervent belief in God and that the division on the basis of community, ritual or theology was not important. The torch lit by Kabir ignited in course of time a wild fire which, carried upon the emotions of sincere seekers of spiritual ecstasy, spread to all corners of the sub-continent.'

Kabir had not spoken in vain, and the names of the saints and thinkers who followed in his footsteps make a distinguished roll: Dadu, Chaitanya, Namdeva, Tukaram, Nanak.

Why did the Muslims refuse to tread the path lighted by such intellects? To them the important question was whether the voice that beckoned them was the voice of Islam or the voice of Hinduism. Their answer was that, though it sounded like the call of Islam, it was a subtle Hindu move to subvert Islam, to absorb the alien element into the Indian *milieu*, and thus to turn the Muslim triumph in India into a defeat. They knew that in the past Hinduism had, by this method, consumed many sects which had arisen within its fold. By preaching the acceptance of a few Islamic values Hinduism, far from compromising with Islam, was actually manifesting its remarkable capacity for synthesis.

Further, any success of such ideas would have led to a decrease in the number of professing Muslims in India. This could not have been a pleasing prospect to a community which was ever conscious of its minority status. Moreover, the emphasis on the spirituality of religion, coupled with a constant reminder of the emptiness and wickedness of ritual, gradually led to laxity in the practice of religion. This neglect was unwelcome both to the orthodox and to the commonality. Formal observance is dear to every religion. It helps solidarity and distinguishes the 'we' from the 'they'. Laxity could, perhaps one day would, lead to irreligiousness and Islam would vanish from the face of India. Had Islam conquered India so that one day it would compromise with the heathen and lose itself in the vast and infidel world of Hinduism?

When the common Muslim argued in this manner no virtues of Bhakti could attract him.

Still another factor worked against the new movement. Its central belief struck at the root of Muslim self-respect. If religion was nothing but spirituality, if Hinduism and Islam were the same, if all religions were the same, what happened to the Muslim's pride in Islam? In the loyalty of the Indian Muslim to his religion neither colour nor race played any part. He was a Muslim because he believed in Islam. Religion was his individuality, his distinguishing mark, his singularity. When this was taken away from him he forfeited all he had. Therefore, he regarded such movements not as attempts at social unity or even as an intellectual quest for conciliation, but as a conspiracy to undermine his religion. For him it was a religious problem, a crisis of belief. The choice lay clear between Islam and compromise. Unhesitatingly he chose Islam. Whatever the cost the Indian Muslim was not prepared to lose his individuality.[1]

The movement for Hindu–Muslim unity thus came to nothing. But it left its marks on several minor things, both social and religious. During periods of communal peace and political calm toleration showed its welcome face. Hindus of some areas were regular visitors of Muslim shrines and other centres of pilgrimage. Some Muslim saints, like Khwaja Hasan Nizami of Delhi, counted Hindus among their disciples. Hindu women prayed at the tombs of Muslim saints and believed that their wishes would come true. Hindus and Muslims were present at each other's religious festivities. Muslims were to be seen in the Dusehra processions. At Holi they threw coloured water on their Hindu friends. Hindus reciprocated by visiting their Muslim friends at Eid and even participating in the Muharram festival.

These might have been minor things, mere drops of good will in the wide waters of antipathy and misunderstanding, and they did not avert a final break-up. But they did exist and it is our duty to record them.

[1] In these paragraphs I have heavily drawn on the excellent treatment in Ishtiaq Husain Qureshi, *The Muslim Community of the Indo–Pakistan Subcontinent (610–1947): A Brief Historical Analysis*, 1962, Chapter V. The passage quoted is on pp. 116–17.

In culture, too, there were strands of unity. Above all, the Urdu language could have, and in some measure did, become a cementing force. It was the spoken tongue of millions of Hindus and Muslims in the Punjab, Delhi, the United Provinces, the Central Provinces and Bihar. Several Hindu names appear in the annals of its literature, from Ratan Nath Sarshar to Firaq Gorakhpuri. Hindu prose-writers and essayists contributed to Urdu journals. Hindu poets recited their verses in *mushairas*. A few of them have been men of distinction in modern poetry. There were well-known Hindu patrons of Urdu literature like Sir Tej Bahadur Sapru. The first comprehensive history of Urdu literature in English was written by a Hindu (Saksena).

This 'Hindu–Muslim' culture bloomed in the United Provinces where diverse cultural traits met and merged to produce a way of life which was neither exclusively Hindu nor exclusively Muslim. In Lucknow and other cities one saw this intermixture in its glory. It extended to many walks of life—dress, language, literature, folk-lore, good living, even parts of food. Friendships crossed communal boundaries (though intermarriage remained an impossibility). One language united those who spoke it. Literary gatherings took no notice of religious beliefs. In normal times there were definite signs of the evolution of a common culture.

But this attempt failed to hold its ground owing to some serious weaknesses in its character. First, it was an urban phenomenon, confined to places like Aligarh, Allahabad, Lucknow and some smaller towns. It did not touch the hamlets, where lack of education continued to breed ill-feeling. Urbanization always unites the city-dwellers in some sort of veiled opposition to the outsiders. There was an element of culture in it, but it was predominantly a question of the urbanites *versus* the countryfolk, not of a conscious effort to evolve a Hindu–Muslim culture. Secondly, even in the cities it was confined to the upper classes. The well-to-do dressed alike, had common culinary tastes, entertained each other, read the same books, lived in similar houses, belonged to the same clubs. They were the upper classes and were aware of it. Less than a century ago they had been united in their allegiance to the court of Oudh. Temperamentally and by upbringing they were courtiers, conscious of their superiority, of their wealth, and, as time passed, of their insecurity. As popular rule approached nearer they closed ranks, and, like all men in fear of an ill wind, magnified their community of interest. It was a closed society whose standards and values did not touch the masses.[1]

The important point is that even this superficial common culture failed to spread. It stayed within the confines of Delhi, Lucknow and Hyderabad. This was due partly to historical reasons (this culture was really a weak and corrupted version of the old Mughul culture of the Delhi imperial court), partly to economic reasons (the poor masses could not partake of this culture of the wealthy: the good example of common living was thus disregarded), and partly to geographical reasons (in a country of India's dimensions currents sent forth from one or two centres died away before reaching the far-away places).

Another weakness was its highly formal character. It put too much emphasis on the external observance of politeness, manners and other graces of good society. The ridiculous length to which such formalities, practised for their own sake, could be taken has become a part of the lore of the U.P. *wala*. This rigidity of formal behaviour, this primness, often coupled with contemptuous references to those outside the pale of this code of conduct ('the Punjabi is a boor'), hindered the spread of this culture to other regions. In the end its mannerisms became an object of kindly ridicule.

Basically the U.P. culture was Muslim in character and content. It was an example of the Hindu upper classes accepting the remnants of the Mughul way of life, not of the Muslims making a compromise with the Hindu environment. Such one-sided borrowing could not make it a genuine movement towards unity. It lacked the solid foundations of a common outlook on life, a common mode of thinking, the awareness of a common past and a common future, an accord on the values of

[1] This phenomenon reproduced itself in several other parts of India. In Hyderabad Deccan the Muslim nobles and the Hindu courtiers of the Nizam were indistinguishable in appearance and other things. In Calcutta or Bombay the urban trader, Hindu or Muslim, had much in common. In the Punjab the rich Hindus, Muslims and Sikhs of Lahore shared many cultural features.

life. That is why it failed to withstand the assault of communal politics. When the times were normal and political controversy was languid there was a show of amity and good fellowship—part genuine, part made-up—and all was well. When prospects of self-rule appeared on the horizon, when one of the parties took over the reins of government, when jobs were to be dispensed, or when a single communal riot broke out, the entire world of civility came tumbling down in dust and smoke.

* * *

Sometimes knowledge increases not so much by giving answers as by asking questions. In this chapter we will ask four leading questions. Was Pakistan inevitable? Could an alternative scheme be substituted for Pakistan? Why did the Muslims of the Hindu provinces support the Pakistan demand? How can the leaving behind of millions of Muslims in the Indian Union be reconciled with the theory that all Indian Muslims constituted one nation and wanted one homeland for that nation?

Some of these questions are hypothetical, others do not lend themselves to a definite answer. No attempt will be made here to simplify matters, for sometimes to simplify is not to clarify. What follows is merely thinking aloud on certain aspects of the Muslim problem in imperial India, the two-nation theory and the creation of Pakistan.

WAS PAKISTAN INEVITABLE?

The point at issue was whether a divided India, with all its flaws, was better or worse than an Indian chaos? Was the unity of India a creation of the British which was destined to disappear with them?

It may be that it was the British determination to introduce a parliamentary form of government in India that led to a demand for partitition. It may also be argued that an early implementation of the federal part of the 1935 constitution would have created a situation where the idea of separation might not have germinated in the Muslim mind. It is possible that there is a direct and causal connection between separate electorate and the creation of Pakistan. It is also possible that the unity of India was a British gift which India was fated to enjoy only so long as the donor was present on the spot.

Perhaps a more rational approach to this question would be to view it against the background of the development of self-government in India. The seeds of Hindu–Muslim discord were sown during the partition of Bengal and the making of the 1909 reforms. The former divided the Hindus from the Muslims; the latter was the first major instalment of a series of measures eventually leading to independence. In other words, the incipience of self-government was coterminous with the appearance of Hindu–Muslim schism. The larger the dose of self-government to India the deeper the Muslim fear of Hindu rule.

Hindu opposition to the grant of separate representation aggravated the situation and made the Muslims look at each advance towards self-rule as one more step towards their thraldom. This process continued until the working of provincial autonomy in 1937–9 told them that the consummation of Indian independence would not bring freedom. It was only then that they began to think of a separate state of their own where independence would be meaningful and freedom a reality.

Perhaps the expedient of communal electorates was neither enough nor effective. Had more drastic safeguards against communal tension been devised and incorporated in the 1935 constitution, Muslims might have shown less fear of democracy and greater willingness to enter a federal union.

Was Congress responsible for the emergence of Muslim nationalism and the creation of Pakistan? We have already touched upon this question, but there seems to be a near unanimous opinion among the knowledgeable that Congress attitude towards the Muslim problem was a major contributory factor. Professor Coupland, Lord Eustace Percy, Sir Stanley Reed, Sir Ivor Jennings, Sir Francis Tuker, Mr. Ian Stephens, Professor Rushbrook Williams, Mr. Penderel Moon and other competent judges of Indian affairs agree that the Congress 'arrogance' and the way in which it worked the provincial governments destroyed all the assumptions on which Muslim acceptance of the federation had been grounded, and so intensified separatism. Sir Ivor Jennings thinks that even as late as 1945 a united India in the shape of a loose federation of Hindu and Muslim States would have been possible if the Hindus had realized that the Muslim demand for a separate Muslim State with Islamic ideals needed to be met. The Congress refusal to see this made the creation of Pakistan inevitable. His latest view is that agreement could have been reached in 1940 or 1942 if the Congress had been willing to concede more to the Muslims.[1]

ALTERNATIVES TO PAKISTAN

When the Muslim mind was evolving the theory of two nations and preparing the demand for a separate State many alternative schemes were formulated. Abdul Latif of Hyderabad, 'A Punjabi', Sir Sikandar Hayat Khan, Sir Firoz Khan Noon and others suggested their own plans. From the British side, too, came some suggestions to solve the Indian problem without the ultimate recourse of partition. Professor Coatman was in favour of re-drawing provincial boundaries and forming a federation of autonomous provinces.[2] Clement Davies, the Liberal leader, thought of something on the lines of the United States, with sovereign provinces, transferring to the centre such rights as they deemed satisfactory, with full right to contract out subject to some sort of plebiscite.[3] Koni Zilliacus suggested a multi-national Indian membership of the United Nations, under which Muslims would be a separate United Nations member and under its protection.[4] Sir Arthur Page's rather impracticable solution was to divide India into predominantly Hindu and Muslim districts and to give them dominion status.[5] Finally, there was Professor Coupland's 'regionalism'. Among the official alternatives were those of Cripps, contained in his draft declaration of March 1942, and of the Cabinet Mission.

It is a fact of great importance that all these schemes came from the Muslim or British sides. The Hindus kept silent. Not

[1] See his *The Approach to Self-Government,* 1956, pp. 45–46, and *Problems of the New Commonwealth,* 1958, pp. 14–15.

[2] John Coatman, letter to *Manchester Guardian*, 25 April 1942.

[3] *H.C. 420, 5S,* 28 July 1944, Cols. 1063–4.

[4] *H.C. 434, 5S*, 5 March 1947, Cols. 547–8.

[5] In *Asiatic Review,* April 1942, p. 160.

one of their leaders gave serious thought to an alternative to partition. They showed remarkable ingenuity in arguing against Pakistan, in pointing out its disadvantages and in predicting a calamitous future for this artificially created State. Rajendra Prased wrote a long book on *India Divided*, but suggested no alternative to it. This is where the weakness of the Congress approach showed its most damaging aspect. Because the Muslim problem did not exist, therefore it offered no obstacle to Indian independence. Because Muslim nationalism was a myth, therefore it merited no attention. The Muslim League was an unrepresentative body which spoke for the minority of a minority, therefore its demands could safely be ignored. This was the cardinal mistake, for which the Congress had to pay the heavy price of partition. Its political short-sightedness was Jinnah's triumph.

Why did the Congress not make an effort to reach some sort of an agreement with the Muslims on the issue of Pakistan? One explanation is that it was convinced that if it stood firm the pressure of events and the logic of history (as the Congress understood it) would force the Muslims to come into a united, unitary India. Another reason was that it never appreciated the strength of Muslim nationalism and dismissed it with such irrelevancies as that the Muslims were converts from Hinduism, or that religious nationalism was a relic of primitive barbarism, or that the Muslims themselves did not realize what they were asking for, and so on. These arguments might have been enough to salve the Congress conscience, but they gave no clue to the political conundrum.

MUSLIMS OF HINDU PROVINCES AND PAKISTAN

It was an interesting feature of Muslim politics in India that the demand for Pakistan received greater support in the Hindu-majority provinces than in the Muslim-majority provinces. The Punjab was predominantly Unionist till the end of 1945, Sind did not take kindly to the Muslim League till 1946, and the Frontier Province maintained its Red Shirts in power right till the Independence Day. In Bengal alone was the Pakistan credo popular, but even there the League following was less resolute and numerous than it could have been. But the Muslims of the Hindu provinces were completely loyal to Jinnah and fully supported the Pakistan idea. What explains this phenomenon?

One reason springs to mind at once. The Muslims of the Muslim-majority areas felt secure in their provinces, though they did not live under a Muslim League Government. The régime did not matter much as long as they were in a majority. They had no fear of a Hindu *raj*. On the other hand, Muslims of the Hindu areas lived in terror, not only of the present but also of the future. They were living, or would live, under a Hindu Government, in which they had no confidence. This was not conducive to a feeling of security. The two years of Congress rule had been a nightmare for them and they would have given their right hand to stop a repeat performance. They would never be a majority and would therefore never rule over themselves. They were in this morass of hopelessness when Jinnah presented them with the idea of a separate State where the spectre of a Hindu *raj* would never materialize. The plan captured their imagination and from that moment they were Jinnah's men.

So far the argument is clear and strong. But—and there is the rub—these Muslims were not going to be a part of Pakistan. It is true that Jinnah used the word 'homeland' for the Pakistan he was demanding, but this was loose thinking. If by a 'homeland' he meant a country which would accommodate all the Indian Muslims (the 'nation'), he should have made it clear that it implied a transfer of population. But he definitely rejected this idea. He neither favoured nor anticipated a wholesale migration of Muslims to the projected Pakistan. On the contrary, he asked them to stay in India and to be loyal to their Government. He wanted them to stay back and not to come to Pakistan. Apparently the word 'homeland' was not used in the normal sense of a country to which all the people demanding it are expected or asked to come.

So it is evident that Muslims of the Hindu areas voted for Pakistan in full knowledge that they would have to remain in India. They fought for a cause which was, strictly speaking, not their cause at all. They strove for the creation of a country which was not going to be their country and in which they were never going to live. Why, then, did they vote for Pakistan?

One explanation is that their struggle in behalf of Pakistan was a sort of vicarious suffering. They wanted Pakistan because at least a major portion of the nation could live in freedom. In psychological terms it was a 'compensation' for them to see that they would be free—'they' here meaning their 'nation', not they themselves. This wore the appearance of sacrifice: they were incurring the hostility of their Hindu neighbours and future masters by agitating for Pakistan. But in fact it was not so. The concept of political retaliation played its part in the situation. It was then widely understood that the presence of a large Hindu minority in Pakistan would assure the protection of the Muslim minority in Hindu India. On one or two occasions Jinnah actually referred to this idea and told the Muslims of Hindu areas that if his Government in Pakistan treated justly with its Hindus there was no reason for the Indian Government not extending full protection to its Muslim minority.

Another explanation is that the emotional wave of propaganda for Pakistan was then at such a pitch that the Muslims of Hindu India gave no thought to their own future. The two-nation theory had enthralled them so completely that it never occurred to them that the creation of Pakistan on its basis would create a problem for them or adversely affect their future. Critical faculties were benumbed in the hurly-burly of events and by the sweep of the nationalist movement. They never considered themselves to be in a position different from that of their co-religionists of the Muslim provinces. This difference was brought home to them only when large scale riots started towards the end of 1946. By then it was too late. They had then gone too far in their support to Pakistan to withdraw from it and were too deeply committed to change their views. It is possible that had they known what was in store for them their enthusiasm for the Pakistan plan might not have been so uncritical.

It is not impossible that Muslims of the Hindu areas neither wanted Pakistan nor believed that it was possible of realization. They supported the idea in the belief, or at least in the attempt, that their pro-Muslim League policy would help create a political deadlock and thus postpone a final settlement leading to British withdrawal. It was in their interest to prolong the rule of the impartial British and to put off as long as possible the rule of the partial Hindu. Pakistan might or might not come, but their interest lay in giving their loyalty to Jinnah and thereby protect their stakes.

THE PRACTICAL SIDE OF THE TWO-NATION THEORY

We have already seen that for multifarious reasons the Muslims of India had come to look upon themselves as one nation. They demanded the creation of a separate State for this nation. But if all Indian Muslims constituted one nation, and if the nation-state of Pakistan was brought into being for them, how do we explain the fact that about forty million members of this nation were left behind and did not become a part of Pakistan? Either Pakistan was meant, or it was not meant, to be a homeland for the Muslims of India. If it was, then these millions should have come to Pakistan so that the whole nation was accommodated in the new State of their dreams. If it was not, then there was no point in claiming that all the Muslims in India were one nation and wanted Pakistan. As matters turned out to be, it seems that the inclusion of all Indian Muslims in Pakistan was not contemplated. If that is correct, then the Muslim League did not want a homeland, but only independence for certain Muslim areas. In theory, therefore, the conception of the two nations had a serious flaw.

Perhaps we can deal with this quandary by looking at the practical side of Jinnah's politics. He felt that a united India under a democratic government would inevitably mean a Muslim minority living for ever under a Hindu majority. How could he avoid this? Safeguards were not enough, and anyway after the British were gone who would guarantee them? The only solution he could think of was that Muslim-majority provinces should make a separate State where Muslims would not have to live under a perpetual Hindu Government. He therefore formulated the Pakistan demand. Then the question arose: how to justify this demand? On what basis should it be made? Modern history supplied the answer: on the basis of nationalism. Muslims were a nation apart and therefore could not live in a united India under the control of another nation. That is how the two-nation theory was born. Without it the

Pakistan demand lost its philosophical meaning. With it the Muslims could at least make out a case for themselves. It is against this background that the strength and weakness of the two-nation theory should be viewed.

CONCLUSION

The formulation of the idea of a Muslim nationality in India started with a relatively small nucleus. Then its influence slowly spread until it reached millions of people. The idea originated with a few individual leaders in various realms of mental and intellectual activity: a Sayyid Ahmad Khan here, an Ameer Ali there, a Shibli at one time, an Iqbal at another. Gradually the different strands of Muslim life and culture in the sub-continent were synthesized. The image of a Muslim India took shape, an image which was simultaneously the cause and the effect of an increasingly coherent intellectual life. The ideals of a culturally united community and of a socially consistent society were accepted by the masses. They were also persuaded of the fact that they shared the same historical background. Thus were laid the foundations of a separate nationalism. This feeling of separate nationalism received an impetus from Hindu opposition to it. Nationalism thrives on opposition. The more it is crushed the more vigorous its rebirth. It is stronger when it is holding an enemy at bay. This is precisely what happened in India. The higher the tempo of Hindu criticism the greater the determination of the Muslims to achieve their goal. The Muslim enthusiasm for Pakistan was in direct proportion to Hindu condemnation of it. Nationalism is a two-fold sentiment: of sympathy towards all within the group and of hostility towards all without it. The solidarity of Muslim India marched with her distrust of all those who stood in her way. Coherence flourished in the face of opposition.

In the final analysis, the idea of Muslim nationalism was more subjective than territorial, more psychological than political; while 'Indian' or Hindu nationalism was more territorial than cultural, more historical than religious. This difference of approach was fundamental, and it is interesting to see that the Muslim theory followed the ideals of the English and French thinkers (e.g. Mill, McDougall and Renan), who have emphasized personal feeling as the first test of nationalism; while the Hindu conception had an affinity with the opinions of German writers (e.g. Herder, Lessing and Wieland), who judged a nationality by its objective marks. The Muslims felt that they were a nation, and by so doing they underlined the subjective factor. The Hindus claimed that India was a nation, and in this they emphasized the objective factor.

BIBLIOGRAPHY

(i) THEORY OF NATIONALISM

Acton, Lord, *Essays on Freedom and Power*, Boston, 1948; London, 1956.

Barker, Ernest, *National Character and the Factors in its Formation*, London, rev. ed. 1948.

Inge, Dean, *England*, London, 1926.

Joseph, Bernard, *Nationality: Its Nature and Problems*, Yale, 1929.

Kohn, Hans, *The Idea of Nationalism*, New York, 1944.

Michels, Robert, *Notes sur les Moyen de Constater la Nationalité*, The Hague, 1917.

Rocker, Rudolf, *Nationalism and Culture*, trans. R. E. Chase, 1937

Royal Institute of International Affairs, *Nationalism: A Report by a Study Group of Members of the Royal Institute of International Affairs*, London, 1939.

Shafer, Boyd C. *Nationalism: Myth and Reality*, London, 1955.

Wells, H. G., *Guide to the New World*, London, 1941.

Znaniecki, Florian, *Modern Nationalities: A Sociological Study*, Urbana, 1952.

For some of the ideas in the Prologue I am indebted to these works.

(ii) OFFICIAL PUBLICATIONS

East India (Reconstitution of the Provinces of Bengal and Assam): *Papers Relating to the Reconstitution of the Provinces of Bengal and Assam*, London, 1905. Cd. 2658.

East India (Legislative Councils): *Representation of Muhammadans on Legislative Councils*, London, 1909. Cd. 4652.

East India (Coronation Durbar): *Announcements by and on Behalf of His Majesty the King–Emperor at the Coronation Durbar held at Delhi on the 12th December 1911, with Correspondence Relating Thereto*, London, 1911. Cd. 5979.

East India (Constitutional Reforms): *Report of Indian Constitutional Reforms*, London, 1918. Cd. 9109 (Montagu–Chelmsford Report).

East India (Constitutional Reforms): *Report of the Indian Statutory Commission*, London, 1930, 2 vols. Cmd. 3568, 3569 (Simon Report).

East India (Constitutional Reforms): *Communal Decision*, London, 1932. Cmd. 4147 (Communal Award).

East India (Constitutional Reforms): *Proposals for Indian Constitutional Reforms*, London, 1933. Cmd. 4268.

East India (Constitutional Reforms): *Elections: Return Showing the Results of Elections in India*, London, 1937. Cmd. 5589.

India (Lord Privy Seal's Mission): *Statement and Draft Declaration of His Majesty's Government with Correspondence and Resolutions Connected Thereto*, London, 1942. Cmd. 6350.

India: *Statement of the Policy of His Majesty's Government by the Secretary of State for India* on June 14 1945, London, 1945. Cmd. 6652.

India (Cabinet Mission): *Statement by the Cabinet Mission and His Excellency the Viceroy*, London, 1946. Cmd. 6821.

India: *Prime Minister's Statement of 20 February 1947*, London, 1947. Cmd. 7047.

India: *Prime Minister's Statement of 3 June 1947*, London, 1947. Cmd. 7136.

India in 1930–31: *A Statement Prepared for Presentation to Parliament in Accordance with the Requirements of the 26th Section of The Government of India Act* (5 & 6 GEO. V, Chap. 61), Government of India, Calcutta, 1932.

(iii) BOOKS

Agarwala, Ratish Mohan, *The Hindu–Muslim Riots: Their Causes and Cures*, Lucknow, 1943.

Ahmad, Jamiluddin (Comp.), *Some Recent Speeches and Writings of Mr. Jinnah*, Lahore, 1952 ed. 2 vols.

All India Muslim League, *Resolutions of the All India Muslim League from May 1924 to December 1936*, Delhi, n.d.

All India Muslim League, *Resolutions of the All India Muslim League from December 1938 to March 1940*, Delhi, n.d.

All India Muslim League, *Report of the Inquiry Committee appointed by the Council of the All India Muslim League to inquire into Muslim grievances in Congress Provinces*, Delhi, n.d. (Pirpur Report).

Amery, L. S., *My Political Life*, Vol. III: *The Unforgiving Years, 1929–1940*, London, 1955.

Andrews, C. F., *Mahatma Gandhi's Ideas, including Selections from his Writings*, London, 1929, 2nd. imp. 1930.

Andrews, C. F. and Mukerji, Girja, *The Rise and Growth of the Congress in India*, London, 1938.

Ansari, Shaukatullah, *Pakistan: The Problem of India*, Lahore, 1944.

Azad, Abul Kalam, *Musalman aur Congress*, Lahore, n.d.

—— *Khutbat-i-Abul Kalam Azad*, Lahore, n.d.

—— *India Wins Freedom: An Autobiographical Narrative*, Bombay, 1959.

Banerji, A. R., *The Indian Tangle*, London, n.d.

Barton, William, *India's North-West Frontier*, London, 1939.

Bhargava, M. B. L., *Political and National Movements in India*, Lucknow, 1936.

Bihar Provincial Muslim League, *Report of the Inquiry Committee appointed by the Working Committee of the Bihar Provincial Muslim League to inquire into some Grievances of the Muslims in Bihar,* Patna, 1939 (Shareef Report).

Bilgrami, Sayyid Husain, *Addresses, Poems and other Writings of Nawab Imad-ul-Mulk Bahadur (Sayyid Husain Bilgrami, C.S.I.),* Hyderabad, 1925.

Birkenhead, Earl of, *Frederick, Earl of Birkenhead: The Last Phase,* London, 1935.

Blunt, Wilfrid Scawen, *My Diaries: A Personal Narrative of Events, 1888–1914,* London, 1932 ed.

Borsodi, Ralph, *The Challenge of Asia: A Study of Conflicting Ideas and Ideals,* Melbourne (Florida), 1956.

Brecher, Michael, *Jawaharlal Nehru: A Political Biography,* London, 1959

Butler, Harcourt, *India Insistent,* London, 1931.

Butt, Abdullah (Ed), *Aspects of Abul Kalam Azad,* Lahore, 1942.

Calpin, G. H., *The South African Way of Life: Values and Ideas of a Multi-racial Society,* London, 1952.

Cash, W. W., *The Muslim World in Revolution,* London, 1925.

Chaudhuri, Nirad C., *The Autobiography of an Unknown Indian,* London, 1951.

Chirol, Valentine, *Indian Unrest,* London, 1910.

—— *India,* London, 1926.

Coatman, John, *Years of Destiny: India 1926–1932,* London, 1932.

Cotton, Henry, *New India,* London, 1907 ed.

Coupland, Reginald, *Report on the Constitutional Problem in India,* Part I: *The Indian Problem, 1833–1935,* London, 1942.

—— *Report on the Constitutional Problem in India,* Part II: *Indian Politics, 1936–1942,* London, 1943.

—— *Report on the Constitutional Problem in India,* Part III: *The Future of India,* London, 1943.

—— *India: A Re-Statement,* London, 1945.

Craddock, Reginald, *The Dilemma in India,* London, 1929.

Crossfield, Henry, *England and Islam,* London, 1900.

Cumming, John (Ed.), *Modern India: A Co-operative Survey of a Century, 1831–1931,* London, 1931.

Durand, Mortimer, *Life of the Rt. Hon. Sir Alfred Comyn Lyall,* London, 1913.

Dutt, Sukumur, *Problem of Indian Nationality,* Calcutta, 1926.

Edwardes, Herbert B., *Our Indian Empire: Its Beginning and End,* London, 1861.

Edwardes, Michael, *A History of India from the Earliest Times to the Present Day*, Bombay, 1961.

Ellan, J. E., *Swaraj: The Problem of India*, London, 1930.

Faruqi, Ziya-ul-Hasan, *The Deoband School and the Demand for Pakistan*, Bombay, 1963.

Fulop-Miller, René, *Lenin and Gandhi*, London, first English ed. 1927.

Garratt, G. T., *An Indian Commentary*, London, 1928.

Gibb, H. A. R. (Ed.), *Whither Islam? A Survey of Modern Movements in the Muslim World*, London, 1932.

Gokhale, B. G., *The Making of the Indian Nation*, Bombay, 1960 ed.

Gopal, Ram, *Indian Muslims: A Political History, 1858–1947*, Bombay, 1959.

Graham, G. F. I., *The Life and Work of Sayyid Ahmad Khan*, C.S.I., London, 1885, rev. ed. 1909.

Gwyer, Maurice and Appadorai, A (Eds.), *Speeches and Documents on the Indian Constitution, 1921–1947*, Bombay, 1957, 2 vols.

Hardie, Keir, *India: Impressions and Suggestions*, London, 1909.

Harrison, Selig S., *India: The Most Dangerous Decades*, Princeton, 1960.

Horne, E. A., *The Political System of British India*, London, 1922.

Huq, A. K. Fazlul, *Muslim Sufferings under Congress Rule*, Calcutta, 1939.

Huq, Afzal (Ahrar), *Pakistan and Untouchability*, Lahore, 1941.

Husain, Azim, *Fazl-i-Husain: A Political Biography*, Bombay, 1946.

Husain, S. Abid, *The National Culture of India*, Bombay, 1961 ed.

India's Problem of Her Future Constitution, Bombay, n.d.

Jennings, Ivor, *The Approach to Self-Government*, London, 1956.

—— *The Problems of the New Commonwealth*, Duke, 1958.

Jones, Thomas, *A Diary with Letters, 1931–1950*, London, 1954.

Kamal Yar Jung Education Committee, *Report*, Calcutta, 1942.

Kenworthy, J. M., *India: A Warning*, London, 1931.

Khan, Aga, *India in Transition: A Study in Political Evolution*, London, 1918.

—— *The Memoirs of Aga Khan: World Enough and Time*, London, 1954.

Krishna, B. K., *The Problem of Minorities or Communal Representation in India*, London, 1939.

Lilly, William S., *India and its Problems*, London, 1902.

Lovett, Verney, *India*, London, 1923.

Low, Sidney, *A Vision of India*, London, 1910.

Lyall, A. C., *Asiatic Studies: Religious and Social*, London, 1882. 2 vols.

MacDonald, Ramsay, *The Awakening of India*, London, 1910.

Madani, Husain Ahmad, *Muslim League Kia Hai,* Delhi, 1945.

—— *Pakistan Kia Hai,* Delhi, n.d.

—— *Makateeb-i-Shaikh-ul-Islam,* Deoband, n.d., later enl. ed. Azamgarh, 1952. 2 vols.

Malaviya, Madan Mohan, *Speeches and Writings,* Madras, n.d.

Malik, Hafeez, *Moslem Nationalism in India and Pakistan,* Washington, 1963.

Mansergh, Nicholas, *Survey of British Commonwealth Affairs: Problems of External Policy, 1931–1939,* London, 1952.

Masani, R. P., *Britain and India,* Bombay, 1960.

Maudoodi, Abul Ala, *Musalman aur Maujooda Siasi Kashmakash,* Lahore, n.d. 3 vols.

—— *Nationalism in India,* Pathankot, 1947.

—— *The Process of Islamic Revolution,* Pathankot, 1947.

—— *The Message of Jamaat-i-Islami: A Contribution towards Islamic Constitution-Making,* Lahore, 1955 ed.

Menon, V. P., *The Transfer of Power in India,* Calcutta, 1954.

Meston, Lord, *India at the Crossroads,* London, 1920.

—— *Nationhood for India,* London, 1931.

Mian, Sayyid Muhammad, *Ulama-i-Haqq aur un kay Mujahadana Karnamay,* Moradabad, 1946–8. 2 vols.

—— *Jamiat-ul-Ulama Kia Hai,* Delhi, n.d.

Mookerji, Radhakumud, *Akhand Bharat,* Bombay, 1945.

Morrison, John, *New Ideas in India during the Nineteenth Century: A Study of Social, Political and Religious Developments,* London, 1907.

Mukerjee, Hirendranath, *India Struggles for Freedom: A History of the National Movement,* Bombay, 1946.

Munshi, K. M., *The Changing Shape of Indian Politics,* Poona, 1946 ed.

Nehru, Jawaharlal, *Glimpses of World History: Being Further Letters to his Daughter written in Prison and containing a Reliable Account of History for Young People,* Allahabad, 1935. 2 vols.

Nehru, Jawaharlal, *A Bunch of Old Letters,* Bombay, 1960 ed.

Niazi, Sayyid Nazir, *Maktubat-i-Iqbal,* Karachi, 1957.

O'Dwyer, Michael, *India as I Knew It, 1885–1925,* London, 1925.

O'Malley, L. S. S., *Modern India and the West,* London, 1941.

Panikkar, K. M. and An Englishman, *Indian Nationalism: Its Origin, History and Ideas,* London, 1920.

Panikkar, K. M. and Pershad, A. (Eds.), *The Voice of Freedom: Selected Speeches of Pandit Motilal Nehru,* Bombay, 1961.

Philips, C. H., *India,* London, n.d.

Philips, C. H. (Ed.), *Historians of India, Pakistan and Ceylon,* London, 1961.

Pillai, C. P., *Pakistan and its Implications*, n.p., n.d.

Punjabi, Kewal L., *Rajendra Prasad: First President of India*, Bombay, 1960.

Pyarelal, *Mahatma Gandhi: The Last Phase*, Ahmedabad, 1958–60. 2 vols.

Qureshi, I. H., *The Muslim Community of the Indo-Pakistan Subcontinent (610–1947): A Brief Historical Analysis*, The Hague, 1962.

Ratcliffe, S. K., *The Resurgence of Asia*, London, 1946.

Rawlinson, H. G., *The British Achievement in India: A Survey*, London, 1948.

Rees, John David, *The Real India*, London, 1908.

Reincourt, Amaury De, *The Soul of India*, New York, 1960.

Ronaldshay, Lord, *The Heart of Aryavarta: A Study of the Psychology of Indian Unrest*, London, 1925.

—— *Life of Lord Curzon: Being the Authorized Biography of George Nathaniel, Marquess Curzon of Kedleston, K.G.*, London, 1928. 3 vols.

Sampurnanda, *Memories and Reflections*, Bombay, 1962.

Satyapal and Chandra, Prabodh, *60 Years of Congress: India Lost, India Regained*, Lahore, 1946.

Schuster, George and Wint, Guy, *India and Democracy*, London, 1941.

Seeley, J. R., *The Expansion of England: Two Courses of Lectures*, London, 1883.

Sen, Sachin, *The Political Thought of Tagore*, Calcutta, 1947.

Setalvad, Chimanlal, *Recollections and Reflections: An Autobiography*, Bombay, n.d.

Seton-Watson, R. W., *The Historian as a Political Force in Central Europe*, London, 1922.

Spear, Percival, *The Oxford History of India*, Oxford, 1958 ed.

Storrs, Ronald, *Orientations*, London, 1943 definitive ed.

Thamankar, D. V., *Lokamanya Tilak*, London, 1956.

Thayer, Philip W. (Ed.), *Nationalism and Progress in Free Asia*, New York, 1956.

Titus, Murray T., *Indian Islam: A Religious History of Islam in India*, London, 1930.

Topa, Ishwar Nath, *The Growth and Development of National Thought in India*, Hamburg, 1930.

Trade Union Congress (British), *Trade Union Congress Annual Report for 1942*, London, 1942.

Tyne, C. H. V., *India in Ferment*, London, 1923.

Waheed-uz-Zaman, *Towards Pakistan*, Lahore, 1964.

Wedderburn, William, *Allan Octavian Hume, C.B.: 'Father of the Indian National Congress', 1829–1912*, London, 1913.

Whitehead, Henry, *Indian Problems in Religion, Education, Politics,* London, 1924.

Williams, Monier, *Modern India and the Indians: Being A Series of Impressions, Notes and Essays,* London, 1878, 3rd. ed. 1879.

Zetland, Marquess of, '*Essayez*': *Memoirs of Lawrence, Second Marquess of Zetland,* London, 1956.

Zwemer, S. W. *et al., The Muhammadan World of Today,* London, 1906.

(iv) ARTICLES

Abbot, Freeland, 'The Jamaat-i-Islami of Pakistan', *The Middle East Journal,* Winter 1957.

Ali, Ameer, 'India and the New Parliament', *Nineteenth Century,* August 1906.

Ali, Shaukat, 'An Appeal from the Muslim World to the British People', *Empire Review,* November 1931.

Archbold, W. A. J., 'Some Indian Problems', *Contemporary Review,* July 1925.

Asiaticus, 'India: Lord Minto's Viceroyalty', *National Review,* November 1910.

Baker, W., 'Reflections on India, 1880–1888', *Fortnightly Review,* August 1888.

Barker, J. Ellis, 'The Future of Asiatic Turkey', *Nineteenth Century,* June 1916.

Barton, William, 'The State and the White Paper', *Empire Review,* January 1934.

Bell, Gertrude, 'Islam in India – A study at Aligarh', *Nineteenth Century,* December 1906.

Blackett, Basil, 'The Economics of Indian Unrest', *Foreign Affairs,* October 1929.

Boggs, T. H., 'England's Problems in India', *Yale Review,* February 1909.

Colvin, E. G., 'The Changing Scene in India', *Nineteenth Century,* May 1919.

—— 'Trial and Error in India', *Fortnightly Review,* February 1932.

—— 'India – The Longer View', *Nineteenth Century,* May 1933.

'Current Events in India', *Empire Review,* February 1902.

Dicey, Edward, 'Islam in Fermentation', *Empire Review,* August 1906.

Elliott, A. C., 'The Unrest in India', *Empire Review,* June 1907.

Garratt, G. T., 'The Third Round Table Conference', *Nineteenth Century,* February 1933.

Gruyther, L. de, 'An Important Indian Institution', *Empire Review,* November 1904.

Keene, H. G., 'Women of Indian History', *National Review,* October 1886.

Lacey, Patrick, 'Deadlock in India', *Nineteenth Century,* July 1937.

'Lord Chelmsford's Viceroyalty', *Quarterly Review,* July 1921.

Machonacie, M., 'The Desirability of a Definite Recognition of the Religious Element in Government Education in India', *Imperial and Asiatic Quarterly Review,* October 1900.

Meston, Lord, 'India Today and Tomorrow', *Nineteenth Century,* March 1932.

Mijatovich, Chedo, 'The Problem of the Near East', *Fortnightly Review,* October 1906.

Morison, Theodore, 'The Hindu–Muslim Problem of India', *Contemporary Review,* June 1931.

O'Dwyer, M. F., 'India under the Congress', *National Review,* July 1939.

Rice, Stanley, 'India: Partition or Unity', *Asiatic Review,* January 1943.

Sharrock, J. A., 'Some Misconceptions about the Unrest in India', *Nineteenth Century,* September 1909.

Smith, Leslie, 'The Congress and Modern India', *National Review,* April 1889.

Srinivasan, S., 'Communal Problem in India', *Empire Review,* January 1941.

Vambery, A., 'Pan–Islamism', *Nineteenth Century,* October 1906.

Williams, L. F. R., 'The Indian Constitutional Problem', *Nineteenth Century,* March 1939.

Williams, Monier, 'Progress of Indian Religious Thought', *Contemporary Review,* December 1878.

Wilson, H. A., 'The Muslim Menace', *Nineteenth Century,* September 1907.

(V) DAILY AND WEEKLY PRESS

Manchester Guardian

Observer

The Times

Economist

New Statesman

Spectator

INDEX